Coded Lyrics
The Poetics of Argentine Rock
under Censorship and Beyond

Liverpool Latin American Studies

Series Editor: Matthew Brown, University of Bristol
Emeritus Series Editor: Professor John Fisher

14 Andean Truths: Transitional Justice, Ethnicity, and Cultural Production in Post-Shining Path Peru
 Anne Lambright

15 Positivism, Science, and 'The Scientists' in Porfirian Mexico: A Reappraisal
 Natalia Priego

16 Argentine Cinema and National Identity (1966–1976)
 Carolina Rocha

17 Decadent Modernity: Civilization and 'Latinidad' in Spanish America, 1880–1920
 Michela Coletta

18 Borges, Desire, and Sex
 Ariel de la Fuente

19 Contacts, Collisions and Relationships: Britons and Chileans in the Independence era, 1806–1831
 Andrés Baeza Ruz

20 Writing and the Revolution: Venezuelan Metafiction 2004–2012
 Katie Brown

21 Marvels of Medicine: Literature and Scientific Enquiry in Early Colonial Spanish America
 Yarí Pérez Marín

22 Colonial Legacies and Contemporary Identities in Chile Revisiting Catalina de los Ríos y Lisperguer
 Céire Broderick

23 Literary Reimaginings of Argentina's Independence: History, Fiction, Politics
 Catriona McAllister

24 Football and Nation Building in Colombia (2010–2018): The Only Thing That Unites Us
 Peter J. Watson

25 A World Without Hunger: Josué de Castro and the Geography of Survival
 Archie Davies

26 Distortion and Subversion: Punk Rock Music and the Protests for Free Public Transportation in Brazil (1996–2011)
 Rodrigo Lopes de Barros

27 The Woodbine Parish Report on the Revolutions in South America (1822): The Foreign Office and Early British Intelligence on Latin America
 Mariano Schlez

28 A City Against Empire: Transnational Anti-Imperialism in Mexico City, 1920–1930
 Thomas K. Lindner

29. Representations of China in Latin American Literature (1987–2016)
 Maria Montt Strabucchi

30. Women's Club Football in Brazil and Colombia: A Critical Analysis of Players, Media and Institutions
 Mark Daniel Biram

Liverpool Latin American Studies, New Series 31

Coded Lyrics
The Poetics of Argentine Rock under Censorship and Beyond

Mara Favoretto

LIVERPOOL UNIVERSITY PRESS

First published 2024 by
Liverpool University Press
4 Cambridge Street
Liverpool
L69 7ZU

Copyright © 2024 Mara Favoretto

Mara Favoretto has asserted the right to be identified as the author of this book in accordance with the Copyright, Designs and Patents Act 1988.

All rights reserved. No part of this book may be reproduced, stored in a retrieval system, or transmitted, in any form or by any means, electronic, mechanical, photocopying, recording, or otherwise, without the prior written permission of the publisher.

British Library Cataloguing-in-Publication data
A British Library CIP record is available

ISBN 978-1-83553-230-0

Typeset by Carnegie Book Production, Lancaster

Contents

Acknowledgements		ix
Introduction		1
1	Once Upon a Time, There Was Rock	9
2	Then, There Was Poetry: The Pioneer Musicians and Their Lyrics	23
3	The Day Words Were Forbidden: Censorship	37
4	Play on Words: Official versus Dissident Language	55
5	Concealed Meaning: Codification of Dissident Messages in Songs	77
6	War of the Words: The Day a War Became an Opportunity	93
7	Words Set Free: Speech and Thought in Post-Dictatorship Songs	107
8	Words Made Eternal: Charly García and the Parody of a Rock Star	127
9	A Cosmos of Words: Luis Alberto Spinetta's Poetry	147
Epilogue		159
Bibliography		161
Discography		167
Index		169

For John Billan

Acknowledgements

I would like to express my sincere gratitude to the Faculty of Arts at the University of Melbourne for their invaluable support during the writing of this book.

I'm thankful to Elizabeth Bryer and Cynthia Troup for their thorough reading and helpful suggestions, and the LUP staff for making this journey enjoyable. My heartfelt gratitude goes out to my family and friends whose unwavering support and encouragement have meant the world to me.

Lastly, I would like to extend my acknowledgement to the artists and musicians who have inspired my work. Your creativity, talent, and passion have been a constant source of inspiration and motivation during my whole career.

Introduction

"There was singing before there were musical instruments,
before there was writing,
and before there was music notation.
There may even have been singing before there was speech."

—Jeanette Bicknell[1]

Rock music developed in South America in contextual conditions that were very different from their English-language counterparts.[2] It is widely known that there were many dictatorships in South America in the 1970s. The particular case of Argentina is enigmatic because the peculiarities that rock took were born out of *a necessity*. When confronted with censorship, musicians faced a dilemma: how might they dissent, reach their audience, and avoid putting their lives at risk, all at the same time? The case of Argentine rock music is probably one of the most outstanding cases of resistance among music genres in South America. Argentina has a long history of contestatory music that gives voice to the displaced, oppressed other. Since the tango of the early twentieth century, performers and the public alike have used the shared performative space of live music as a platform for resistance, as a form of public dialogue, and as a basis for solidarity. This is what this book is about: how and why Argentine rock came to be, with a focus in language. Through examining the particular case of Argentine rock and its lyrics, this book will explore how language can be used to construct and shape resistance. It will show that censorship in Argentina led to unexpected outcomes,

---

1 Jeanette Bicknell, *Philosophy of Song and Singing: An Introduction* (New York: Routledge, 2015), p. 1.
2 Pablo Vila, and Paul Cammack, "Rock Nacional and Dictatorship in Argentina," *Popular Music* 6 (2): 129–48, 1987.

with the case of Argentine rock lyrics being one of the most compelling examples of the power of art to creatively resist totalitarianism.

Rock critics and academics have offered useful and illuminating insights into the ways in which rock music originated and developed in other parts of the world. Works by Frith (1983, 1998),[3] Grossberg (1984),[4] Middleton (2006),[5] and many others are central to the understanding of rock as the central manifestation of post-war mass culture and to its analysis as a form of mass cultural activity. Yet these ideas cannot be applied to every country that saw the emergence of rock in the 1960s and 1970s, as is the case with rock in Argentina. Although several Argentine musical genres have been the object of academic research and literary analysis, Argentine rock, which reached its popularity peak and became a symbol of national identity in the 1980s, is the one that has received the least scholarly attention.[6]

In order to understand the "explosion" of Argentine rock it is essential to acknowledge that the military dictatorship, in a way, "collaborated" with its popularisation. It is not an exaggeration to emphasise that Argentine rock flourished because of the military repression and censorship. Rock musicians at the time found themselves bound by a common goal: defeat censorship policies and convey messages of protest against the regime's violence. In Pablo Vila and Paul Cammack's words, Argentine rock represented "an oppositional cultural expression of a specific social actor, youth".[7] It is indeed possible to talk about Argentine rock before and after the dictatorship. As in many censorship cases, the results of these regulations were unexpected because they fuelled the creativity of artists, and instead of crushing dissidence, they favoured the development of a musical genre that not only occupied the political space of opposition to the regime, but also became one of the major popular music genres in Argentina today.

Over time, Argentine rock carved out a new space. It had a clear counter identity and an ideology that distinguished it from other South American youth genres of the time. Popular music is a nucleus around which discursive practices can form, providing alternatives to the official version. This book focuses on Argentina's authoritarian decades and the post-dictatorship period, and in particular on the lyrics of the *Argentine rock*

---

3 Simon Frith, *Sound Effects: Youth, Leisure, and the Politics of Rock* (London: Constable, 1983) and, by the same author, *Performing Rites: On the Value of Popular Music* (Cambridge MA: Harvard University Press, 1998).
4 Lawrence Grossberg, "Another Boring Day in Paradise: Rock and Roll and the Empowerment of Everyday Life," *Popular Music: A Yearbook* 4: 225–58, 1984.
5 Richard Middleton, *Voicing the Popular: On the Subjects of Popular Music* (London: Routledge, 2006).
6 Oscar Conde, *Poéticas del rock* (Buenos Aires: Marcelo Héctor Oliveri Editor, 2007), p. 99.
7 Vila and Cammack, "Rock Nacional and Dictatorship in Argentina," p. 129.

music genre, to explore the struggle between state and public over identity, language, and perception as negotiated around the medium of rock. This is not a musicological study; rather it is an investigation of language and culture. The purpose of this study is not to explain the history of Argentina or of rock, both of which have been amply discussed elsewhere. It is rather to elucidate what this study understands as the collaborative authorship of an alternative set of practices, articulated through the interaction of many individuals and institutions, including state, artists, and public, the fine and blurry line that intends to separate reality from fiction.

Chapter 1 outlines the historical and political context where this phenomenon developed. Far from the freedom of expression and youth movements that were taking place in the US and in Europe, Argentina was cyclically burdened by authoritarianism and censorship. In the vastly populated field of Argentine rock, there are two musicians that emerge as the main pioneers and, arguably, are considered national idols in the popular consciousness: Charly García (1951–) and Luis Alberto Spinetta (1950–2012). Chapter 2 portrays the first two most iconic bands of Argentine rock: Almendra and Sui Generis, the former led by Luis Alberto Spinetta and the latter by Charly García. Chapters 8 and 9 will deal with them individually in further detail. Chapter 2 explores the first three albums produced by Sui Generis, the first band to use coded language as a weapon of the weak. In fact, it is at this time that composer and band member Charly García developed a particular style of lyrics. He became an allegorist. By borrowing the same rhetorical strategy that the military officials used in their eloquent speeches, and putting it to new ends, Charly used allegories to criticise the regime and subvert the use of language tropes. In a way it was like showing them that musicians were smarter. The band not only mastered the use of allegory but used it better than the military officials in their discourse to speak out against them. And the censors did not get it. In the following chapters, García's lyrics also occupy a prominent space precisely because of his importance in the genre, and his main role in Argentine popular culture from the start of his career until now. As for Almendra, Luis Alberto Spinetta built the base of Argentine rock's aesthetics and poetic content. One of the promoters of the idea of singing rock in Spanish, his exemplary ethics and eccentric personality might have also contributed to his stardom and to the fact that the Argentine National Day of the Musician is celebrated on Spinetta's birth date.

Chapter 3 analyses the case of censorship during the most recent dictatorship regime. However, censorship did not start with the "Process of National Reorganisation", as the military Junta called their government; musicians had been dealing with it for several years when the military officials seized power again in 1976. Therefore, they had already started to develop a particular approach to writing the lyrics of their songs. This peculiar style intensified and further developed under the Process as censorship intensified as well. As Diana Taylor puts it, "nation-ness was resemanticised. The ideal citizens were those who self-consciously controlled their... every word".[8] The machinery of censorship imposed by the regime was a distinct one as there was no official organism or office to which work could be submitted for approval. Its guidelines were blurry, confusing, and vague. Consequently, nobody knew exactly what could or could not be said. This caused the development of self-censorship, as out of fear, producers and editors censored their artists themselves.[9] However, censorship was not *always* blurry. There was a list of prohibited words and some "blacklists" of forbidden artists circulated among TV and radio stations. Interestingly, some theatre productions, with apparent "subversive content" were not censored. This was what Hernán Invernizzi calls the "impact theory". Examples such as Teatro Abierto plays, which were only attended by a few dozen people, were not thought to have the same "impact" as a published book or a broadcast/recorded song, which had the potential to "impact" thousands. Examples of "freedom of expression" such as Teatro Abierto would serve the regime as a defence when questioned in an international forum.[10] In sum, this chapter explores the dynamics and shades around censorship and the turns that were taken, in order to comprehend the context and conditions in which the rock movement developed and flourished.

In Chapter 4, we turn to the rhetorical pillars of the regime. The military Junta seemed obsessed with language. Their discourse was heavily loaded with medical metaphors, such as "we are the surgeons who will operate on society to extirpate the cancer it is suffering from", meaning they wanted to eradicate communism.[11] Their official communiqués were adorned with literary devices and presented a messianic message, speaking about God, love, trust, faith, and family values. At the same time, people were disappearing, and the youth were targeted as the main "enemy". This chapter specifically traces the machinations of the so-called Process of National Reorganisation, as it sought to control the thought of the nation by controlling perception and image. Not coincidentally, both are key factors in the construction of identity, and both were manipulated as means to the ultimate end of recreating a national identity in a "pure" form—eliminating subversive elements of youth culture. Indeed, the military discourse was elaborate and playful, and one of the main rhetorical strategies used by the military officials was allegory. A previous study of their allegorical themes reveals they had a carefully planned and hidden agenda, and their messages revolved around the "Western and

---

8 Diana Taylor, *Disappearing Acts: Spectacles of Gender and Nationalism in Argentina's "Dirty War"* (Durham: Duke University Press, 1997), p. 95.
9 To read about how censorship operated, see Hernán Invernizzi, *"Los libros son tuyos": políticos, académicos y militares: la dictadura en Eudeba* (Buenos Aires: Eudeba, 2005); also, Hernán Invernizzi, and Judith Gociol, *Un golpe a los libros: represión a la cultura durante la última dictadura militar* (Buenos Aires: Eudeba, 2005).
10 Mara Favoretto, personal interview with Hernán Invernizzi and Judith Gociol, Buenos Aires, 26 November 2007.
11 Ricardo Piglia, *Crítica y ficción* (Barcelona: Anagrama, 1986), p. 36.

Christian values" they claimed to defend vigorously.[12] Admiral Emilio Massera was the orator of the Junta, and his speeches were carefully crafted. Marguerite Feitlowitz studied their language, which she called a "lexicon of terror", and used examples of Massera's speeches to illustrate the glossary she compiled. For instance, in one of his many addresses to the public, Massera warned his audience to be wary of words. They are "unfaithful", he said. And "the only safe words are *our* words".[13]

Within this "obsession" with words, rock musicians suffered the effects of censorship that cut not only their long hair but also the lyrics of their songs. For example, the album *Instituciones* (Institutions),[14] by Sui Generis (1974), saw its lyrics transformed and censored so much that composer Charly García decided to change its title to *Pequeñas anécdotas sobre las instituciones* (Little Anecdotes about Institutions) to reflect such reduction.

Chapter 5 examines the struggle over national identity through scrutinising the response of the audience and strategies of listening developed by the youth. My analysis focuses on the interrelationship between the fans, music, and musicians of Argentine rock in several kinds of musical events, para-musical texts in the form of rock magazines, and the negotiation of meaning that took place in the realm of image and identity. The leaders of Argentina's dictatorship of 1976–83 tried to manipulate the image of youth, and thereby redefine the social space of the nation. Yet official negation of youth identity was countered by affirmations based on the identities that centred around rock. This section explores the coded language in the most popular songs performed by the bands La Máquina de Hacer Pájaros (The Bird-making Machine) and Serú Girán. It deals with the struggle over expression and focuses on language. The military dictatorship wanted more than just to create a new nation by means of its "Process of National Reorganisation". It wanted to create a whole new reality. The rock songs produced and performed during the same period depict a whole world view, based on values that are completely opposite to those of the regime, constituting an alternative view.

Yet, in a surprising turn, things were about to get better for Argentine rock musicians. As outlined in Chapter 6, during the short war (2 April–14 June 1982) between Argentina and the United Kingdom over the islands known as Malvinas by the former and the Falklands by the latter, Argentine rock music was given its best opportunity to flourish. The military dictatorship decided to ban all songs in English—after all, it was the language of "the enemy". Consequently, on many radio and TV stations there was an empty space that

---

[12] See Mara Favoretto, *Alegoría e ironía bajo censura en la Argentina del Proceso (1976–1983)* (Lewiston NY: Edwin Mellen Press, 2010), pp. 11–70.

[13] Marguerite Feitlowitz, *A Lexicon of Terror: Argentina and the Legacies of Torture* (New York: Oxford University Press, 1998), p. 19. Unless otherwise acknowledged, throughout this book all translations into English of quoted material are mine.

[14] Sui Generis, *Pequeñas anécdotas sobre las instituciones* (Microfón/Sony BMG, 1974).

had previously broadcast Anglo rock and now needed to be filled with music belonging to the same genre so as not to lose its audience. Furthermore, the regime decided to seek the support of the youth—their target since the start of the dictatorship—and Argentine rock was conveniently branded "national rock".[15] Suddenly the regime reached out to those they considered "subversive" and summoned them to become "supporters" of the regime. This chapter explores how censorship created an opportunity for local rock musicians, transforming the local rock scene by favouring its growth. It shows how rock musicians not only made the most of this opportunity, but also used it as a weapon against the regime that had thought it could count on them in its nationalistic campaign against the United Kingdom.

Chapter 7 briefly shows some aspects of post-dictatorship rock and the main new trends. It was the end of censorship and the report published by the Comisión Nacional de los Desaparecidos (National Commission on the Disappearance of Persons, or CONADEP) detailed the confirmed disappearance of thousands of people, and documented the repressive role played by the dictatorship between 1976 and 1983. The new democratic context and the influence of international trends in music in the 1980s can be easily identified in the new lyrics performed by new bands. This chapter explores some of the new aspects of the production of rock song lyrics at this time: the transition songs, songs that talk of freedom and songs that voice resentment.

The final two chapters deal with the two national rock pioneers introduced in Chapter 2, Luis Alberto Spinetta and Charly García. After dissolving the foundational bands discussed in Chapter 2, Almendra and Sui Generis, which nowadays are attracting a considerable amount of research attention and historical revisits, both pursued solo careers and became "national idols" in Argentine popular culture. As well as having different styles, they managed their stardom in distinct ways. Whereas Charly construed a parody of a rock star, Spinetta built a private and protective shield, hiding himself from the public eye while writing encrypted lyrics that constructed a mythical world in which to seek solace.

Chapters 8 and 9 serve as windows into the distinctive rhetorical strategies and songwriting styles employed by Charly García and Luis Alberto Spinetta. Our aim is to gain a comprehensive understanding of their diverse approaches within the realm of the genre.

In Chapter 8, we delve into Charly García's intriguing journey, initially gaining fame for his political resistance during the dictatorship era. After a thorough examination of his songs in the preceding chapters, we scrutinise how García navigated the challenges of cooptation in the democratic period. In his quest to avoid being reduced to a mere commodity in the music industry, García ingeniously constructed a parody of himself as a rock star,

---

15 Miguel Grinberg, *Cómo vino la mano: orígenes del rock argentino* (Buenos Aires: Gourmet Musical Ediciones, 2008).

a theme that would define his career under democracy. This self-portrayal as a national icon is mirrored in his songs, which thematically incorporate all the elements contributing to this status, including a distinctive logo, a formidable adversary, a compelling mission, and a set of guiding principles.

Moving on to Chapter 9, our focus shifts to Luis Alberto Spinetta, whose poetic approach addresses profound existential matters and endeavors to reconcile the dichotomy between humanity and the cosmos, offering solace in the face of existential angst. Spinetta's lyrical creations are marked by their intricate nature, frequently enveloped in layers of symbolism and metaphor. Within his work, he employs a poetic strategy that seamlessly integrates chaos reminiscent of the cosmos, infusing it with profound depth and significance, thus fashioning an undeniably captivating artistic journey.

In sum, this book tells a different story of the history of rock. Lyricists such as García, Spinetta, and many others around the world, in different languages, should be given as much attention as their Anglo counterparts. Let us start exploring why.

CHAPTER ONE

Once Upon a Time, There Was Rock

"Cuando comenzamos a nacer"

—Charly Garcia

"Canta palabras, canta y se torna luz"

—Luis Alberto Spinetta

Rock music in Argentina began as an "imposed" phenomenon. Cultural industry producers saw a business opportunity in Argentina, a new market for rock. At first, they imported rock from elsewhere, before pushing a local version that closely adhered to the same mass-market models. Yet it appears that these apparently cynical investments in manufacturing a local scene overlooked what would prove to be Argentine rock's most valuable assets: the feelings and creativity of a whole generation. The outstanding popularity of the film *Rock Around the Clock* in 1957, as well as Bill Haley's successful visit to Buenos Aires,[1] confirmed that a wide audience existed for this new genre. Less predictably, what started as a commercial enterprise would soon transform into a political arena. The market opened for local musicians who embraced the rock phenomenon, but most of these youngsters would soon distance themselves from the entertainment industry and the translated versions of Anglo hits. Instead, as this volume will demonstrate, they composed songs that told the stories of a generation of people living under repression, in circumstances where the freedom of the 1960s in the Anglo world was just a dream for the Argentine youth. Crucially, this repression would make the lyrics of Argentine rock unique. Their complex, coded nature meant a whole new language that drew on sophisticated literary devices was created, transforming rock into a means of resistance and the songs themselves into small, ingenious works of art.

---

1 Victor Pintos, *Tanguito. La verdadera historia* (Buenos Aires: Planeta, 1993), p. 32.

For these reasons and others, while the origins of Anglo rock have some bearing on the emergence of Argentine rock, in telling the story of rock in Argentina it is vitally important to take steps towards decolonising cultural studies. The Anglo-centric study of rock, which flies in the face of rock ideology's emergence in many different parts of the world, may have contributed to Bob Dylan's Nobel Literary Prize win in 2016. While this win was undoubtedly well-deserved, it highlighted the troubling fact that many outstanding lyricists whose songs are not sung in English were overlooked. To name only Latin American composers, Chico Buarque (Brazil), Silvio Rodríguez (Cuba), and Luis Alberto Spinetta (Argentina) would have been serious—even, perhaps, more deserving—contenders. If all other languages in which rock songs have been written were taken into consideration, the list would be lengthy.

Moreover, in the Spanish-language version of his book *De la cultura rock* (2012), Claude Chastagner contends that, starting in the 1960s, Argentina became a major rock music scene in Latin America, one of the first to break free from the Anglo influence.[2] Chastagner goes even further and suggests a reverse influence, that of Latin American music on Anglo-Saxon hegemonic rock.[3] Indeed, as we will see in the present volume, Argentina has contributed an outstanding case of resistance through popular music, providing a riveting example of what can happen when freedom of expression is crushed. Unlike their counterparts in the UK and US, young Argentine rock musicians were forced to find ways to express themselves in a hostile, repressive environment. In fact, and perhaps surprisingly—certainly in direct contrast to the censors' aims—censorship fuelled an enormous amount of high-level creativity among rock musicians. Unexpected, sometimes-startling results came out of the game of cat and mouse that the musicians played with the censors, the many twists and turns of which will be explored in Chapter 7.

Undoubtedly, the origins of rock in Argentina were associated with the cultural industry and massive consumption of a youth-targeted type of music. At that early stage in the 1950s, this music was not yet known as "rock" but as "música beat", and it occupied a peripheral, marginal position.[4] The process of differentiation from commercial, manufactured rock, started by the musicians who would found the basis for Argentine rock, became more visible in the 1970s, when the word "movement" emerged as a self-descriptor employed by the youth involved.[5]

Some rock historians pinpoint the origins of Argentine rock to the mid-1950s, when Eddie Pequenino's performances, as well as a new generation of artists who had begun to popularise rhythm and blues and rock and

---

2 Claude Chastagner, *De la cultura rock* (Buenos Aires: Paidós, 2012), p. 11.
3 Chastagner, *De la cultura rock*, p. 12.
4 Claudio Díaz, *Libro de viajes y extravíos: un recorrido por el rock argentino, 1965–1985* (Unquillo: Narvaja, 2005), p. 35.
5 Díaz, *Libro de viajes y extravíos*, pp. 35–36.

roll, were gaining traction. As was simultaneously happening in the US and the UK, new social actors emerged in the Southern Hemisphere in the form of young people who were dissatisfied with the establishment and who had started to create new codes of identification that included this nascent music genre. Yet in Argentina, the process by which rock and roll developed into a form of expression for the youth was markedly different. In this case, rock and roll did not evolve from pre-existent forms of popular song, but instead started out as a commercial opportunity seized upon by the record companies, which inaugurated a new market for what they labelled "progressive music". Local producers, motivated by the success of Anglo musicians, wanted to replicate the models that had proved so lucrative abroad.

In this context, the new "rock business" started in Argentina with *El Club del Clan*, a TV show that featured performances by the first singers of rock songs in Spanish. That new movement was called "nueva ola" and then "música beat".[6] Broadcast between 1962 and 1964, *El Club del Clan* assiduously tailored its content to the middle-class audience that would purchase the company label's records, which made for pop stars and pop songs that were exceedingly manufactured. Song lyrics generally revolved around trivial themes, romance, and fun dance moves.[7] The youth were now divided into two camps: "rockers", who shared hippie and vanguardist ideals, and *"chetos"*, consumers from the middle and upper classes.

Yet in the existing bibliography about the origin of rock in Argentina, most authors coincide in pointing out a completely different phenomenon. This phenomenon is far removed from commercial opportunity, and its aesthetics part significantly from those of the Anglo models, inaugurating a novel formulation of rock music based on the construction of codes and ideological concepts. Perhaps surprisingly, those authors' views are not incongruent with the fact that rock music had thoroughly commercial beginnings in Argentina, or that local artists embraced the genre by performing local versions of Anglo hits. This aesthetics of encryption and ideology emerged in response to the political context. "Authentic" and original bands followed on from those strategic attempts to manufacture a commercial product, and these bands were a genuine expression of the youth, complete with a unique language. This was not just the Spanish language, but a system of metaphors, allegories, nonsense, and play on words that would not only distinguish the genre, but also enabled dissidence in censorship conditions, as we will see in the next chapters.

In order to explore the conditions that gave rise to the particularities of Argentine rock, it is essential to understand a three-fold crisis that shook the country. Díaz describes it as a *hegemony crisis* that took place in different

---

6 Díaz, *Libro de viajes y extravíos*, pp. 17–19.
7 For example, "Despeinada" by Palito Ortega was about how messy his girlfriend's hair looked. Sung by Violeta Rivas, "Qué suerte" was about a lucky night for a girl longing to meet the boy she liked.

but interrelated spheres. The most important was the increasing loss of legitimacy suffered by previous governments through their failure to unite the population, which, affected by repression, had become divided along ideological lines. Compounding this was the chronic underfunding that was damaging various cultural expressions, as well as the censorship constraints impacting literature production. In sum, he contends that in the 1960s, the homogenising discourse in nationalistic fictions was replaced by historiographical debate. People no longer accepted "one" truth; instead, they started to question perceptions of the past and the present that circulated among society.[8]

As we will see, young people in Argentina were at the forefront of this questioning of perceptions. They found a very particular, very sophisticated way to express themselves. Because the political context during the 1960s and 1970s was one of censorship and persecution of the youth, rock songs came to adopt a unique style and to work as a real "weapon of the weak". This secret weapon was fashioned from coded language in the form of metaphors, allegories, nonsense, and irony. It would prove extraordinarily successful. In Claudio Díaz's view, "it was music for the youth, made by the youth, but this time it did not talk about love, it wasn't fun, and in many cases it wasn't even music to dance to".[9]

The pioneers who defied language

The first rock bands in Argentina in the 1960s still sang most of their songs in English.[10] Luis Alberto Spinetta (1950–2012), one of the country's first rock musicians, explained in an interview that rock sung in Spanish was not considered of high quality at the time, as it risked comparison with music performed on *El Club del Clan*, which was, to borrow his term, "crap". In other words, to sing in the "language of The Beatles" was a way to project an image of quality and style.[11]

Argentine rock, a genre that was striving to differentiate itself from "música beat", started to be referred to as such in 1965.[12] According to Polimeni, on 2 June 1966, the main members of the band Los Beatniks, Pajarito Zaguri and Moris Biravent, persuaded the general director of an international record company that it was worth recording a few rock songs in Spanish. The executive thought they were referring to new translations of

---

8 Díaz, *Libro de viajes y extravíos*, p. 32.
9 Díaz, *Libro de viajes y extravíos*, p. 21.
10 Sergio Pujol, *Las ideas del rock: genealogía de la música rebelde* (Rosario: Homo Sapiens Ediciones, 2007), p. 169.
11 Juan Carlos Diez, *Martropía: conversaciones con Spinetta* (Buenos Aires: Aguilar, 2006), p. 170.
12 Silvia Kurlat Ares, "El lenguaje de la tribu: los códigos del rock," *Revista iberoamericana* 73: 267–86, 2007, at p. 267.

Anglophone rock songs, but they explained that they meant new Argentine songs.[13] Thanks to this conversation, Los Beatniks became the first band to record an Argentine rock single with a major label. They recorded two songs: "Rebelde" (The Rebel) and "No finjas más" (Stop Pretending).[14] Argentine rock journalist Miguel Grinberg recalls his first impression of Los Beatniks when he saw them perform live: "[Theirs was] a vigorous way to make music that had something different: it was replete with reality".[15] "Replete with reality" references, at least in part, the fact that the songs were in a language the audience could understand and engage with. This was the first revolution: a change of language, which was also a *toma de posesión*, or a marking of territory. Musicians were making rock music in Argentina. They were making it for Argentines, about Argentine reality. It followed that the language needed to be the local vernacular. The objective, as Grinberg explains, was not to seize the political power of the country; it was to seize the creative power of a whole generation.[16]

Little by little, Argentine rock carved out a new space. It had a clear countercultural identity and an ideology that distinguished it from other South American youth genres of the time. Its countercultural identity can be chiefly attributed to the cultural and socio-political conditions out of which the music genre arose. A new generation of pop artists were questioning reality through their vanguardist productions and ideas, in part because, during the relatively short 1963–66 democratic government of Arturo Illia, the arts were given the chance to flourish at universities such as the University of Buenos Aires (UBA) and educational institutions such as Instituto Di Tella. These pop artists' work was "replete with reality" too, though it was a reality that was expressed through alternative modes of representation that included surrealism. And a new local sound was developing within that context. While it took its aesthetic cues from Anglo rock, Argentine rock came to incorporate local flavours and rhythms and, vitally, it embraced a new way of writing song lyrics. This second and most important language revolution was one of coded lyrics, with rock lyricists drawing on rhetorical strategies such as metaphor, allegory, nonsense, and surrealism to embed a multiplicity of meanings in their songs. This encouraged great freedom of interpretation, and it meant that the audience was called on to play an active role in meaning making. This multiplicity of meanings meant that Argentine rock was no longer simply "replete with reality" but rather replete with *multiple, alternative* realities.

The artists and musicians of the era frequented Buenos Aires bars La Cueva and La Perla. While they were labelled "hippies" and adhered to the

---

13 Carlos Polimeni, *Bailando sobre los escombros: historia crítica del rock latinoamericano* (Buenos Aires: Editorial Biblos, 2002).
14 Los Beatniks, *Rebelde / No finjas más* (Columbia Records, 1966).
15 Grinberg, *Cómo vino*, p. 48.
16 Grinberg, *Cómo vino*, p. 8.

international movement, they preferred a local name: *náufragos*, or castaways, a term that referenced their lifestyle—they would "crash" (or shipwreck) in one place for a few days, then move along to the next. Castaways sported necklaces, denim, and colourful clothes, and they subscribed to the free-love lifestyle.[17] Men were identified by their long hair,[18] a feature that would soon count as reason enough to be escorted to a police station for the night, where their hair would be forcibly cut. Eventually, the term "castaway" became popular enough that it replaced "hippie".[19]

Between 1955 and 1983, Argentina experienced a long period of political instability. Aside from a few democratic interruptions (Arturo Frondizi's government in 1959 and Arturo Umberto Illia's in 1963), for three decades the country was governed by dictatorship regimes committed to eliminating Peronism from the political landscape.[20] International events, including the Cuban Revolution led by the Argentine Che Guevara in 1959, fuelled political polarisation in a society already divided along Peronist and anti-Peronist lines. The "Revolución Libertadora" (1955–58) was a de facto government, followed by the elected president, Arturo Frondizi. Some of his political decisions, such as meeting Che Guevara personally on his arrival to his native land, not supporting the economic blockading of Cuba, and his friendship with the Peronist Party, generated discomfort in the military forces. The 1963 elections brought Arturo Illia to the presidency. He faced a strong opposition, and on 29 June 1966, a new coup d'état installed Juan Carlos Onganía as de facto president. With the excuse that they "threaten[ed] the values of the Argentine people", this new dictatorship persecuted the castaways. Long-haired young men were imprisoned and humiliated, while young women were taken for a "proper measurement" of the length of their miniskirts, in an effort to combat what was considered "pornography".[21]

Late one night in 1967, local artist Tanguito played the first line of a song he had been working on. In the restrooms of La Perla bar, he showed it to fellow musician Litto Nebbia:[22] "I am abandoned in this crappy world…".

---

17 Grinberg, *Cómo vino*, p. 71.
18 Grinberg, *Cómo vino*, p. 61.
19 Juan Ignacio Provéndola, *Rockpolitik: 50 años de rock nacional y sus vínculos con el poder político Argentino* (Buenos Aires: Eudeba, 2015), p. 64.
20 Peronism (named after Perón) is a political party that is now one of the principal ones in Argentina. It is based on leftist ideas, social justice, economic independence, and political sovereignty, and positions itself as opposed to capitalism.
21 Horacio Delbueno, "Rock nacional: rebelde me llama la gente. Contexto sociohistórico," in *Yo no permito: rock y ética en Argentina durante la última dictadura*, by Ramón Sanza Ferramola and Horacio Belbueno, 9–32 (San Luis: Nueva Editorial Universitaria, 2009), p. 23.
22 Juan Carlos Kreimer, Carlos Polimeni, Guillermo Pintos, and Gustavo Álvarez Núñez, *Ayer nomás: 40 años de rock en la Argentina* (Buenos Aires: Musimundo, 2006), pp. 24–25.

Nebbia grabbed the guitar and started singing some lines, modifying them and adding others. That was the birth of "La balsa" (The Raft).[23] It was a song as a "raft", constructed by two castaways to describe the feeling of their generation:

> Estoy muy solo y triste acá en este mundo abandonado
> tengo una idea, es la de irme al lugar que yo más quiera
> me falta algo para ir, pues, caminando yo no puedo
> construiré una balsa y me iré a naufragar
> tengo que conseguir mucha madera
> tengo que conseguirla de donde pueda,
> y cuando mi balsa esté lista partiré hacia la locura
> con mi balsa yo me iré a naufragar

> I feel so lonely and sad here in this abandoned world.
> I have an idea: I want to go to the place I like best
> I can't go on foot, I need some means of transport
> I'll build a raft to sail away and shipwreck
> I need to find lots of wood, from wherever
> When my raft is ready, I'll sail away to madness
> On my raft, I'll sail away and shipwreck

The song was released on 3 July 1967.[24] An instant hit, 250,000 copies of the single were sold in one year, which was a sales record at the time. According to Kreimer and colleagues, part of the song's success was due to the line "On my raft, I'll sail away and shipwreck" because young Argentines identified strongly with it.[25] The castaways had their first bonding hymn, a song that united them all in a generational feeling.

The foundational metaphor of "the raft", as well as its association with the castaway movement, would set the tone for most Argentine rock songs written from that point forward. The metaphors that comprised this allegorical song invited an array of interpretations. What was the raft, exactly? It could have been an idea, or a drug, or exile, or music. It could have been each of these things but, more than anything, it was the start of a coded language in rock, a new means of communication. This first Argentine rock hit would pave the

---

23 Los Gatos, *La balsa / Ayer nomás* (TNT, 1967).
24 "The composition of La Balsa was surrounded by a certain mystery. It is known that it was written in the Perla del Once bar by Litto Nebbia and Tanguito. However, different voices took care to spread divergent legends and various anecdotes about the way and the moment in which it was created. Those narrations and the premature and never fully clarified death of Tanguito contributed to turning it into a mythical text": see Cecilia Flachland, *Desarma y sangra. Rock, política y nación* (Buenos Aires: Casa Nova Editores, 2015), p. 30.
25 Kreimer et al., *Ayer nomás*, p. 26.

way for a plethora of songs to come, in part because the political context was about to deteriorate even further.

Though the new music found an increasing number of sympathisers among mainstream listeners, the authorities did not look upon it quite so favourably. Added to this, not all the youth were "castaways". In October 1967, a group of Catholic and nationalistic young people, at a roundtable organised in a bookstore, decried Argentine hippies as easy targets for communism and zionism.[26] They demanded that the SIDE (State Intelligence Service) publish documents about the activities of these "corrupted" youths. In January 1968, the FAEDA (Argentine Federation of Anti-communist Democratic Entities) publicly declared in a parade down Buenos Aires' main street that they were against hippies because they were how communism was infiltrating the country.

Indeed, there was a noticeably clear trend of connecting the "música beat" movement to the infiltration of communism, even though, in those times, other genres such as nueva canción Argentina were much more political. Argentine rock was interested in broader issues, such as the "system", freedom, human rights, and love. It was a countercultural movement, inspired by Anglo rock. Yet the political context and censorship obliged musicians to continue to shape their lyrics in a sophisticated, coded way. That is what would come to distinguish Argentine rock from the rock that came into being in the rest of the world.

The process of negotiation between the musicians and the producers began. In Luis Alberto Spinetta's band, for example, one of the guidelines was to sing in both Spanish and English, though soon the Spanish language would take over the country's rock territory without so much as a backward glance.

Though the late 1960s were years of freedom in some parts of the world, it was a time of repression for the Argentine youth. Miguel Abuelo (1946–88) was singing "throw away your armour, to be as light as the air means you are not thinking. Everything that ties you up is your murderer, all that is tying you up is not peace" ["Ya arroja tu armadura, ser el aire no es pensar. Todo lo que ata es asesino, todo lo que ata no es la paz"] ("Oye niño", 1968).[27] This was his way of asserting that the "peace" promoted in the official discourse was, in fact, a fallacy. "To be as light as the air" and avoid thinking indicated the lightness of the "nueva ola" songs performed on *El Club del Clan*,[28] the literary content of which was trivial entertainment. "Tying you up" alluded to repression and warned the listener about the killings that

26 Provéndola, *Rockpolitik*, p. 61.
27 Miguel Abuelo, *Los solistas de Mandioca* (Talent, 1970).
28 *El Club del Clan* was an Argentinean musical television program from the 1960s, which was broadcasted in several Latin American countries (with local versions being made in some of them). The program brought together a group of pop singers who sang in Spanish (something unusual for the time) and achieved enormous popularity.

were already happening by 1968. "Being the air" meant surviving without asking questions, living in a cloud of lies, "not thinking". This same idea of "lightness" and poor commitment was expressed in the song "Mariposas de madera" (Wooden Butterflies),[29] in which Abuelo sings: "butterfly with wings of water, do not try to escape, when I look for you I can't find you, when I find you, you are not there" ["Mariposas de alas de agua no te quieras escapar. Si te busco no te encuentro, cuando te encuentro no estás"] (1970). This poetic line, with its surrealist images, describes a devastating feeling of emptiness, of feeling lost in a context that was as terrifying as it was uncertain. The poetic voice yearns for freedom through the symbolic image of the butterfly, though its wings are not flight-efficient: made of wood or water, they are either heavy or intangible.

Luis Alberto Spinetta also mentioned freedom in his songs, and his poetry was, like Miguel Abuelo's, concerned with the education of the youth and the need to liberate them from the constraints of a repressive system. In his song "Todas las hojas son del viento" (All Leaves Belong to the Wind)[30] he gives advice on bringing up children. He suggests looking after children's minds, preserving them from drugs and never repressing them. The metaphor he uses for the title and lyrics of the song compares a person to a leaf on a tree, powerless against the wind. The powerful wind can change its strength, its direction, and its consequences while, conversely, the leaf is at the wind's mercy, helplessly hanging from the tree, unable to choose its own direction. This metaphorical image is perhaps representative of a sample of society and the context of the moment. The tree can be interpreted as the community; the leaves, its members; and the wind, the power that rules uncontrollably. All we can do is look after the leaves, or the children, as best we can; the rest is beyond our control. We will return to Spinetta and his songs in later chapters.

The 1970s: The arena becomes violent

Onganía's de facto presidency weakened and the military forces replaced him with Roberto Levingston, in the first instance, and, nine months later, with Alejandro Lanusse. Meanwhile, Juan Domingo Perón was negotiating his return to the country, and the military were trying to assure a smooth transition back to democracy. Between 1968 and 1970, the two main guerrilla groups, the ERP (Popular Revolutionary Army) and the Montoneros, among others, started readying themselves for what would turn out to be social and political chaos.[31] The 1970s became a violent political arena, and rock concerts were the main target of raids and anti-guerrilla operations. High numbers of attendees were detained as "suspects". This situation inspired

---

29 Miguel Abuelo, *Buen día, día* (Interdisc, 1984).
30 Pescado Rabioso, *Artaud* (Talent, 1973).
31 Provéndola, *Rockpolitik*, p. 72.

many songs in which the youth expressed feeling unjustly repressed and persecuted.

In 1970, Moris (1942–), a former founding member of Los Beatniks, released his solo album *30 minutos de vida* (30 Minutes of Life).[32] The title of the LP seemed to indicate that "life" was to be found in rock music, because in the "real" world there was persecution and death. The album contains several seminal songs in Argentine rock. "El oso" (The Bear) is an allegory in which a bear and a tiger, captives in a circus, lament their sad lives entertaining the audience. One day the bear manages to escape and become free again. The second song, "Ayer nomás" (Just Yesterday), was the original version of the same song, which had been modified due to censorship restraints in order to be included on a single with his band Los Gatos (1967). Among the remaining six songs on the album, two of them are outstanding. "De nada sirve" (There's No Point)—7:43 minutes long—was a sort of existentialist manifesto delivered in a stream-of-consciousness style, a flow of ideas and feelings in which the poetic voice claims there is no point escaping oneself, and feels trapped in this world, with no way out. Gender is also a topic that was defied in some songs in Argentine rock, from its early days. "Escúchame entre el ruido" (Listen to Me amid the Noise) is probably the first song in Argentine rock that discusses masculinity. Besides criticising society, education, and the establishment in general, the song makes a strong stand against sexism. It denounces the "macho" culture that indicates that "to be a man" one cannot cry, must use women as objects, and must engage in fights. This is probably one of the first songs in Argentine rock to discuss sexism and less rigid performances of gender, something that, in a conservative country in the early 1970s, was adventurous and risky. In sum, *30 minutos de vida* was certainly "replete with reality": it was a reality that a whole generation claimed as their own, and a philosophy of life that distanced itself from the hegemonic culture.

The subscribers to this new philosophy of life continued to grow in numbers. Rock music festivals increased in popularity. The first "Acusticazo" (1972) is today considered historic and was held in the Teatro Atlantic, which has since been demolished. Performers at the festival included Litto Nebbia, León Gieco, David Lebón, Raúl Porchetto, Edelmiro Molinari, and one of the first female voices, Gabriela. The BA Rock Festival in 1972 was quite different from the festivals that would come in later years. It was a peaceful concert and the police were nonplussed about the hippies who attended, not viewing them as troublemakers. These were the years of daytime outdoor concerts, which, as rock musician Miguel Cantilo recalls, were spaces of relaxation and non-reaction.[33] Yet after 1973, there was clear intent to politicise these concerts and, consequently, things changed. The Peronist Party

---

32 Moris, *30 minutos de vida* (TNT, 1970).
33 Ezequiel Abalos, *Historias del Rock de Acá: primera generación* (Buenos Aires: Editora AC, 1995), p. 128.

that was in power in 1973 organised a concert at the Argentino Juniors Soccer Club with the intention of creating a connection between rock and politics. They were unsuccessful, as rockers such as Cantilo refused to be associated with the government. When the government realised it could not use rock as part of its politics, it decided to fight it.[34] In 1973, Luis Alberto Spinetta wrote a manifesto and handed it out in printed form at three concerts where he performed. The text was also published in *Rolanroc*, a short-lived newspaper, in 1974. In his manifesto, Spinetta made clear that Argentine rock "was born from an instinct" and expressed Argentine rock ideology in clear terms:

> Rock is not just a certain rhythm or melody. It is the natural impulse to elucidate, through a total liberation, the deep knowledge that the average man is otherwise unable to access because of repression. Rock dies only for those who always tried to replace that instinct with expressions of the superficial. As such, what comes from them still carries repression, and only stimulates external and counterrevolutionary change.[35]

In his manifesto, Spinetta, who would become one of the most important leaders of the rock movement in Argentina (see Chapter 9), insisted on the deep internal change that, in his view, rock music facilitated. He highlighted that "superficial" forms of expression could only bring about repression and therefore only stimulated external change. For him, the only valid change should be an internal one, and he was not interested in politics but in larger, broader issues. However, most Argentines were deeply interested in politics. In fact, the 1970s were highly political times in Argentina. There was a brief return to democracy in 1973. The dictatorship called Revolución Argentina was over, and Héctor Cámpora was elected president, only to resign a few months later when Juan Domingo Perón returned to Argentina from his exile. The formula Perón–Perón was a winning combination in the new elections, with Juan D. Perón as president and his wife, María Estela Martínez, better known as "Isabelita", as vice-president. Perón died in 1974 and subsequently his wife became the first female president in history. The polarisation of the left and the right reached new heights and the Anti-communist Argentine Alliance (AAA)[36] became an extreme right-wing paramilitary group that prosecuted and killed hundreds of artists, politicians, and intellectuals who spoke out against the government.[37] Those were days of repression, violence,

---

34 Cantilo in Abalos, *Historias del Rock*, p. 128.
35 Juan Bautista Duizeide, *Luis Alberto Spinetta: el lector kamikaze* (Buenos Aires, 2017), p. 34.
36 Minister López Rega, Isabelita's right hand, was the leader of this group.
37 According to official statistics, between 1973 and 1976, during democratic times, 1,358 people were killed: 66 were military officials, 136 were state policemen, 34 were federal policemen, 677 were civilians, and 445, according to their labelling, were "subversives". See Eduardo Blaustein, and Martín Zubieta, *Decíamos ayer: la prensa argentina bajo el Proceso* (Buenos Aires: Colihue, 2006), pp. 88–89; this volume

bombs, killings, and censorship; the country descended into a state of utter chaos. Miguel Abuelo's song "Tirando piedras al río" (Throwing Stones into the River)[38] represented the general mood accurately, though in a highly coded way:

> No todas son rosas en el campo del rey
> No todas las rosas del campo son del rey
> No todos los reyes saben mucho sobre rosas
> No todas las rosas quieren saber de algún rey.
>
> Not every flower is a rose in the king's land
> Not every rose in the land is the king's
> Not every king knows much about roses
> Not every rose wants to have much to do with the king.

In the song, roses and kings do not have a great relationship. The metaphor of "the king" can be straightforwardly interpreted as a wielder of power. "The roses"—vulnerable, pure, beautiful—perhaps stand for the people. While there is only one king, the plural form of "roses" seems to indicate the masses, the "*pueblo*". The first line of this stanza signals that some of the members of the government were corrupt, or worse; the second points out people's autonomy and freedom of choice; the third warns about how disconnected from reality and everyday life some members of the government had become; and the final one reminds the audience that there were many people who did not subscribe to Perón's politics, as well as potentially pointing to the anarchist movement of the time. In these few lines of the song, by playing on the relationship between just two symbols, the concepts of corruption, freedom, ignorance, and anarchism are thematised. The song title hinted at how the audience should interpret the lyrics: when one throws a stone into the river, it produces ripples, waves, movement. Miguel Abuelo's song was indeed trying to create ripples in the political landscape of the convulsed Argentina of the 1970s.

According to Díaz, the bands that would eventually be considered the pioneers of Argentine rock gave a strong impression of breaking the mould of the industry, and they staged a generational confrontation with social rules and institutions. This rupture and this confrontation gave rock its foundations. It was an attitude that generated the conditions of its progressive marginality. In fact, even though there was a major first sales success with Los Gatos, it would take until the 1980s for similar successes to occur. The reception that the first rockers helped generate came from a faithful but

---

is a vast compilation of newspaper and magazine articles, covers, and quotes that comprises the main press outlets during the time of the dictatorship, 1976–83. In the present study, we are referring to those reproductions often, as a source of useful and reliable information.

38 Miguel Abuelo & Nada, *Miguel Abuelo & Nada* (Moshe-Naïm, 1975).

small audience, and for years the rebellious attitude of the earliest rock meant they were sanctioned by the industry in the form of exclusion from radio and television broadcasting, limited editions, and some censorship.[39]

Among the pioneer bands, the next chapter will explore the lyrics of the albums of the first two bands that made the greatest impact: Sui Generis and Almendra, fronted by Charly García and Luis Alberto Spinetta respectively. Throughout this book, we will revisit the songs by these two main musicians, whose output is considered the most outstanding in Argentine rock.

Let's explore, then, how poetic language started to animate the lyrics of rock songs in Argentina, in the hands of its main representatives.

---

39 Díaz, *Libro de viajes y extravíos*, p. 28.

CHAPTER TWO

Then, There Was Poetry
The Pioneer Musicians and Their Lyrics

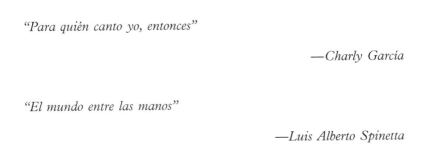

"*Para quién canto yo, entonces*"

—*Charly García*

"*El mundo entre las manos*"

—*Luis Alberto Spinetta*

Titans of Argentine rock Charly García and Luis Alberto Spinetta only ever composed one song together. "Rezo por vos" (I Pray for You)[1] was part of a larger project that they abandoned after being rattled by a freak event. A clue to that event is buried in the song itself, in the curious line, "I burnt my curtains and I burst into flames for your love" ["Y quemé las cortinas y me encendí de amor"]. One day, Spinetta and García were at a TV studio recording the song when an assistant burst in to tell Charly his apartment was on fire.[2] Apparently, a recorder that the two had left on had short circuited, causing the nearby curtains to go up in flames. Somewhere between excitement and desperation, Spinetta lamented that the whole thing was his fault, to which Charly responded, "Shut up, idiot!", throwing an ashtray at him in an effort to get him to stop feeling guilty.[3]

Yet perhaps this freak event was an excuse, rather than a reason, for Argentine rock's two most important composers to cut short their

---

1 Charly García, *Parte de la religión* (Sony BMG, 1987).
2 Laura Ramos, and Cynthia Lejbowicz, *Corazones en llamas: historias del rock argentino en los '80* (Buenos Aires: Clarin Aguilar, 1991), p. 95.
3 Roque Di Pietro, *Esta noche toca Charly: un viaje por los recitales de Charly García (1956–1993)* (Buenos Aires: Gourmet Musical Ediciones, 2017), p. 376.

collaboration.[4] While Charly's life was characterised by a lack of routine, not a few excesses, and a rock-and-roll lifestyle, Spinetta had a family and was very involved in the day-to-day upbringing of his four children. Though they admired, loved, and respected each other, their personalities and their dissimilar lifestyles probably pushed them apart.

Separately, then, García's Sui Generis and Spinetta's Almendra changed Argentine rock forever. Among the pioneers, these bands were unique in bringing poetry and sophistication to rock song lyrics. While chapters 8 and 9 will take a closer look at the particularities of these rock musicians' personas and their individual qualities, let us confine our analysis for now to the revolutionary songs of their earliest bands.

Sui Generis (1970–75)

The remarkable case of Sui Generis, while fascinating in terms of the contribution they made to Argentine music, is also an opportunity to study some of the complex processes that have taken place in Argentina's recent history.[5] Sui Generis—meaning "unique" or "in a class of its own"—is a fitting name for what was arguably the most influential band in the history of Argentina. Though there have been other musicians of importance in the same period, including Almendra, Manal, and Los Gatos, the popularity of Sui Generis was unparalleled. Indeed, it is not inappropriate to divide Argentine music into that which came before Sui Generis and that which came after, for this band marked an abrupt shift in the way language was used in popular song.

Sui Generis was born from the union of Charly García's band To Walk Spanish and Nito Mestre's The Century Indignation. The first of Charly and Nito's rock bands to record in a studio, Sui Generis would be commemorated as one of the main pioneers of Argentine rock. Two life-sized bronze statues of the members of this duet were even erected in the tourist city of Mar del Plata.

Before Charly García became widely known as a musician and influenced the popular music scene, a development that will be expanded upon in later chapters, Argentine rock was starting to forge a unique local identity. As outlined in Chapter 1, Los Gatos expanded the expressive capabilities of the simple *música beat* of the day through adding poetic metaphor, while, as we will soon see, Almendra fused the surrealist poetry of Luis Alberto Spinetta with urban music. At the time, some of the songs that Charly composed with his friend Alejandro Correa were in English; once translated

---

4 The song was recorded by Spinetta on his album *Privé* (Interdisc, 1986), and by García on his album *Parte de la religión*, released the following year. The moment when they recorded together in the studio while Charly's apartment caught fire has been documented in a demo; see Di Pietro, *Esta noche*, p. 376.
5 Julián Delgado, "El show de los muertos: música y política en el grupo de rock argentino Sui Generis," *A contracorriente* 13 (3): 18–49, 2016, at p. 21.

into Spanish, they became part of the Sui Generis repertoire. For example, "Seminare"[6]—a song that, when it was recorded years later, would become a youth anthem—contains part of a song that Charly wrote aged sixteen.[7]

Charly García composed most of Sui Generis' songs. Contrary to what is often supposed, political references in Charly's songs did not begin with the coup d'état of 1976—which was when Argentine rock reached its peak—but instead could be observed as early as his compositions for Sui Generis. In fact, his experience with military service[8] was decisive because it inspired him to write "Canción para mi muerte" (Song for My Death),[9] a song that would lead him to success with Sui Generis.[10]

In the Sui Generis era, not only the songs were political;[11] the stage was also decorated with militant slogans. Indeed, the concerts functioned as a space of dissent for young people.[12] At the time, García also wrote "Juan Represión" (Jo Repression)[13] and "Botas locas" (Mad Boots),[14] songs that, because of their explicit references to the army, would not be recorded until many years later. Yet, at times, the first chords were played at concerts, functioning as a kind of wink to the audience, a reminder of the existence of songs that could not be played. In fact, on *Adiós Sui Generis I*, which was recorded live, on track seven under the title of "Zapando con la gente" (Jamming with the People),[15] the first chords and lines of "Botas locas" and Charly's introductory phrase are heard: "This is a warning [*aviso*]: I was part of a crazy army, I was twenty years old and had very short hair, but, my friend, there was some confusion because to them I was the crazy one" ["Esto es un aviso: Yo formé parte de un ejército loco, tenía 20 años y el pelo muy corto, pero mi amigo hubo una confusión porque para ellos el loco era yo"]. This was probably a preview of an idea. The word "aviso" in Spanish has a

6 Serú Girán, *Serú Girán* (Music Hall, 1978).
7 Daniel Chirom, and Charly García, *Charly García* (Buenos Aires: Libreria y Editorial El Juglar, 1983), p. 32.
8 Until its abolition in 1994, under Carlos Menem's democratic presidency, military service was compulsory for all Argentine young males.
9 Sui Generis, *Vida* (Microfón/Sony BMG, 1972).
10 Chirom and García, *Charly García*, p. 47.
11 To read more about *rock nacional* as a resistance movement, see: Pablo Alabarces, *Entre gatos y violadores: el rock nacional en la cultura argentina* (Buenos Aires: Colihue, 1993); Néstor García Canclini, editor, *Cultura y pospolítica: el debate sobre la modernidad en América Latina* (México: Consejo Nacional para la Cultura y las Artes, 1995); Sergio Pujol, *Rock y dictadura: crónica de una generación (1976–1983)* (Buenos Aires: Booket, 2005); Pablo Vila, "Argentina's 'Rock Nacional': The Struggle for Meaning," *Latin American Music Review / Revista de música latinoamericana* 10 (1): 1–28, 1989.
12 Chirom and García, *Charly García*, p. 54.
13 Sui Generis, *Pequeñas anécdotas sobre las instituciones*.
14 Sui Generis, *Adiós Sui Generis II* (Microfón/Sony BMG, 1975).
15 Sui Generis, *Adiós Sui Generis III* (Microfón/Sony BMG, 1996 [recorded live in 1975]).

double meaning: it refers both to a warning and to an advertisement. Here, the "warning" is they censored me, and they accused me unfairly, while the "advertisement" is of a song that would be recorded in the future, predicting the end of a repression that would not last forever. Thus, the warning spoke of a "confusion" that was both sides of the same coin: the madness, fictitious or real, of both soldier Charly and military army.

Sui Generis produced three albums in three consecutive years. Five main themes can be discerned on these studio albums: a utopian view of (physical) free love; a re-examination of life experiences, including a rejection of traditional values; youth solidarity; a criticism of some institution or aspect of society (such as the bourgeoisie or marriage); and, finally, a more specifically targeted criticism of some aspect of the authoritarian regime and/or the repression it inflicted. On the first album, the distribution of themes is heavily weighted toward general anti-establishment themes, and there is no discernible reference to the political system at all. The second is more evenly weighted, and by the last of the band's three albums, a clear majority of songs reference aspects of the military–authoritarian power structure.

Vida in 1972

Their first album, *Vida* (Life),[16] released in October 1972, surprised the audience, the critics, and the market by selling 200,000 copies.[17] The band's success was partially based on the image its members projected: they were long-haired, laid-back young musicians, and they told a story with every song. Their style, in some respects resembling those of Bob Dylan, Simon & Garfunkel, and Crosby, Stills, Nash & Young, was characterised by acoustic songs with simple melodies and harmonies and a substantial poetical component.[18] The poetics in the songs of Sui Generis spoke to a generation of people who loved rock music but also had an interest in literature—European, American, and Latin American—and were hungry for meaningful lyrics. Sui Generis' songs referenced existential issues, questioned sexual repression, and expressed love and respect for freedom and beauty.

In combination, the music and lyrics of Sui Generis songs created a theatrical, but also intimate, atmosphere. Appealing directly to the sensitivity and life experience of a vast portion of the youth in Argentina at the time, their first songs spoke of folk values, everyday experiences, and the discovery of love. However, as we will see, the content of the lyrics would change over time. They would shift to the political realm and the language would become coded so that dissident messages could pass unnoticed by the censors. The

---

16 Sui Generis, *Vida*.
17 Valeria Manzano, "'Rock Nacional' and Revolutionary Politics: The Making of a Youth Culture of Contestation in Argentina, 1966–1976," *The Americas* 70 (3): 393–427, 2014, at p. 409.
18 Delgado, "El show de los muertos," p. 22.

band's experience with censorship before the 1976 coup was crucial because it meant they developed astute strategies to deal with language expression during the PRN (Process of National Reorganisation), as we will see.

As mentioned, *Vida* was released in 1972. The black-and-white photo on the album cover showed the two young band members Nito Mestre and Charly García sitting on the floor, leaning against an empty wall, as if it were a *tabula rasa*. The happy faces of both friends appeared on the back of the album, superimposed on an urban image featuring grey roofs. One of the songs included in this album, "Cuando comenzamos a nacer" (When We Begin to Be Born), emphasises the essential idea shared by teenagers trapped in a conservative education system:

> Cuando comenzamos a nacer,
> la mente empieza a comprender
> que vos sos vos y tenés vida.
> ...
> y comenzás a preguntar
> y conocés a la mentira.
>
> When we begin to be born
> Your mind starts to understand
> that you are yourself, and you have life.
> ...
> you start asking questions
> and you get to know lies.

This song poetically summarises the process of growing up and discovering the world: taking steps towards self-recognition as an individual, learning to differentiate between fantasy and reality, and encountering the world of adults. This discovery of "adolescent–adult" is accompanied by disappointments and pleasures: lies, repression, and also love.

Beside gender challenges and existential and identity issues, Sui Generis' songs reflected the convulsive atmosphere of the time. "Amigo vuelve a casa pronto" (Come Home Soon, My Friend) in a way predicts the arrival of tougher times for young people on the political stage: "We know it's going to rain hard soon, better stick together this time" ["Sabemos que pronto va a llover fuerte, mejor estemos juntos esta vez"]. While after the elections in 1973 there was a three-year democratic period, the status quo clearly pointed towards the possibility of another coup d'état.

Confesiones de invierno in 1973

After a first album that marked, in many ways, a stage of self-discovery, in the second album, *Confesiones de invierno* (Winter Confessions),[19] the tone

---

19 Sui Generis, *Confesiones de invierno* (Microfón/Sony BMG, 1973).

of the lyrics is more outward looking. Yet the cover of the album suggests a different tone: it features Juan Gatti's colourful drawing of Charly and Nito's smiling faces. The back cover depicts a landscape of clouds, a rainbow, and snow-covered hills, evocative of a dream country that the artists are loath to leave. The inside cover photo shows an idyllic scene of a group of friends sharing a picnic in the forest. "Winter" is apparently present only in the lyrics of the songs. Yet a key song sounds alarm bells, hinting that the visual art of the cover should be viewed in an ironic light: "Tribulaciones, lamentos y ocaso de un tonto rey imaginario, o no" (Tribulations, Laments, and Twilight of a Silly Imaginary King, or Maybe Not) is an anti-authoritarian allegory seemingly evocative of the French revolution.

"Tribulaciones" is certainly a complex allegory that encourages multiple interpretations. One of the characteristics of allegorical writing is the way it generates a profusion of potential readings, which, rather than cancel each other out, coexist on parallel levels.[20] On a subjective level, this song may be seen as depicting a child's fantasy world falling apart as he discovers the harsh and cruel reality of the adult world ("my mansion today is ashes" ["mi mansión hoy es cenizas"]). Charly once said that this was "an ironic song: I put myself in the place of the king".[21] Doing so would mean occupying a privileged position, since he would be living "on the top of a hill, from the palace you could see the sea" ["Vivía en la cima de la colina, desde el palacio se veía el mar"], although it would be an undeserved privilege: "I was the king of this place although I did not know it very well" ["Yo era el rey de este lugar aunque muy bien no lo conocía"]. This king could represent a teenager who lives in an ideal or fantasy world and has not yet opened his eyes to what is happening around him in a social and political sense. The arrival of "them, brutal heartless people who destroyed our world" ["Llegaron ellos, gente brutal sin corazón que destruyó el mundo nuestro"] seems to point to the destruction of idealism when it clashes with a devastating reality.

At a political level, it seems that Charly predicts what will happen a few years later with the military coup ("Until one day they came" ["hasta que un día llegaron ellos"]). The title of the song is striking, since it ends with "or maybe not", leaving the song open to meaning the very opposite of what it says. Maybe "the silly imaginary king" is not a product of the imagination or a subjective allusion, but a direct reference to the political situation of the time. "Imaginary king" could imply that power is not really in the hands of those in government but is instead a temporary arrangement. It should be remembered that while Charly's political songs are generally associated with the last military dictatorship (1976–83), this was not exclusively the case. The so-called Argentine Revolution (1966–73)—the dictatorship led by Juan Carlos Onganía (1966–70), Marcelo Levingston (1970–71), and Alejandro

---

20 Mara Favoretto, *Charly en el país de las alegorías: un viaje por las letras de Charly García* (Buenos Aires: Gourmet Musical Ediciones, 2014), pp. 159–70.
21 Chirom and García, *Charly García*, p. 54.

Lanusse (1971–73)—was in place at the time when young Charly was growing up and composing songs like this one.

Therefore, this song can be interpreted from a contrary standpoint, especially when considering the suggestive "or maybe not" of the title. The first-person narrator who tells the story could be a dictator, a "king", who foolishly used and abused his power. He ignored the hunger of his people and believed that his power had been granted to him by a superior being ("I was the divine light" ["Yo era el amor, la luz divina"]), a possible direct reading of the relationship between the church and the right-wing coup d'état. The "revolution", in this case, would be that of the people who pushed for elections in 1973 when Héctor Cámpora (1909–80) took over as president. The king in the song might be quite blurry. Is the king a fool? Is the king the real villain? Indeed, the variety and multiplicity of possible interpretations only serve to underscore the audience's freedom. Whereas freedom of speech and expression could be curtailed, nobody could monitor or control freedom of private individual thought.

Pequeñas anécdotas sobre las instituciones in 1974

The third and final album, *Pequeñas anécdotas sobre las instituciones* (Little Anecdotes about Institutions),[22] returns to a black-and-white cover. On this opportunity, Juan Gatti's drawings represent the "institutions" that the songs criticise. This time, Charly and Nito are shown without the smiling faces of the two previous albums. In one of the photos, they are standing separated, as if in mid-air, against a black background, with a timid halo of light over them. In another they appear back-to-back, in the middle of a deserted street, between old buildings with shuttered windows. Thus, the visual art of the album is loaded with anguish and signs that indicate the devastation, oppression, and atmosphere of confinement expressed in the lyrics—"there are four houses without windows" ["son cuatro casas sin ventanas"] ("Tango en segunda" [Tango in Second Gear]).

The evolution of a coded language in Argentine rock lyrics can be traced through examples from this paradigmatic album. Comparing the first versions of some of the songs Charly García composed with the heavily modified products that were eventually released reveals a shift from direct/descriptive rational discourse toward oblique/suggestive poetic discourse. The album was originally titled "Institutions". Yet the effect of pre-coup censorship was so drastic that it came to be titled using a phrase that, as indicated, translates as "Little Anecdotes about Institutions". This was Charly's tongue-in-cheek way of referring to the severely diminished content of his lyrics, which became "little anecdotes" instead of the whole stories initially intended. The album that musicians Charly García and Nito Mestre had planned did

---

22 Sui Generis, *Pequeñas anécdotas sobre las instituciones*.

not eventuate, because censorship pressure demanded numerous changes. According to the artists, this pruning had deleterious effects on the quality of what would be Argentina's first concept album. Charly García explained that the original idea was to have an array of songs referring to different institutions: there was going to be a song about the police, a song about the army, another one about the family, and so on.[23]

As a child, Charly was fascinated by Greek mythology, legends, and ancient poems such as *The Iliad* and *The Odyssey*. References to this reading are evident in his songs, especially at this stage, when the socio-political context was oppressing him. His fascination with this type of literature seems to have been the inspiration for a record where "institutions" such as marriage, censorship, and power appear parodied. The legend of the founding of Rome inspires him to think of "a she-wolf that looks after me when I start to take off" ["Así es la loba que me cuida cuando empiezo a despegar"] ("Tango en segunda"), imagining the arrival of a day of liberation. The story of Cassandra, a character from Greek mythology who is considered mad because of her capacity to predict the future, inspired one of the most outstanding songs on this album: "El tuerto y los ciegos" (The One-eyed Man and the Blindmen). This song not only refers to the ability and willingness to open our eyes to the context that surrounds us, but also talks about predicting the future: "I only tell you about those things you may miss out on" ["solo te cuento las cosas que se te pueden perder"]. In Charly's song, Cassandra is welcome although "there are only a few of us who can *still* see you" ["Aunque siempre seamos pocos los que aun te podamos ver"].

The interpretation of Charly's allegorical songs, much like Cassandra's predictions, would be delayed in time, since at first only the sharpest receivers would tune into the message and find its possible meanings. The rest would be attracted by the beauty and poetry without inquiring beyond the words' immediate connotations. Indeed, Daniel Chirom remembers that when asking Charly if the album had been financially successful, he responded that, when people listened to it, they did not like it, and it was only with the passage of time that the album began to be understood in "another way".[24] This perhaps points to the difficulty of interpreting allegorical texts. The parody in "El Show de los muertos" (The Show of the Dead) was probably not received the way it is recalled now, several decades after the death squads were killing people in the streets in Argentina. The song thematises death in several forms and timidly slips in a statement: "algo anda mal" ["there's something wrong here"]. The last song of the album, "Para quién canto yo entonces" (Who Do I Sing for, Then), clearly differentiates between us and them: "I sing for these people because I am also one of them. They write things and I provide them with melody and verse. Because when they shout, the others come, and so

---

23 Miguel Angel Dente, *Transgresores: Spinetta / García / Páez* (Buenos Aires: Distal, 2000), p. 68.
24 Chirom and García, *Charly García*, p. 61.

then they remain silent" ["Yo canto para esa gente porque también soy uno de ellos. Ellos escriben las cosas y yo les pongo melodía y verso. Si cuando gritan vienen los otros y entonces callan"]. Despite the multiplicity of interpretations and the ambiguous lyrics, it becomes quite clear that there is a "them" and "death" as signalled by "they fall silent". The weapon denouncing these acts seems to be song ("I sing for these people"). Language is probably the best, if not the only, tool against imposed language constraints.

Nowadays, language is being challenged in Argentina because of its gender limitations. Currently, across the entire Spanish-speaking world there is a move towards adopting more inclusive language. The main issue is that nouns in Spanish are saddled with a gender, and when several nouns of different gender are mentioned together, the masculine takes over as the grammatically correct choice. In recent years, different countries have developed a variety of strategies to overcome this constraint. Indeed, gender equality has become an important topic in Latin American and Spanish discussions, and Argentina is a pioneer in legislating those human rights.

Yet before the gender equality and gender identity laws (2012) and the push for an inclusive language in Argentina (2018), which came many years after Sui Generis' music, the Argentine mainstream maintained a conservative view on gender. As early as Sui Generis, young Charly had tried, with little success, to express more directly his disagreement with "what it meant to be a man" according to traditional social norms. For example, some characteristics of the male characters in Charly's songs disturbed defenders of the national "manhood". One example is "Natalio Ruiz, el hombrecito del sombrero gris" (Natalio Ruiz, the Little Guy in the Grey Hat),[25] included on this album. In addition to the suggestive diminutive "little man" used to describe him, Natalio Ruiz is a figure that is no longer: "Where are you now? What has happened to you and your little grey hat?" ["Y ¿dónde estás?, ¿a dónde has ido a parar? ¿y qué se hizo de tu sombrerito gris?"]. As a representative of past times and obsolete ideas, Natalio Ruiz—the song's protagonist—is buried in Recoleta Cemetery in Buenos Aires.

Another example of untraditional manhood is represented by Mr Jones ("Mr Jones o pequeña semblanza de una familia tipo americana" [Mr Jones or a Small Semblance of an American Family]),[26] who is a murderer. Far from being the patriarch who looks after his family, he murders his mother and his wife. In Charly García's songs, these men, grey, dumb, representatives of old ideas, or even cruel murderers, are opposed by other men, romantic, everyday heroes including the captain who "leaves his cap and serves tea with lemon" ["deja la gorra y sirve té con limón"] when his beloved Mariel arrives ("Mariel y el capitán" [Mariel and the Captain]).[27] The Captain not only serves his lover tea instead of the other way around, he also takes off his cap, a symbol

---

25 Sui Generis, *Vida*.
26 Sui Generis, *Confesiones de invierno*.
27 Sui Generis, *Vida*.

of rank on the hierarchical power scale. Serving tea is perhaps significantly less representative of an assertive manhood than serving a glass of whiskey.

Sui Generis was unique. Their songs are now part of the popular canon in Argentine music. These songs are widely known by several generations, and it is not uncommon to see parents, children, and even grandchildren singing some of them together at family events. These songs became anthems that everybody sang at school camps, friends' parties, and Christmas family celebrations. The popularity they garnered had to do with their poetry, their music and the shared feeling of community and belonging experienced by a politically embattled generation.

Almendra (1968–71)

Luis Alberto Spinetta (1950–2012) was an eccentric and charismatic artist. He was one of the foremost pioneers of Argentine rock in the late 1960s, and was an advocate of singing rock in Spanish. Talking about that time with Juan Carlos Diez, he explains that music

> brought people together in a new language, in a new way of capturing the Argentine reality. It wasn't that a strategy was devised to demolish a certain cultural structure; instead, it was the consequence of people coming together. Ethically, people felt connected enough to listen not only to Almendra but to the bands and soloists of the time, and to give themselves the pleasure of attending festivals to listen to their favourite bands. All together they gathered and started enjoying events that had no precedents here in Argentina.[28]

Without a doubt, Spinetta was an eclectic artist who participated actively in this era in various ways: with his drawings, his music, his lyrics, his performances on stage, his manifesto, his ideas, and his commitment to respecting himself as an artist, which was an ethical example for many. "El Flaco", as he was to be called, believed in the revolution of eclecticism. For him, "we need to generate a creative maelstrom that destroys all boundaries" ["tiene que crearse una vorágine creativa que rompa con todo"].[29]

The first song recorded by Spinetta's first band, Almendra, on their 1968 single, was "Tema de Pototo" (Pototo's Song),[30] in which the poetic voice takes loneliness as its subject, comparing it to a feeling of emptiness. Its lyrics are accessible, with clear analogies. The second song introduces more encrypted, unpredictable lyrics, and in them the audience is invited to glimpse some of this artist's life philosophy. Of course, for the song to convey meaning, the audience must actively participate in its interpretation: "Where are you and the roses? And why do you want so much time to wither? I have

---

28 Luis Alberto Spinetta in Diez, *Martropía*, p. 183.
29 Grinberg, *Cómo vino*, p. 110.
30 Almendra, *Tema de Pototo / El mundo entre las manos* (RCA, 1968).

asked the wind to tell you: there is little time left, it can wither" ["Y tú y las rosas dónde están? Y tú ¿por qué quieres que marchite tanto tiempo? He mandado al viento a decirte, queda poco tiempo, puede marchitarlo"] ("El mundo entre las manos" [The World in Our Hands]). The play on words involving the wind, time, and what withers, which is conjugated in first- and second-person singular, is quite confusing, but at the same time it clarifies that both voices (I and you) perceive time in a subjective way: while for one there is "so much" time, for the other, time is scarce ("there is little").

The role of the audience, then, is active, because, as Spinetta would later state in his 1973 manifesto, he is convinced that "whoever receives this must definitely understand that projects on Argentine rock are born out of instinct".[31] Instinct is human beings' purest and most elemental quality. To be born from "an instinct" overrides any filter, philosophy, idealism, system, or government. Instead, it implies that "being" depends exclusively on individual freedom. It is clear then that Spinetta considers his music a raw, visceral expression, which must be received and interpreted in the same way, and in a free and active way.

The second single (also 1968) included "Hoy todo el hielo en la ciudad" (Today All the Ice in the City),[32] a song that has rebellious and political connotations, where the poetic voice's distant position, as an observer, is clear. The metaphors used come from nature (ice covers the city):

> Cuando la luz ya no puede llegar
> la gente en vano se pone a rezar
> no es el diluvio, no es el infierno
> voy a perforar el hielo
> voy a remontarme al cielo
> para observar hoy todo el hielo en la ciudad.

> When the light can no longer reach us
> people begin to pray in vain.
> It's not the flood, it's not hell
> I will pierce the ice
> I'm going to rise up to the sky
> So I can observe all the ice in the city today.

The reference to the political context is almost impossible to ignore, the atmosphere is so disastrous that it is compared to flood and hell (biblical images) while the people pray "in vain". We know that the role of the church's leadership, very close to the government of the time, was questionable. The poetic voice is detached from the rest of society and "rise[s] up to heaven" to observe from a distance "the ice" that freezes, paralyses, and immobilises fellow citizens. Then, even before his first long-play album, the young

---

31 Luis Alberto Spinetta in Grinberg, *Cómo vino*, p. 110.
32 Almendra, *Hoy todo el hielo en la ciudad / Campos verdes* (RCA, 1968).

Spinetta clearly expresses that his intention is to "pierce the ice and rise up to the sky", objectives from which he would not depart throughout his entire artistic career, and which he invites us to share.

The cover of Almendra's first album is today a symbol for Argentine rockers, an icon that needs no further reference.[33] The drawing of a sad clown, dressed in pink, with a plunger on his head, apparently trying to extract something from his brain, and with its cold red nose, probably caused by that "ice in the city", was by Luis Alberto Spinetta himself. This anguished visage included the word "Almond" on the clown's shirt, which seemed to bring a little sweet energy to his sad look.

This album contains one of the songs for which Spinetta is best known, with romantic poetic images and a surrealist tinge. The song is about a girl who has paper eyes, rayon skin, honey breasts, a chalk heart, and a sparrow's voice, and suggests not running to her because "your time is today" ("Muchacha ojos de papel" [Paper Eyes Girl]). Surrealist poetry continues in "Color humano" (Human Colour): "cotton seas without tides" ["mares de algodón sin mareas"]. According to this song, "we do not know what a human being is today" ["somos seres humanos sin saber lo que es hoy un ser humano"] and it is precisely through unimaginable images that subvert reality that humans will be able to wake up, "sublimating ourselves" ["sublimándonos"] and letting ourselves be carried away by those cotton seas that are not governed by the tides but, instead, defy physical laws.

Continuing with the same socio-political climate that was glimpsed in a song called "Hombres de hielo" (Ice Men), the songs that follow allude to repression. "Figuración" (Figuration) empathises with those who go out on the street and "lose their minds" ["pierden la cabeza"]: they are no longer "men" even though "the world continues under the sun… everything goes on under the sun…. There are trees just as yesterday… streets as yesterday… lights as yesterday" ["el mundo sigue bajo el sol, todo bajo el sol, debajo del sol… calles como ayer, luces como ayer"]. The world is described as something real and immutable.

That same feeling of devastation and loneliness in the middle of an unwelcoming city is described in "Ana no duerme" (Ana Doesn't Sleep). The protagonist of this song entertains herself by doing impossible activities such as touching her shadow and playing "with nothing" ["juega con nada"], and, unable to sleep, she counts the lights as if they were sheep. While she waits for daylight, alone in her room, her hope transmutes into perhaps waking up "over the sea" ["sobre el mar"]. The sea, as in "Color humano", is an image that provides a feeling of peace, immensity, and stability, something that obviously neither Ana nor any of the other characters in these songs find in the city. "Fermín", like Ana, turns and spins even more, but his room is in a hospice. Fermín, who has apparent conflicts with reality, is destined to die

---

33 Almendra, *Almendra* (RCA, 1969).

in that hospice and his death is again associated with the eternal image of the sea. The song ends with a clear wink to the traditional song "Mambrú se fue a la guerra (no sé cuándo vendrá)", which tells the story of a warrior (the Duke of Marlborough in the original French song) whose loved ones wait for him but who never returns; instead, the only thing that comes back is news of his death. It is usually included in children's songbooks when in fact it would be better placed in horror stories. The relationship between Mambrú and Fermín is madness: the madness of war, the madness of hospice, and the madness of teaching such a song to children. On the contrary, Spinetta composes a much more beautiful song for them, in which "the world is chocolate" ["el mundo es un chocolatín"]. Without denying reality ("in the gardens of a place that you will never find when awake" ["en los jardines de un lugar que jamás despierto encontrará"]), "Plegaria para un niño dormido" (Prayer for a Sleeping Child) describes the dream and the fantasies of a child whom nobody should wake up ("let him continue dreaming happiness" ["déjenlo que siga soñando felicidad"]), in a place where child labor does not exist ("destroying polishing cloths, moving away from evil" ["destruyendo trapos de lustrar, alejándose de todo mal"]). Without a doubt, "Plegaria para un niño dormido" is much more suitable as a nursery rhyme than "Mambrú se fue a la guerra".

Almendra II (Almendra, 1970)

The cover of Almendra's second album shows the band members surrounded by a green geometric labyrinth.[34] This maze seems to represent the world and the cosmos, with its forms and its eternity. Or perhaps it references the political context of the time, a tangled and undecipherable reality. Alternatively, it could represent both things, as well as all the others conjured by Almendra listeners willing to let their imaginations run wild. In fact, lyrics of a political nature, as well as constant reference to a much broader context—to an eternal cosmos—abound in this album. The green labyrinth proposed on the cover invites its audience to imagine, to fly away, to travel to infinity. This journey is also suggested in the title of the first song: "Toma un tren hacia el sur" (Take a Train down South). Its lyrics warn that the exile is coming: "Wear the red beret... buy dulce de leche, take a train towards the south, you will do well there". If we think that this was a premonitory reading of all the artists who would soon join the lines of the political exiles (in red berets), the suggestion to buy "dulce de leche" (Argentina's typical caramel) has to do with what represents belonging to a society, the roots to the land and local customs. Where is the south? Is it a geographical south, an imaginary south, an ideological south? The south is always an end, a pole, never a centre where directions are negotiated and mixed. Going south also

---

34 Almendra, *Almendra II* (RCA, 1970).

means embarking on a journey to find your own boundaries and experiment with your own limits, without forgetting who you are and where you come from (the land of "dulce de leche").

The semantic map of this album traces a path that will be repeated throughout the artist's discography. There is an ideology, a particular philosophy that he will never depart from, and a lyrical aesthetics that will only be refined and explored repeatedly. It is interesting to see that at the beginning of Spinetta's career, when he finds success with Almendra, he registers his disgust with fame, his rejection of the "idealisation" of artists, in the song "En las cúpulas" (On the Domes), in which he states "nobody place me on a single dome... heroes never rise... Let's knock the domes down to the ground, so that there is not one more next to the trees" ["Hoy nadie me siente en la cúpula... nunca los héroes se levantan... Tiramos a tierra las cúpulas, que no quede una sola más al lado de los árboles"]. It follows that there is no place for both in the natural world (fame and the trees; materialism and nature).[35]

In sum, Charly García and Luis Alberto Spinetta would build the base of Argentine rock's aesthetics and poetic content. While their approaches differ and their careers have been marked by opposing styles and marketing choices, they now stand side by side in Argentina as the pioneers of this movement and genre.

Yet, as the next chapter will explore, both musicians, along with all artists at the time, had to deal with a machinery of censorship. A system that had bizarre and puzzling particularities, which, surprisingly enough, fuelled the artists' imaginations in their quest to dissent without getting caught. Let's move on, then, to the villainy of censorship and its boomerang effect.

---

35 Mara Favoretto, *Luis Alberto Spinetta: mito y mitología* (Buenos Aires: Gourmet Musical Ediciones, 2017), pp. 78–81.

CHAPTER THREE

The Day Words Were Forbidden
Censorship

"... hasta que un día llegaron ellos"

—*Charly García*

"Una vez vi que no cantabas y no sé por qué"

—*Luis Alberto Spinetta*

In 1974, Charly García wrote "Botas locas" (Mad Boots).[1] In it, he speaks about a "crazy army" where the game is simple: "they always throw insults, I always keep quiet" ["ellos siempre insultan, yo siempre callado"]. The song that brought its composer lots of trouble with the police was describing the feelings of a soldier while serving the then-compulsory military service (abolished in 1995). An interesting turn occurred when García, questioned by the police about the song lyrics, changed them on the spot, singing a new version in which the army was, instead, praised. This quick thinking saved his life, but not the life of the song, which would not be recorded until 1994. His idea of the "mad boots" was not confined to his imagination. Things were going to get extremely bizarre in the next few years.

In a memorandum distributed in 1981, the government said the following:

The ministry proposed to step up its gathering of information, not only because it is a requirement of the National Executive Power, but also because it is psychologically convenient to accelerate the eradication of terrorist ideologues. The reality of the sectoral spectrum shows us that, although terrorist activists were eliminated, ideological activists still remain at the tertiary and *secondary* levels.[2]

---

1 Sui Generis, *Adiós Sui Generis II*.
2 Darío Marchini, *No toquen: músicos populares, gobierno y sociedad: de la utopía a la*

As told by Sergio Pujol, the Subsecretary of Culture of the City of Buenos Aires, Francisco Carcavallo, presented his cultural plan with these words:

> Culture has been and will be the highest means for the infiltration of extremist ideologies. In our country, the channels of artistic–cultural infiltration have been used through a deforming process based on protest songs, exaltation of artists and extremist texts. This is how they manage to influence a sector of youth, nonconformist by nature, inexperience or age.[3]

Those basic ideas were the rationale behind the kidnapping of nine teenagers in September 1976, an event widely known as "La Noche de los Lápices" (The Night of the Pencils), depicted in a famous film of the same name, directed by Héctor Olivera in 1976. The nine teenagers were members of the Student Union of La Plata, involved in a peaceful campaign seeking benefits for students, such as a waived public transport fee. They were all brutally tortured and only three survived. These sixteen- and seventeen-year-olds endured electric shocks on their genitals, food deprivation, brutal rapes, and torture, all because the military Junta saw them as sympathisers of left-wing ideologies, enemies of the country and of their "Christian and occidental values".

And yet, despite such brutal acts, which were shrouded beneath a "Christian values" mantle, the military dictatorship (1976–83), whose modus operandi this chapter will explore, considered itself heroic. They had embarked upon a messianic crusade to save the country from what they called "subversion" and "terrorism". For them, the "subversives" were not only those enrolled in leftist groups such as unions, student centres, or political parties, but also those who opposed their views or had alternative ideas. Argentine scholar Julia Risler explains that the propaganda showed a good image of the government action, billing it as the new as opposed to the past and as the guarantee of a return to normality. It sought the broad adherence of the inhabitants to the regime, and had as a framework of action the presence of a permanent threat that functioned as a warning to the population: they would receive punishment or sanctions in the face of possible forms of subversion.[4] Meanwhile, as we will see, the censors operated using covert strategies that would only come to light decades later.

The case of censorship in Argentina during the PRN has been extensively studied by Andrés Avellaneda,[5] David William Foster,[6] Daniel Balderston,

---

persecución y las listas negras en la Argentina 1960–1983 (Buenos Aires: Catálogos, 2008), p. 253, my emphasis.
3 Pujol, *Rock y dictadura*, p. 22.
4 Julia Risler, *La acción psicológica. Dictadura, inteligencia y gobierno de las emociones 1955–1981* (Buenos Aires: Tinta Limón, 2018), p. 186.
5 Andrés Avellaneda, *Censura, autoritarismo y cultura: Argentina 1960–1983*, 2 volumes (Buenos Aires: Centro Editor de América Latina, 1986).
6 David William Foster, *Violence in Argentinean Literature: Cultural Responses to Tyranny* (Columbia: University of Missouri Press, 1995).

Tulio Halperín Dongji, Francine Masiello, Marta Morello-Frosch, Beatriz Sarlo,[7] and Reina Roffé,[8] among others. One of the first to address this topic was Avellaneda, according to whom the salient feature of the censorship apparatus was the absence of a censor committee or a censorship office. This lack of a centralised, official body dedicated to reviewing artists' works did not mean that censorship in Argentina of the period was light or negligible; far from it. Instead, officials were able to deny that censorship existed when addressing the international community while simultaneously fomenting a sense of uncertainty about what could and could not be published at home.

In his analysis of censorship in Argentina, Avellaneda suggests that "in order to understand how cultural production is affected by censorship, an analysis of its discourse is not enough; it is also essential to understand the mechanism that includes or excludes the producer of that culture, the specific organisation that allows or denies expression".[9] In agreement with this idea, Roffé adds that no one knew who the censors were or how they operated. This lack of information led to, in her words, "a real psychosis".[10] This "psychosis", a side effect of Argentina's particular breed of censorship, activated self-defence mechanisms in artists, writers, and educators. Censorship's lack of clear guidelines fostered self-censorship.

Building on Avellaneda's observation, Roffé identifies a coexistent system of "paracensorship" at work. Community organisations that supported the regime acted as what she calls "ghost juries": anonymous decision-makers in positions of power who decided whether publications upheld military-regime values and, in cases where the answer was no, acted swiftly to ensure the offending publication was removed from circulation or never published in the first place. Roffé considers that the Inquisition in the Middle Ages was more coherent than these ghost juries, who included publicists, librarians, booksellers, and editors, and most of whom were not acting in an organised way, but out of fear, according to their personal interpretations of what exactly constituted military-regime values. Often, she explains, a simple edict, even if it included no institution representative or officer signing it, sufficed for a text or book to be removed from the public eye.[11]

This type of censorship created an atmosphere of fear and paranoia, and because of it, many artists, writers, and musicians resorted to self-censorship or internal exile.

Invernizzi and Gociol elaborate upon the constant feeling of insecurity experienced by writers and editors: "On several occasions Argentine

---

7 Daniel Balderston, et al., *Ficción y política: la narrativa argentina durante el proceso militar* (Buenos Aires: Alianza Editorial, 1987).
8 Reina Roffé, "Omnipresencia de la censura en la escritora argentina," *Revista iberoamericana* 51 (132): 909–15, 1985.
9 Avellaneda, *Censura, autoritarismo*, p. 186.
10 Roffé, "Omnipresencia," p. 909.
11 Roffé, "Omnipresencia," p. 909.

publishers demanded clear rules of the game. They wanted to know what was allowed and what was prohibited, to plan their projects within the permitted margins. But they never got an answer. They only heard, like the whole of society, that in Argentina there was no prior censorship and that, therefore, the law was abided. It was a perverse truth. It was not about prior censorship, strictly speaking, but something worse".[12]

The discovery of secret archives in 2000 opened a new line of enquiry in the study of how censorship operated during the PRN. Research carried out by Hernán Invernizzi and Judith Gociol, published in 2000, is essential reading for anyone wanting to understand this apparatus. Invernizzi and Gociol not only discovered that the censorship agency existed clandestinely, but that its readings were highly sophisticated and sometimes even verged on paranoia. The regime's strategy had been to leave no trace of its actions, their tactic to "disappear" not only the bodies of the victims of repression, but also any documents that corroborated acts of censorship.

Operation censorship

In 1966, de-facto president (1966–70) Juan Carlos Onganía instituted a series of laws to protect the country from the spread of communism. Hernán Invernizzi notes that the National Defence Law (16.970/66), in particular, was so vague that it opened up the idea of national defence to include all sorts of "arbitrariedades legitimadas" (legitimised arbitrariness). This arbitrary nature of Argentine censorship was further legitimised when the military government of 1976 implemented the Actas del Proceso, a series of "supra-constitutional" acts, which gave the military "enormous censorial powers".[13]

The regime considered these documents "supra-constitutional" and constituted their legal system above any other law. They legitimised them via article 23 of the national constitution, which refers to what happens to constitutional guarantees in the case of a coup d'état. According to the military government's interpretation, this article allowed for censorship, though there is no explicit mention of censorship in the actual text of the constitution.[14]

---

12 Invernizzi and Gociol, *Un golpe*, p. 74.
13 Invernizzi and Gociol, *Un golpe*, p. 59; p. 64.
14 Constitución Nacional de la República Argentina (Capítulo Primero: Declaraciones, derechos y garantías): "Artículo 23. En caso de conmoción interior o de ataque exterior que pongan en peligro el ejercicio de esta Constitución y de las autoridades creadas por ella, se declarará en estado de sitio la provincia o territorio en donde exista la perturbación del orden, quedando suspensas allí las garantías constitucionales. Pero durante esta suspensión no podrá el presidente de la República condenar por sí ni aplicar penas. Su poder se limitará en tal caso respecto de las personas, a arrestarlas o trasladarlas de un punto a otro de la Nación, si ellas no prefiriesen salir fuera del territorio argentino". ("Article 23. In case of internal commotion or external attack that endangers the exercise of this Constitution and of the authorities created

Despite these laws permitting the regime to censor, no specific censorship law was known to the public. Avellaneda and Invernizzi and Gociol agree that a legal system that justified censorship did not exist. To overcome this inconvenience, the military authorities created the abovementioned Actas del Proceso. Invernizzi and Gociol explain that the Junta repeatedly declared that (pre-publication) censorship did not exist in Argentina and that Article 14 of the national constitution guaranteed freedom of expression. Certainly, between 1976 and 1983, there was no committee that would approve or reject media, art, or publications in an act of pre-publication censorship.[15] When newspaper and magazine editors asked for clear guidelines on what was prohibited, they received no response.[16] Despite this, everybody knew that language was controlled and monitored. If dissidence were to exist, it had to find a cunning way to dissent.

On the day of the coup, the military Junta publicly announced the main objectives of their de facto regime:

- Validity of Christian moral values, national tradition and the dignity of the Argentine being (ser nacional).
- Validity of national security, eradicating subversion and its causes.
- Creation of an education system aligned with the country's needs, the nation's objectives and aimed at consolidating the values and aspirations of the Argentine being.[17]

In order to achieve their objectives, the first major step of the Junta was, indeed, censorship. However, as already explained, the case would present complex particularities. To start with, it was ambiguous. As stated above, there was no censors' office *per se*, at least not a publicly known one. Argentine essayist Beatriz Sarlo describes the apparatus of censorship in this way: "Censorship operated via three tactics: unawareness, which begets rumour; exemplary measures, which beget terror; and half-words, which beget intimidation".[18]

The "unawareness" Sarlo describes was a hotly debated topic for several years in Argentina. Before 2000, most scholars who investigated this

> by it, the province or territory where the disturbance of order exists will be declared in a state of siege, suspending there the constitutional guarantees. But during this suspension, the President of the Republic will not be able to condemn himself or apply penalties. His power will be limited in such a case with respect to persons, to arrest them or transfer them from one point of the Nation to another, if they do not prefer to leave Argentine territory".) https://www-congreso-gob-ar.translate.goog/constitucionParte1Cap1.php.

15 Favoretto, *Alegoría*, p. 26.
16 Invernizzi and Gociol, *Un golpe*, p. 74.
17 Blaustein and Zubieta, *Decíamos ayer*, p. 29.
18 Saúl Sosnowski, *Represión y reconstrucción de una cultura: el caso argentino* (Buenos Aires: Eudeba, 1988), p. 101.

case of censorship agree that lack of information was a key to its success. Indeed, the uncertainty generated by the absence of clear guidelines caused self-censorship and paranoid fear, as "anything" could be deemed suspicious or subversive. Fear was fuelled whenever books that contained Marxist ideas were confiscated, and when thousands of titles were burned and schools and public libraries continuously inspected in what Sarlo calls "exemplary measures".

Sarlo explains that censorship worked "at every conceivable level with great tactical skill. As a terrorist regime (where legality is marked by the arbitrary nature of power), the patterns of censorship were only partially known by those on whom the censors operated. ... Subjected to this system of indeterminacy, education and print mass media chose to stay beyond the danger line, thus proving the effectiveness of a game based on laws only known by the military leader who presided over each of the instances".[19]

However, the censors were not only military officials. The combined actions of librarians, editors, publishers, and the general public, all guided by the same fear, supported the repressive regime. Some non-governmental organisations, such as groups associated with the church, cooperated with the regime and in doing so formed part of the abovementioned "paracensorship system". These associations, or, as Roffé calls them, "morality leagues", supported the regime and acted as the "ghost jury" mentioned earlier.[20] They actively participated in the control of the media and contributed to advertising campaigns that supported the dictatorship. Some of them were Liga de Madres de Familia, Liga de Padres de Familia, Instituto de la familia, Movimiento Familiar Cristiano, Obra de Protección a la Joven, Unión Internacional de Protección a la Infancia, and Obras Privadas de Asistencia al Menor. They had close ties with each other and worked collaboratively, forming what Althusser calls the "state ideological apparatus".[21] Because most of the institutions that were part of the paracensorship system were Catholic, those who attacked the regime's ideas were seen as also attacking God.

---

19 Sarlo in Sosnowski, *Represión*, p. 104.
20 Roffé, "Omnipresencia," p. 909.
21 Althusser distinguishes between the repressive apparatuses of the state, which use force, such as the army, the government, the prisons, and the police; and the ideological apparatuses of the state, which disseminate the ideology of government, such as the media and educational and religious institutions—see Louis Althusser, "Ideology and Ideological State Apparatuses (Notes towards an Investigation)," in *Lenin and Philosophy and Other Essays*, translated by Ben Brewster (London: NLB, 1971), p. 121.

Church and state

In order to succeed, the regime needed the consent and support of the main sectors of Argentine society, such as the Catholic Church. There was a deep division in the Catholic community at the time: those who were accomplices of the state and those who resisted it. The second group included members who suffered repression, and some were even disappeared. Officially, the church expressed its unconditional support for the regime. On the first page of newspaper *Clarín*, on 16 May 1976, the episcopate published a pastoral letter in which they explicitly highlighted that the role of the state is to rule as mandate of authority.[22] As a result, church and state formed a united front: they supported, justified, and praised each other. By their alliance with the church, the military men ascended hierarchically, claiming spiritual licence for their actions. This way, they gave the appearance of not only being "military men", but of also playing a spiritual, messianic role.

The agreement between the state and the church was made clear to the public in different ways: some priests spoke of it during their homilies or while preaching, and the media often mentioned it as well. For example, when reports of possible conflicts between the institutions started to circulate, the magazine *Carta Política*, directed by journalist Mariano Grondona, responded by publishing an article that included powerful rhetorical questions and metaphors that were aimed at protecting the alliance:

> What will remain in Argentina without the sword or without the cross? Who will want to remain in history as the one who deprived the country of one of them? Argentina is Catholic and military. At this time there is no greater responsibility than taking care of that "and".[23]

As expressed in the second article in the Argentine Constitution, Catholicism is the official religion of the country. Many members of the ecclesiastic power pyramid praised and supported the regime as if the military Junta were crusading to protect the Catholic community against the Marxist threat. In fact, the Argentine Church's hierarchy is among the most conservative in Latin America.[24] The role it played during the military dictatorship was essential precisely because it is the official state religion, according to the constitution. Undoubtedly, in a Catholic society, the words pronounced by the priests at Sunday mass have an intense influence over parishioners. Many bishops were aware of what was happening in the country but remained silent. Others, such as Monseñor Tortolo, invited parishioners to "cooperate positively" with the regime, prophesying the coming of a "purifying process".[25]

---

22 Blaustein and Zubieta, *Decíamos ayer*, p. 123.
23 Blaustein and Zubieta, *Decíamos ayer*, p. 142.
24 Emilio Fermín Mignone, *Iglesia y dictadura* (Buenos Aires: Colihue, 2013), p. 11.
25 Mignone, *Iglesia*, p. 25.

44   CODED LYRICS

While around the world some groups had started to question the Argentine government about the fate of the disappeared[26] and the human rights violations,[27] some members of the church actually justified those acts. Such was the case of Archbishop Quarracino, who in 1976 stated that "in a war situation, the limits of Ethics enter an umbra".[28] Note the language used: an "umbra". The Argentine Church officially supported the regime and justified their acts by pronouncing phrases such as Quarracino's during their homilies. It even looked as if politics was replacing the evangelic mission of the church, with the high-ranked church representatives reinforcing such a move. According to Mignone, who investigated the role of the church during those years, the bishops and the apostolic nuncio were aware of what was truly happening regarding the crimes against humanity in Argentina.[29] More disturbingly, within the military vicary, the priests who visited police stations, jails, and military quarters cooperated with repression:[30]

> "Son," he (Father Felipe Perlanda Gómez, chaplain of the prison services) said to one of the detainees who complained about the torments to which he was subjected, "what do you expect if you do not cooperate with the authorities who are interrogating you?".[31]

The prisoners had to say confession before they were shot. The report written by CONADEP includes a large number of testimonies that prove that the priests not only justified torture, but also played an enabling role: through spiritual counsel, they helped the repressors accept the legitimacy of their violations of human dignity. "They even composed sacrilegious prayers. In one of them they said: 'By the skill of my hand, may my shot be accurate'".[32]

Fortunately, not all sectors of the church agreed with the regime nor with the highest-ranked church members. The Catholic Church, as an institution, had to deal with a series of internal conflicts. There was a clear division between a left-wing movement called "Movimiento de Sacerdotes del Tercer Mundo", whose ideas favoured social work, and those sectors of Catholicism

---

26 "In Argentina there are no mass graves and each corpse has a coffin. ... Disappeared? ... You know that there are disappeared people who today live peacefully in Europe...": Cardinal J. C. Aramburu to the Roman newspaper *Il Messagero*, 12 November 1982, reprinted by *La Nación* (Buenos Aires), 12 November 1982—see Blaustein and Zubieta, *Decíamos ayer*, p. 516.

27 Human rights were also among the topics discussed by Monsignor Octavio Derisi, rector of the Catholic University, when in an interview published in the magazine *Somos* (155), on 7 September 1979, he formulated the rhetorical question: "How can the United States, a country that has had one million abortions in a year talk about human rights?": Blaustein and Zubieta, *Decíamos ayer*, p. 302.

28 *Clarín, suplemento especial* (Buenos Aires), 24 March 1976, p. 14.

29 Mignone, *Iglesia*, p. 17.

30 Mignone, *Iglesia*, p. 36.

31 Mignone, *Iglesia*, p. 38.

32 Mignone, *Iglesia*, p. 40.

which remained traditional, aristocratic, and nationalistic.[33] Consequently, it would be unfair to argue that the totality of the church supported the dictatorship, as there was a considerable number of dissidents within the institution. Moreover, these dissidents suffered the same repression that affected every sector of society. As stated by Invernizzi and Gociol, church authorities rarely disagreed with the dictatorship in public, although they held private discussion with the military authorities in an effort to reach verbal agreements.[34]

Admiral Emilio Eduardo Massera would embellish his speeches with what he considered "Christian values". He portrayed the Junta as the owner of the only possible creed, and their role as one replete with messianic qualities. Just a year after the coup, Massera spoke eloquently to *Revista de la Familia Cristiana*:

> General Videla, Brigadier Agosti and I, all of us members of the Military Junta, supreme organ of power in Argentina, are not only Catholic, but practising Catholic. As such, we are well aware of the limits of temporary power and the sense of responsibility of an institution that has God as a Teacher who said: "My Kingdom is not from this world..." When we act as Political Power, we are still Catholic. When Catholic priests act as Spiritual Power, they are still citizens. It would be an arrogant sin to expect the former or the latter to be flawless in their opinions and decisions. However, we all act based on love, which is what sustains our religion, there are no problems between us and I can assure you that our relationship is optimal, as it should be among Christians.[35]

In that speech, Massera refers to the omnipotence of the Junta. The close ties between both institutions—church and state, which Massera calls "Spiritual Power" and "Political Power"—are evident in the quote above. Massera claims that his actions are guided by love. However, there are other quotes by Massera himself that contradict these ideas. For instance, he said "We will not fight to the death, we will fight until victory, whether that be beyond death or this side of it".[36] This heroic invitation to combat beyond death, far from assuring freedom and security to the population, incited fear and promoted self-censorship.[37] While Massera claims to be humble, not arrogant or

---

33 Invernizzi and Gociol, *Un golpe*, p. 151.
34 Invernizzi and Gociol, *Un golpe*, p. 154.
35 Claudio Uriarte, *Almirante Cero: biografía no autorizada de Emilio Eduardo Massera* (Buenos Aires: Planeta, 1991), p. 138.
36 Uriarte, *Almirante Cero*, p. 140.
37 Videla, speaking with English journalists, reproduced by *La Prensa* (Buenos Aires), 18 December 1977: "A terrorist is not only considered as such for killing with a weapon or planting a bomb, but also for mobilising other people through ideas contrary to our Western and Christian civilisation": Blaustein and Zubieta, *Decíamos ayer*, p. 222.

almighty, the Junta he represents has absolute power over the country. His words seem to recall the temporal binary of earthly power versus spiritual authority which attracted lengthy debates among theologians.[38]

Disappearing acts and the impact theory

In order to conceal their illegal repressive actions and crimes against humanity, the Junta created the figure of the "disappeared". Through this euphemism, they suggested that there were people who had "disappeared" themselves; that is, people who were hiding from the authorities. To make someone "disappear" was an act of total impunity; if there was no proof of the crime, no offender could be brought to justice. Therefore, by means of this strategy, they not only murdered people, but also destroyed any evidence of their procedures, which included kidnapping, torture, and death squads. The military officials clandestinely and routinely made tens of thousands of people disappear.[39] In order to fulfil this task, they needed to build concentration camps and detention centres where they could keep the prisoners.

There is a clear analogy between this modus operandi and the way censorship operated. Both processes were clandestine, sometimes even paranoid. All evidence had to be destroyed, no traces left. The censorship office was run by the intelligence officers who, on a daily basis, would write a report on "media behaviour".[40] Because the military authorities did not want their "enemy" to have access to any of their strategies and procedures in their fight against subversion, the list of prohibited artists, books, and publishers was not published. Only some individuals could have access to the "blacklists",

---

38 Albano Harguindeguy, Internal Affairs Minister, told *La Nación*, published 22 September 1979: "We have not confessed to the Inter-American Commission on Human Rights. We have limited ourselves to stating the facts. Argentina only confesses before God": Blaustein and Zubieta, *Decíamos ayer*, p. 316.

39 According to the Comisión Nacional de los Desaparecidos (National Commission on the Disappearance of Persons, or CONADEP), there were more than 30,000 people disappeared during the dictatorship. Many of those people were not politically engaged and were very young: see CONADEP, *Nunca Más (Never Again). Report of the National Commission on the Disappearance of Persons*, translated by Writers and Scholars International Ltd (Buenos Aires: Editorial Universitaria de Buenos Aires, 1984), http://www.desaparecidos.org/nuncamas/web/english/library/nevagain/nevagain_001.htm.

40 According to Invernizzi, during the 1960s and 1970s, eighty percent of the books imported into Spain came from Buenos Aires, and Latin American schools used Argentine texts. However, at the end of the 1970s, the Argentine book industry was on the point of collapsing due to military policies: see Invernizzi and Gociol, *Un golpe*, p. 58.

which contributed to the blurry censoring system.[41] This was, in fact, a clever way of ensuring power. The military authorities believed that keeping their actions secret and mysterious was a way to confuse the "enemy", and in this way make that enemy easier to defeat.

Of course, the idea of "disappearing" all traces of culture is not new. The Spaniards, in their process of colonisation, burned the libraries of the Mayans and the Aztecs, as well as the khipus of the Inkas, so today comparatively little remains of the laws by which they were governed, their literary production, religious texts, history, and worldview. During the dictatorship, when a book was banned, the directors of public libraries were given the order to "destroy" not only all copies of a title, but also all traces of its existence (files, archives, notes, and inventories). This way, any physical evidence that might remind the public who visited those libraries of the books' existence disappeared along with the books themselves. Not only were they absent from the shelf, in other words, it was as if they had had never been there. While this process meant the actual burning of many books, thanks to a handful of librarians who buried and hid some of the books they were supposed to burn, nowadays researchers can clarify the reasons behind the censors' decisions.[42]

Until the year 2000, researchers believed that the main feature of the censorship system during the period 1976–83 had been the lack of organisation and the absence of an official publication control office.[43] However, a serendipitous event followed by further research shed new light on the modus operandi of censorship in Argentina. In March 2000, completely by chance, an employee of the Ministry of Internal Affairs found some boxes in the cellar of the former bank Banade, which had been shut down in the 1990s. Those boxes contained an archive of about 600 documents, a total of 4,000 pages that provided evidence of censorship operations. Until then, all analytical studies about censorship in Argentina had presumed that a formal and organised system had not existed. This new evidence found in the cellar of the abandoned bank building changed our understanding of what really happened during those years and how the "disappearing technique" really worked.

The disappearing technique was applied to people, books, and art, as well as to any documentation that could be used as evidence of the regime's actions. It was comparable to Decree NN (Nacht and Nebel: Night and Fog), the decree of physical elimination of resistance in Nazi Germany

---

41 Internal Memorandum No. 44 of the newspaper *La Voz del Interior* (Córdoba) addressed to the Editorial Secretariat, cited in *Nunca Más* (Buenos Aires: Eudeba, 1996, 4th reprint), p. 368, reads: "CORDOBA, 4/22/76. Due to the disposition of our leadership and by directive of the III Army Corps Command on this date, complaints from relatives of alleged detainees who wish to know their whereabouts should not be published": see Blaustein and Zubieta, *Decíamos ayer*, p. 120.
42 Invernizzi and Gociol, *Un golpe*, pp. 98–99.
43 Invernizzi and Gociol, *Un golpe*, pp. 98–99.

during World War II, under which the enemy was eliminated without any record being kept of the fact. After the discovery of the Banade archives in Buenos Aires, new research also fuelled debate about the role of culture during the dictatorship and how the military officials were, in fact, acutely aware of the importance of culture when manipulating public opinion. In 2005, Hernán Invernizzi published *"Los libros son tuyos": políticos, académicos y militares: la dictadura en Eudeba*, an exhaustive research study confirming the hypothesis of the existence of a systematic plan for cultural repression during the military dictatorship. This plan included the fields of education, cultural expression, and the media. It was an organised system, with its own buildings, staff, laws, decrees, a generous budget, and vast resources from the censorship apparatus. All documents produced by this system were top secret, and they were strictly for internal use. Invernizzi confirms that there was a team of civil professionals that contributed to the promotion of the dictatorship's ideals and values. These professionals, instead of destroying Eudeba—Editorial Universitaria de Buenos Aires—used it to further the dictatorship's propaganda. In his book, Invernizzi discloses a secret agreement between the publishing house, led by General Corbetta and the Ministerio del Interior's General Harguindeguy. This memorandum of understanding explicitly established that the former would publish a series of books as directed by the latter. These books would not be differentiated in any way, so that the public could not possibly identify them as deliberately selected by the regime. Dozens of titles belonging to neoliberal and conservative authors clandestinely infiltrated the Eudeba collection. This was not a random choice. Eudeba was one of the most prestigious publishing houses in the Hispanic world and the biggest university publisher in the world in the 1960s: "Instead of destroying it, they decided to put its prestige to their own ends and used it to promote the ideas they wanted to foster in society".[44]

In addition to the disappearance of people, the dictatorship regime also disappeared indigenous history, images, and language. In 1977, the Estado Mayor General del Ejército (EMGE) wrote the Special Report No. 10 (*Informe Especial No. 10*) which had clear guidelines regarding the control of cultural production.[45] To achieve their goals, the authorities created the Dirección General de Publicaciones (DPG), which had police-like power to enforce the law and was backed up by the military. Another step in their control process, then, was the creation of a committee that developed criteria to regulate the mass media. The Special Report No. 10 included a definition of what the military leaders considered "culture", which, in their words, was "conceived through the Hispanic-American legacy". This view ignored the

---

44 Pablo Montanaro, "Eudeba era muy peligrosa para los militares. Entrevista a Hernán Invernizzi," *Rio Negro Online* (Buenos Aires), 6 February 2006, https://www.rionegro.com.ar/columnistas/eudeba-era-muy-peligrosa-para-los-militares-DFHRN06020616061003.
45 Invernizzi and Gociol, *Un golpe*, p. 33.

indigenous history of Argentina, adding ancient aboriginal cultures to the list of "disappearing" acts.

There were two complementary and inseparable infrastructures that operated the acts of disappearance during the dictatorship: on one side, the prisons and detention camps; on the other, a sophisticated apparatus that controlled education and culture.[46] On some occasions, the prohibition of a book was accompanied by an official report that outlined the reasons and criteria for its ban. On others, no routine methodology was followed, such as the previously mentioned agreement between Eudeba and the Ministerio del Interior.[47] Formally, there was no pre-censorship between 1976 and 1983. Publishers were allowed to launch books without having to submit any application for permission to a censorship committee. However, as stated previously, *there were* censorship committees, though they acted post-publication: they carefully read every published text in the country, looking for anything suspicious. The committees were clandestine and, to date, their members have been kept secret. The "disappearing technique", explains Invernizzi, is still a hypothesis, because we still do not know for sure who those censors were:

> Not having been able to identify them does not mean they have disappeared or that the blacklists have been disappeared. I imagine that all of them had negotiated their non-appearance as a condition of their contribution because they were semiologists, anthropologists, academics, lawyers, and none of them wished to remain associated with such activities because they knew that the dictatorship sooner or later would come to an end, unlike their careers.[48]

Culture was at the very core of the regime: the authorities regularly monitored newspapers, magazines, TV and radio shows, and even university programs in order to "protect culture".[49] The professional teams who acted as censors carried out a sophisticated and painstaking reading of everything that was published. They analysed the content as well as the potential "impact" on the audience. Invernizzi adds:

> In the documents that we have investigated, the phrase 'impact or recipient, or impact sector' always appears. The first thing they look for is the ideological content; second, to whom it is addressed; and third, putting those two things together, what result it could have. These are

---

46 Invernizzi and Gociol, *Un golpe*, p. 15.
47 Invernizzi and Gociol, *Un golpe*, p. 179.
48 Favoretto, personal interview with Invernizzi and Gociol.
49 A letter signed by the General of Infantry José Antonio Vaquero explains the problem of subversion in society as follows: "As long as subversion is not combated in the cultural sphere, it may continue with the recruitment of juvenile minds": see Invernizzi, *"Los libros son tuyos"*, p. 44.

sophisticated mechanisms that belong to reading professionals; and the reading that they undertake has to do with science, it takes into account the impact index. There were military men who were experts in public opinion research, experts in marketing research. Let's not underestimate those readings.

As was mentioned before, the military authorities were not as interested in destroying the cultural apparatus as they were in using it to their advantage. Their project sought to replace critical thought with an ideological hegemony designed by them. This was made very clear to the general public, as in every public speech they stated that their basic motivations aligned with "Christian values" and the "complete eradication of subversion". There were words and expressions that the military considered as subversive and of dangerous ideological content, such as "class struggle", "sexual freedom", "theology of liberation", and "unionisation". Authors such as Marx, Engels, Che Guevara, Lenin, Trotsky, and Mao were taken as signs of questioning Western and Christian values and were therefore considered dangerous and subversive. The official rhetoric was construed by means of a careful choice of words around something called the "Argentine being" ("ser nacional"). The next chapter will explore these rhetorical strategies in detail.

The investigation carried out by Invernizzi also highlights that censorship was not consistent. Not everything that was "subversive" in the censors' eyes was banned. Because they analysed the "impact" of each cultural expression, some drama plays, which were only attended by a relatively small audience, were not censored. They were allowed because they served a larger purpose: they could be deemed proof of freedom of expression when international organisations questioned the conditions for artists in Argentina. This inconsistency can also be seen in the different ways publishing houses were treated. For example, while some publishers suffered severe measures including the incarceration of editors, the Catholic publishing houses were invited to "meetings" to "discuss" their releases in a very diplomatic way (personal interview). Added to this, while sometimes the team of specialists, after carefully assessing texts, signed formal reports or recommendations, at other times there was no formal procedure at all.[50] Such was the case for some Eudeba books, which were simply listed in documents under titles such as "out of stock" or "discontinued" ("*Libros fuera de comercio*"; "*Libros detenidos por funcionarios civiles*"). Invernizzi underlines the Eudeba case because, more than the military censorship, it was the scholars running the publishing house who acted as censors in their own right.[51]

The field of education was quite different from the literary one. There was a special committee that existed prior to the dictatorship, the main function of which was to control and oversee the books used in schools. "Operación

---

50 Invernizzi, *"Los libros son tuyos"*, p. 69.
51 Invernizzi, *"Los libros son tuyos"*, p. 83.

Claridad" (Operation Clarity) was the title of a document that was given to teachers in schools with the aim of assisting them in the identification of possible "subversive" colleagues, books, or any type of ideology influenced by Marxism that could pose a threat to the objectives of the National Reorganisation Process. There was a list of "permitted authors", which meant that if teachers wanted to include someone else who did not appear on that list, moved by terror, they were unlikely to risk making a wrong decision. This feeling of insecurity also resulted in self-censorship. During the dictatorship, school and university curricula were carefully revised, and the "behaviour" of teachers and professors was routinely monitored. Leftist books used in high schools such as *ERSA: Estudio de la Realidad Social Argentina* were replaced with a new series called *Formación moral y cívica*. In 1977, all schools received a booklet titled *Subversión en el ámbito educativo, conozcamos a nuestro enemigo* (Subversion in the Educational Field: Knowing Our Enemy). It highlighted the role of teachers as "saviours of the motherland" and the importance of identifying the enemies of the nation, so that future generations would be protected. However, more than a booklet with guidelines, this document worked as indoctrination. It offered a detailed description of how subversion operated:

a) Subversive action is developed through ideologically motivated teachers who influence the minds of impressionable young students, encouraging the development of rebellious ideas or behaviours, which will be transformed into action at higher levels.

b) ... Marxist publishers pretend to offer "useful books" for development, books that accompany the child... that help him not to be afraid of freedom, that help him to love, to fight, to affirm his being...

c) Ideological action intensifies as the children grow older... tending to modify the scale of traditional values (family, religion, nationality, tradition, etc.).

Furthermore, on 11 October 1977, the Secretary of Education published Resolución No. 44, in which it was explained how to detect subversive infiltration in schools. It lists a series of indicators that signal the destruction of traditional conceptions of family and paternal authority, modification of the traditional set of values (family, religion, nation, tradition, order, and hierarchy), opposition to private property, alternative interpretations of history, and the use of religion as a means to promote social class distinction.[52]

Children's literature was also targeted by censorship. There was an assessment committee called Consejo Nacional de Educación that acted as a pre-censorship office so that new books could be submitted for approval before publication.[53] To give one example, Elsa Bonermann's *Un elefante*

---

52 Invernizzi and Gociol, *Un golpe*, p. 104.
53 Invernizzi and Gociol, *Un golpe*, p. 110.

ocupa mucho espacio was banned because the animals in the story went on strike.[54] The author had been granted the Hans Christian Andersen Award for this book by the International Board on Books for Young People. However, for the military censors, the story promoted values that contradicted the common good. Of the many cases Invernizzi and Gociol studied, Noemí Tornadú's book *Dulce de leche* is worth mentioning because it was banned for having an open ending. This type of reading, according to the censors, could lead children to imagine an ending that might not be appropriate. They also criticised the pessimistic tone in the story, especially because they believed that pessimism was "subversive".[55] Some Catholic children's books were also censored.[56] Their justification was always of similar content: "not aligned with the aims of the Process of National Reorganisation".[57]

By 1974, from the 50 million books printed each year in Argentina, the number decreased to 41 million in 1975, 31 million in 1976, and 17 million in 1979.[58] These statistics are evidence of the decline of production and publication of books during the military dictatorship.

The boomerang effect of censorship

The censor is an intrusive reader who infiltrates the mind of the writer, influencing the writer's thoughts and challenging freedom of expression. Undoubtedly, artists have the skills to create alternative paths in their texts to defy both the censor and the audience. In doing so, they find themselves in a labyrinth attempting to solve their dilemma: how to overcome their own fear, which leads to self-censorship, and how to express their ideas while overcoming the two main obstacles of official censorship apparatuses and social paracensorship, especially when these were infested with Catholic doctrine that deemed the reading of non-recommended texts sinful?

The "cultural strategy" of the military regime seems to have failed. Perhaps the cultural battle, quite different from the armed battles, was lost by the military Junta. During the dictatorship, the unexpected outcomes caused by censorship and paranoid censorship prepared the ground for the emergence of several types of literature and dissident forms of expression. Some scholars have talked about "the divided literature", referring to the one

---

54 In the resolution that prohibits this children's book it is said that the cause of this determination was the "need to guarantee the Argentine family their natural and sacred right to live according to our customs and traditions"—see Invernizzi and Gociol, *Un golpe*, p. 111.
55 Invernizzi and Gociol, *Un golpe*, p. 126.
56 Among the banned Catholic books were *Dios es fiel* by Beatriz Casiello, *Introducción a la sociología* by Duilio Biancucci, and the *Biblia latinoamericana*, all published by Editorial Guadalupe (Invernizzi and Gociol, *Un golpe*, p. 154).
57 Invernizzi and Gociol, *Un golpe*, p. 154.
58 Invernizzi and Gociol, *Un golpe*, p. 58.

produced within Argentina and the one published overseas.[59] However, a vast majority of the population remained unaware of these types of dissidence for a long time, partly because they were not regular consumers of these kinds of cultural product. Added to this, the mediocrity of hegemonic entertainment and the make-believe reality imposed by the regime were alienating and misleading.

Side by side with operation censorship, the military Junta inundated their speech with expressions such as "human rights" and "Christian values". Right from the start of the dictatorship, they presented themselves as highly organised, tidy, prudent, and firm in their decisions, adopting, at the same time, the image of a protective and disciplinary father. Their approach was indeed paternalistic; it did not allow any kind of dissidence, and thus silenced alternative views. Any resistance to their authoritarianism was intercepted or destroyed.

One of the unexpected and surprising consequences of censorship in Argentina during the military dictatorship, and probably one of the most outstanding cases of female struggle in Latin American history, was that of the Mothers of the Plaza de Mayo. Because they were not allowed to publish their claims in the media, these women created an alternative and original resistance movement. Another consequence, and the main topic of this book, was the development of coded forms of expression as response to the rhetoric of the imposed ideology of the regime. The lyrics of rock songs sourced language tropes such as allegory, irony, nonsense, surrealism, and play on words in a game of cat and mouse, where the censors were provoked but never given explicit proof of dissent. Rock musicians, as subsequent chapters will explore, beat the censors with one of their own weapons: words.

It could be concluded, then, that the repressive system only enjoyed partial success, for there was dissidence that it could neither control nor repress. This resistance was highly sophisticated and of outstanding literary quality, and, far from the mediocrity of the hegemonic cultural production,[60] it contributed not only to the development of political rhetorical tools, but also enriched national culture with quality art. It is possible then to think of two different levels of temporality in the resistance to the regime: (a) a social dissidence, which was immediate and faced immediate consequences; and (b) a literary dissidence, produced at the same time but the consequences of which were carried into the future. In the long term, when these literary texts are revisited and reinterpreted while keeping in mind the context in which they were created, they are further understood as resistance texts. Yet the case of Argentine rock, in particular what was called "rock nacional" during the dictatorship, presents both temporalities together. The concerts were the

---

59 Sosnowski, *Represión*, pp. 16–19.
60 For example, the films produced and directed by Palito Ortega, the saga of the "superagents" by Víctor Bo, Ricardo Bauleo, and Julio de Grazia, the "blue commandos" of Emilio Vieyra, and the musicals by Enrique Carreras.

social spaces where consequences were immediate—people taken to prison, police raids, disappearances—while the lyrics of the songs proved to be a "safe space" where both artists and audience could express dissent together, in complicity, and yet walk away free.

CHAPTER FOUR

Play on Words
Official versus Dissident Language

"Tengo los muertos todos aquí, ¿quién quiere que se los muestre?"

—*Charly García*

"Usualmente, solo flotan cuerpos a esta hora"

—*Luis Alberto Spinetta*

The military Junta, as well as destroying physical bodies and breaking the identity structures of many sectors of Argentine society, created a rhetoric of terror that was built on an obsession with language. Their discourse was heavily loaded with medical metaphors, such as the oft-repeated "we are the surgeons who will operate on society to extirpate the cancer it is suffering from", meaning they wanted to eradicate communism.[1] Rear Admiral César A. Guzzetti elaborated further for *La Opinión* on 3 October 1976:

> The social body of the country is contaminated by an illness that in corroding its entrails produces antibodies. These antibodies must not be considered in the same way as [the original] microbe. As the government controls and destroys the guerrilla, the action of the antibody will disappear... This is just the natural reaction of a sick body.[2]

The Junta's official communiqués were adorned with literary devices and presented a messianic message, speaking about God, love, trust, faith, and family values. At the same time, people were disappearing, and the youth

---

[1] In her highly regarded study titled *Poder y desaparición*, Argentine scholar Pilar Calveiro explains that the concentration camps were the "operating room" where said surgery was carried out; they were also, without a doubt, the testing ground for a new ordered, controlled, terrified society: see Pilar Calveiro, *Poder y desaparición. Los campos de concentración en Argentina* (Buenos Aires: Colihue, 2001), p. 11.
[2] Quoted in Feitlowitz, *A Lexicon*, p. 38.

were targeted as the main "enemy". The official discourse was plagued with ambiguity in the form of metaphors and euphemisms that invited confusion. Yet the communiqué that announced the coup d'état was clear and unilateral, making sure the general public understood that there was only one alternative in the face of chaos and anarchy.

When power was seized in March 1976, it was broadcast with messianic expressions such as "the Armed Forces of the nation, committed to their inalienable duty, have assumed the executive power of the state".[3] In the same press release, the military authorities stated that their aim was to "put an end to the subversive flagellum" and to carry out a "complete observance of the ethical and moral principles of justice, the holistic approach to a humanity that observes their rights and dignity: this way, the Republic will unite the Argentines and recover their national being". They also add that "all represented sectors of the country *must* feel clearly identified" and that "there is a *fighting* role for each citizen. It is a tough and urgent task which will require *sacrifice*" (our emphasis). The rhetoric of the press release combines toughness with service: "the Process will be conducted with absolute strength and vocation of service, ... we will defeat subversive delinquency, be it covert or overt". The document authors, Jorge Rafael Videla, Eduardo Massera, and Orlando Agosti, finish their communiqué with a salutation invoking "God's help".

Right from these very first official texts, the main rhetorical elements that would form the basis of the military discourse throughout the whole dictatorship period can be identified. This discourse references Catholic concepts such as "sacrifice", "vocation", "service", and "flagellum". Besides these words, the basic pillars of the construction of the official discourse are formed by allegories: the sick body, the Christian and Western family, union of all citizens, and a common enemy that the whole of Argentina needs to defeat in a war that, according to the military authorities, is inevitable.

Allegorical and religious texts

One could claim that a Catholic audience is quite familiar, in a sense, with allegorical texts. The Bible, the parables, and the stories of the saints all include allegorical elements, and as such it is not far-fetched to affirm that the Argentine population of the period was accustomed to encountering allegory, and was therefore well placed to interpret it. It is interesting to note that, in 1971, the rock band Vox Dei released an album called *La Biblia*,[4] which was a rock opera based on their own interpretation of the sacred text. The musicians submitted the lyrics to church officials, who approved the recording and broadcasting of the work. Raúl Porchetto, in 1972, released

---

3 Blaustein and Zubieta, *Decíamos ayer*, p. 96.
4 Vox Dei, *La Biblia* (Disc Jockey, 1971).

his first album called *Cristo rock*,[5] a rock opera based on the figure of Jesus. It is no coincidence that the Argentine military discourse was based on expressions about Christian and Western values, family, love, duty, and morality. The military officials' speeches had a messianic tone emulating that of a priest addressing the devotees assembled at mass, and, just as was done in the Christian texts with which they were so familiar, they put allegory to use, for example by describing subversion as a societal cancer.[6]

In their speeches and interviews, the military Junta also usually used metaphoric expressions, often with a messianic tone as well. Videla, for example, explained that *"weeds had grown and hence the national style was being taken over"*.[7] These words, which come from ecological phenomena, are used by Videla to describe events that are as far from nature as possible. The weeds he refers to are crime or terrorism and the overflow is the internal chaos in the country at the time. The choice of these two metaphors is by no means unsophisticated. Weeds are generally eliminated by "violent" means, preferably by attacking their very roots so they have fewer chances of growing again. The complete destruction of weeds is often preferred. Overflows are usually contained by means of retaining walls, rocks, and impenetrable barriers. Therefore, violence and concentration camps seem to be justified as "naturally necessary".

The main rhetorical pillars of the military discourse can be categorised around five main themes: the sick body, family, union, the "ser nacional", and the enemy. For the military regime, the "enemy" (subversion, dissidents, Marxists) causes a "disease" to the "great Argentine family" which is "united" by the single, ideal "ser nacional".[8] The only possible way to "save" (messianic tone) the members of that nation–family is to protect that unilateral "ser nacional" based on "Christian and Western values"; therefore, it is inevitable to undergo "surgery with no anaesthetic" (dictatorship, censorship, repression, death squads). This chapter explores those rhetorical pillars in order to grasp a deeper understanding of the verbal context in which Argentine rock flourished and why musicians developed language tropes to show the regime that "the enemy" was not going to be defeated with words. There was a real "war of words" and some cunning skills were needed to win.

Medical metaphors: The sick body

The regime authorities had embarked on a "political crusade": they spoke about the presence of "cancer" in Argentine society. They self-identified as "surgeons" who had come to "cure" the country, to "extirpate the cancerous

---

5 Raúl Porchetto, *Cristo rock* (Microfón, 1972).
6 For the reader interested in a full study of the military discourse, see Feitlowitz, *A Lexicon*.
7 Blaustein and Zubieta, *Decíamos ayer*, p. 128, my emphasis.
8 Favoretto, *Alegoría*, pp. 41–60.

cells and operate with no anesthesia". They construed a medical discourse around the concepts of disease, cure, tumour, surgeons, and sick bodies, making sure the message was that they were here to "save lives".

In keeping with this medical discourse, when the military Junta published their "Reglamento", it clearly stated that they were the "supreme organ of state".[9] Just a month later, newspaper *La Opinión* published an interview with Miguel Tato, a cinema censor, who said that "Censorship, if well applied, is *hygienic*. And highly *healthy*, like *surgery*. It *heals* and *disinfects* the *unhealthy* particles, *extirpating* bad *tumours* that *sicken* the screen and *contaminate* the audience".[10] This medical fiction draws a particular relationship between politics and science, at the same time as it favours an interpretation of the facts that implies cause and consequence. It describes a sick body affected by a growing cancerous tumour (subversion), which suggests that the body must suffer mutilation of some of its parts as the only way to survive. Marguerite Feitlowitz studied the language of the torturers in their "interrogation room", which was better known as the "surgery".[11] The program used to "recycle" prisoners was called a "process of recuperation". By means of that procedure, they tried to rescue some of the detained so that they could serve the armed forces in their crusade.[12] Torture was known as "treatment" or "intensive therapy". Argentine critic and writer Ricardo Piglia says that by using this type of medical language, the military built a fiction, a version of reality: "The theory of the foreign body that had penetrated the social fabric and that it should be extirpated began to circulate. What was going to be done to the victims' bodies in secret was anticipated publicly. Everything was said, without saying anything".[13]

The medical metaphors were not only used by the military authorities. Some members of the church adopted the same rhetoric. For example, Monseñor Adolfo Tortolo said, "the warm blood of our martyrs will be the vital plasma of our renewed Argentina".[14] Monseñor Tortolo's expression is quite sophisticated as it combines medical discourse with biblical concepts. According to him, the dead are "martyrs" that constitute the "plasma" that

---

9 *Clarín* (Buenos Aires), 26 March 1976, p. 1.
10 Blaustein and Zubieta, *Decíamos ayer*, p. 118, my emphasis.
11 Feitlowitz, *A Lexicon*, p. 57.
12 The recovery process had been designed by Admiral Massera and Captain Acosta. In an interview carried out by Feitlowitz, one of the survivors of the ESMA explained: "Acosta believed that if he gained the good will of those [of us] being 'recuperated', that would help him win a political history [after the dictatorship]. In our conversations with him, we were constantly having to simulate a change in our personal scale of values... This duality demanded a great deal of psychic and nervous energy, and added to the constant tension of our situation": see Feitlowitz, *A Lexicon*, p. 58.
13 Piglia, *Crítica*, p. 36.
14 Blaustein and Zubieta, *Decíamos ayer*, p. 144.

will bring "life" back to the country. From that we can deduce that there must be some death in order for there to be life for everyone.

Included in this rhetoric, which "diagnosed" a sick image of Argentine society, there seemed to be an uncorrupted and "healthy" institution that was as yet uncontaminated: the armed forces. It seemed to be the only institution that could succeed in eradicating disease and fighting against the subversive virus. As such, no community group or "organism" could self-manage or self-heal, as subversion had penetrated every space in the social fabric under different guises. The "cancer" metaphor seemed to work so well for the military discourse because one of the disease's characteristics is that it may spread unnoticed to different organs without actually interfering with the normal functioning of the body for a while. Besides, the treatments that existed at the time, such as chemotherapy, surgery, and radiotherapy, presented aggressive, nasty side effects that damaged the body in different ways. This devastating vision worsened when a more personal and emotional touch was added: the whole country was compared to a big loving family.

The country as one big family and the role of women

Though apparently simple, the comparison of the country to one big family was, in fact, quite complex. Citizens, as members of that great family, were asked to cooperate with the Process to "purify" the siblings who had erred. The government was identified as the father figure, who, in a conservative society, is the head of the household, the person who metes out orders and makes decisions.[15] This comparison allowed the military Junta to justify repression on many occasions. As head of the household, their duty was to maintain order, praising or punishing family members as needed.

An example of this paternalistic rhetoric can be seen in Massera's Message to Citizenship, in August 1978, when he officially retired as admiral, where, among other things, he said:

> Power is a pact with loneliness, although I tried to permanently break it whenever I could. Many times, coming home late at night, I would see lights on through your windows and wonder who lived there, how the decisions we had made that day affected you, to what extent I was complying with my obligation to watch over the destiny of my compatriots,

---

15 Some members of the church supported this paternalistic idea, such as Monseñor Adolfo Tortolo, who, in an interview published by *Para Ti* women's magazine on 28 June 1976, said: "the great Argentine family, our Nation, is wounded and bleeding... More than one family is sunk in bitterness because of someone who left, someone who did not know how to overcome their passion or someone who left home because of the seduction of a criminal adventure, sometimes": see Blaustein and Zubieta, *Decíamos ayer*, p. 132.

and I would have liked to enter each house and speak to you, and listen to you, and ask you about your joys and disappointments....[16]

Both General Videla and Admiral Massera fit the image of the good, strong, tough-loving father who guarded the well-being of his family. They made sure they established a strong institutional partnership with the Catholic Church. The two entities, "God and the Motherland", were always mentioned in their speeches. For instance, in 1980, at a public inauguration of the Livestock Market in his home town, Mercedes, Videla spoke of

> that Regiment of which my father was chief, and from whom I received, along with his example, a permanent source of inspiration and support. Here, finally, my family have always resided, the family that has been for me a permanent school of faith, a melting pot of civic virtues and a temple of love.[17]

General Videla married his first and only girlfriend when he was twenty-three years old. His life revolved around his family and the army.[18] For example, in his Christmas message in 1977, Videla spoke to the Argentine family using "usted", a formal use of the second-person singular in Spanish. However, he switched to the informal Argentine "you" form ("vos") when in his speech he wanted to address the youth, whom he described as "emotionally unstable and morally idealistic". Videla finished his public address in the following terms: "I summon everyone, in national union, within our families, face to face with Baby Jesus, to scrutinise our own conscience".[19] His message draws on the family, union, the instability of the youth, and God, all usual rhetorical elements in the military discourse.

Jorge Rafael Videla faced the jury between 1983 and 1985. He was sentenced to life imprisonment and perpetual absolute disqualification. If the penalties for the charges against Videla were cumulative, he would have had to spend 10,248 years in prison.[20] During the trial, prosecutor Julio César Strassera said that what was interesting about Videla was the fact that he insisted on affirming that certain things, which had been proven, never happened, as if he could deny reality be means of words:

> The hollow references of General Videla affirming that he is responsible for everything but that the events did not happen expose an elemental way of thinking that, giving a magical value to words, intends to use them to make the reality that one wants to deny disappear.[21]

---

16 Uriarte, *Almirante Cero*, p. 212.
17 Blaustein and Zubieta, *Decíamos ayer*, p. 123.
18 Blaustein and Zubieta, *Decíamos ayer*, p. 211.
19 Blaustein and Zubieta, *Decíamos ayer*, p. 226.
20 María Seoane and Vicente Muleiro, *El dictador: la historia secreta y pública de Jorge Rafael Videla* (Buenos Aires: Sudamericana, 2016), p. 607.
21 Seoane and Muleiro, *El dictador*, p. 605.

Admiral Emilio Eduardo Massera was also married at a noticeably young age, perhaps because a single officer would be looked upon with suspicion as regards his sexuality. Uriarte, the author of Massera's unauthorised biography, explains that "the military caste tended strongly to reproduce itself on the basis of 'society's primary cell: the family, which the school study manuals taught to defend together with order, Christianity and the Fatherland'".[22] Uriarte remarks that divorce was quite rare among military men because it lowered their prestige and ruled their family status as "irregular". Adultery was quite common and accepted among both men and their wives, although discreetly hidden away. A trait shared by the wives of military men, according to Uriarte's study, was their immaturity. They acted as childish, submissive wives for whom their husband was the head of the family. "The childishness of the women predisposed their husbands to adultery and gradually confined the women to the place of a curious servitude, where the husband was everything but their wives managed domestic tranquility and stability".[23]

Within this great state family, the role of women was indeed quite traditional. They were asked to fulfil their vocation as mothers. Their role as mothers was constantly highlighted as being responsible for the education and ideology of their children. For example, the media published an "Open Letter to Argentine Mothers" inviting them to reflect on their motherhood and their role as such:

> What are they doing to our children? What infernal machine achieves such a brainwashing...? ... We insist: mothers have a fundamental role to play... One of the key targets of the enemy is your child, your child's mind.[24]

Moreover, in a Catholic country, the Virgin Mary is presented as the feminine ideal, as an example of motherhood. Yet, as Marina Warner thoroughly studied, the twin ideal (mother by way of immaculate conception) represents an ideal that is of course unobtainable:[25] "Mary establishes the child as the destiny of woman, but escapes the sexual intercourse necessary for all other women to fulfil this destiny".[26] Such an impossible and unobtainable ideal, in Warner's words, drives women into a "position of acknowledged and hopeless yearning and inferiority".[27]

A thorough look at the covers of magazines and newspapers shows quite different coverage when the so-called subversives who were caught and/ or died were women. The photos were in black and white and their female condition was highlighted. This is evident in headlines such as "Young

---

22 Uriarte, *Almirante Cero*, pp. 35–36.
23 Uriarte, *Almirante Cero*, p. 37.
24 Blaustein and Zubieta, *Decíamos ayer*, p. 130.
25 Marina Warner, *Alone of All Her Sex. The Myth and Cult of the Virgin Mary* (London: Vintage, 2000), p. 337.
26 Warner, *Alone*, p. 336.
27 Warner, *Alone*, p. 337.

Woman who Planted Bomb Previously Convicted" (*La Prensa*, 19 June 1976, p. 1) and "Fleeing Woman Shot Down before She Could Swallow the Poison She Was Carrying" (*La Razón*, 3 December 1976, p. 1), among others. In *Clarín*, on 3 December 1976, under the headline "Subversion Suffered Casualties Record", the text describes the male responsible for a terrorist organisation and, interestingly, states that "his concubine, nicknamed Mimí, was responsible for indoctrination".[28] With that phrase the author of the text casts aspersions on this woman not only through mentioning her "concubinage" (de facto status), which for the Catholic Church was a mortal sin, and her nickname, reminiscent of sex workers and criminals, but also through emphasising that she was responsible for the "indoctrination". The person in charge of indoctrinating others is supposed to be someone who has studied the theory. It is not hard to deduce from these examples that, for the official ideology, women should not be educated more than necessary, because too much theory could become a dangerous tool. Instead, women should look after their children and protect them from the enemy.

Indeed, women seem to form a special, separate group under the lens of the Process. In an article in *Gente* on 9 June 1977, titled "Subversion: These Women Have Won the War Too", there is a dramatic and emotional description of the sorrows of mothers who had lost their children in the so-called dirty war. In contrast, the Mothers of the Plaza de Mayo were called "crazy" (locas) by the regime. What was the difference between one mother and the next? Wouldn't they share the same pain? Did *Gente* mean that some mothers suffered more than others? How could it be thought possible to measure the pain of mothers according to their children's occupations? *Gente* went on to explain: "high-ranking military women, soldiers, firefighters, police, executives, employees. All of them had to face the war. You all lost something unrecoverable... You *too* won the war".[29] If women were not considered a separate group, the use of "you too" (ustedes también) would not be necessary in the text.

The role and responsibility of women was highlighted on a regular basis in women's magazines such as *Para Ti*. For instance, Lucrecia Gordillo signed an article in which she alluded to an "international boycott" of Argentina by American senators. She encouraged all Argentine women to unite and fight for human rights and the forging of a new country. The author titled her article "We, women, are responsible for our children's country".[30] Such a statement should be understood in context, given that the magazine targeted a female audience. In other contexts, mothers were the ones to be blamed. When questioned about the disappeared by Japanese journalists, Videla

---

28 All these articles are published in Blaustein and Zubieta, *Decíamos ayer*; see p. 131; p. 161; p. 165; p. 166.
29 Blaustein and Zubieta, *Decíamos ayer*, p. 198, my emphasis.
30 Blaustein and Zubieta, *Decíamos ayer*, p. 244.

indirectly blamed subversives' mothers or wives, alluding to their responsibility and vulnerability:

> We understand the pain of that mother or wife who has lost her son or husband, about whom we cannot offer any news, whether because they clandestinely joined the ranks of subversion, or because they were seized by *cowardice* and were unable to maintain their subversive attitude, or because they have disappeared by changing their name and clandestinely leaving the country, or because their *extremely mutilated body*, impacted by explosions and gunfire in *a confrontation*, could not be identified, or *due to excessive crowd control measures*.[31]

Videla's comment refers to mothers' and wives' pain, but he does not address the male relatives of the disappeared. This fact underlines the female "weakness" and vulnerability, and the sexist popular expectation that men do not cry.

On the one hand, the Madres de Plaza de Mayo are censored, misunderstood, considered "crazy", and indirectly blamed for not educating their children properly. On the other, the media bombardment, in particular from the magazines targeting a female readership, highlights the relevance of the role of women as supporters of the PRN. These images are sending a message to the audience that may condition the reception of news regarding the death of children. This seems to be a manipulative move. While being a mother of a disappeared is construed as a crime, being the mother of a soldier or military official is an honour. The aesthetic distance between the imposed, "correct" interpretation that seeks to eliminate any other form of reading and to limit readers' freedom is therefore deliberately restricted.

Union: Team allegory

National union not only depended upon the comparison of the country to a large family. Sports provided another useful analogy. For a family to function properly, the union of its members is essential. The military authorities chose a strategy whose success, taking into account Argentines' passion for soccer, was guaranteed.

The 1978 soccer World Cup, hosted by Argentina, was an opportunity for the regime to exploit citizens' love for this sport in service of their political aims. It proved to be the most efficient strategy to achieve national union. Right from the slogan "25 million Argentines will play in the World Cup" ["25 millones de argentinos jugaremos el mundial"], everyone was called on to share a common goal. President Videla personally invited the population to become part of the team: "achieving these goals requires a long and shared effort" (*Clarín*, 18 April 1976, headline, p. 1). Another major publicity

---

[31] Blaustein and Zubieta, *Decíamos ayer*, p. 220, my emphasis.

campaign stated, "In the World Cup, you play as an Argentine". Indeed, the soccer World Cup and Argentina's victory allowed the Junta to reinforce the idea that "union" was the key to success. The performance of the national team of soccer players fuelled feelings of national pride.

The soccer World Cup was exploited in two ways: first, to distract people from the atrocities the regime was committing; second, to unify the population and transform the sports passion into a feeling of social and political success. Moreover, it was used to send an international audience an image of the country different from the existing one at that particular moment, as General de Brigada Antonio Luis Merlo expressed in an interview published by *La Opinión* on 16 November 1976:

> The 1978 World Cup will have two fundamental purposes beyond football itself: to show abroad an Argentine image that has been deformed by foreign interests and to unite the country's inhabitants around an event that is everyone's heritage, without exclusions.[32]

The triumphalist discourse, evident in newspapers, magazines, and publications of the time, played a major role in uniting a country that had been dealing with frustration, anger, and pain for some time. It was utilised as a compensation mechanism, as a new start, in keeping with a process of reorganisation. The most effective tool this mechanism put to use was, indeed, sport. Soccer is the most accessible, popular, and beloved sport for Argentines, and Argentine soccer attracts world-wide attention due to its skillful players. During the 1978 soccer World Cup hosted by Argentina, many citizens were distracted from the socio-political status quo, absorbed as they were by the games. Argentina won the Cup and this triumph was translated into national pride, pride for "being Argentine", words that were used and overused in the media. President Videla presented himself as one of the main supporters of the national team, attending several matches and celebrating each goal. This move was successful in that it attracted popularity. Suddenly he seemed like a likeable guy. Videla has been known by his staid, sober, cold, and serious-minded profile. These televised images of the president emotionally engaging with an Argentine passion contributed to building a human side to the man, making him more accessible and closer to the people he governed. When interviewed, Videla assured them that "I have not done it for political reasons because it would be wrong to capitalise on the success that really belongs to the people".[33] However, in the broadcast message at the end of the World Cup, his political use of the event becomes clear:

> That cry of Argentina that arose unanimously from our hearts, that unique celestial and white flag that flew in so many hands, are signs of a *profound*

---

32 Blaustein and Zubieta, *Decíamos ayer*, p. 160.
33 Blaustein and Zubieta, *Decíamos ayer*, p. 258.

reality that exceeds the limits of a sporting event. They are the voice and the banner of a nation that, in the fullness of its dignity, has found itself.[34]

Interestingly, Videla's words attribute national unity to soccer. It was through soccer, according to him, that the nation managed to come together and find itself. In the rhetoric of the president's speech, what Christian and Western values alone were not able to achieve was possible thanks to a popular sport.

In 1979, Argentina won the youth soccer World Cup. This new sports success was used as yet another symbol of national unity. During this championship, a young Diego Maradona emerged as a popular idol. Videla saw his charm and popularity and publicly spoke to him in the following terms: "I want to convey my pleasure to you, as captain, ... in a team-like feeling that shows us all what Argentines can do when they dedicate themselves to working together".[35] Some popular radio presenters adhered to this "uniting feeling". For example, José María Muñoz became political during his soccer report: "Let's all go to Avenida de Mayo and show the gentlemen of the Human Rights Commission that Argentina has nothing to hide". The members of the Inter-American Commission on Human Rights were at the OAS headquarters—located on Avenida de Mayo—and at that time they were preparing to go to the National Congress to present their findings to the military Junta.[36]

The analogy between "the team" and "the nation" works in a patriarchal context. In a soccer team, leadership is in the hands of a male—in 1978, the soccer World Cup that Argentina won had no women players. The colours of the national team's shirt are those of the Argentine flag, a national symbol that unites the whole population. The result is a "team" in which men (soccer players) are active and women (all of them) are passive, though they are unconditional supporters. Videla's use of the team allegory effectively evokes the shared passion for soccer, recalling an event that made a strong imprint in peoples' lives, as well as being intended to extend that feeling beyond the sport. The 1978 World Cup was, at least for most Argentines, a historic moment filled with positive emotions and feelings of national belonging. By encouraging Argentines to transpose these positive feelings of belonging to the political figure of the Junta, the military leaders garnered more support than could have been gained by means of almost any other strategy.

However, unity was an illusion. Argentina was divided in two. On one side was a merry Argentina celebrating sports successes; on the other was a sad and desperate Argentina holding long lists of disappeared as they queued outside the OAS to present their claims. The contrast calls to mind Rosario's Archbishop Monseñor Guillermo Bolatti, who said: "Each country must regulate human rights. It should not be foreigners who come to tell

---

34 Blaustein and Zubieta, *Decíamos ayer*, p. 262, my emphasis.
35 Blaustein and Zubieta, *Decíamos ayer*, p. 305.
36 Blaustein and Zubieta, *Decíamos ayer*, p. 306.

us what we have to do".[37] That same week, the popular magazine *Gente* published an open letter to the Inter-American Commission for Human Rights, in which they assured "You come to this country invited by the national government".[38] These incoherent or contradictory messages, both from supporters of the regime, reveal the discomfort caused by the presence of the Commission.

Undoubtedly, the 1978 World Cup was a powerful and unforgettable event in Argentina's popular history, mainly because of the strong sense of belonging experienced by Argentines. Evidence of this can be found in the publicity campaigns of the time: for example, in *Clarín* (1 June 1978) under the title "I Feel Proud", signed by "an Argentine citizen", the author enumerated the reasons for his national pride. Among them, he made a special mention of all people who, through their various jobs, had contributed to the success of the event, acting as hosts to thousands of international visitors. The last of the eighteen items in this enumeration simply stated, "I am proud of being an Argentine". Videla himself, at the end of one of the main matches that ensured the trophy cup stayed in Argentine hands, made the most of the opportunity to say: "Our players showed the courage, emotion and desire to win that the Argentine people have in *all aspects*".[39]

Historical allegories

In order to achieve the homogeneity of the great state family or the great national team, the population had to be unified ideologically. The traditional concept of "ser nacional" (national being) was redefined by the political discourse and brought to the centre of the military leaders' ideology. In Feitlowitz's words,

> To the Gentlemen of the Coup, el ser nacional resonated with divine purpose, with the country's grand destiny. It reinforced the message that the coup was tantamount to normalisation, integration. The expression also served to locate the Process within each Argentinean: to resist the Process was to deny one's self.[40]

The myth of the "ser nacional" was based on what the military men considered "tradition" and became an essential component of their speeches. The regime ruled, emphasising national unity and vehement nationalism while imposing their policies through violence, censorship, and a discourse based on myths. Their idea of the national being was used to unify people and to manipulate public opinion by means of patriotic rhetoric, such as the sentiment expressed by Lieutenant Hugo Pascarelli in March 1977: "Our

---

37 Blaustein and Zubieta, *Decíamos ayer*, p. 308.
38 Blaustein and Zubieta, *Decíamos ayer*, p. 310.
39 Blaustein and Zubieta, *Decíamos ayer*, p. 254, my emphasis.
40 Feitlowitz, *A Lexicon*, p. 21.

fight knows no moral limits. It is beyond good and evil".[41] To be "beyond good and evil" presupposes a messianic role in a sublime, epic conceptualisation of the regime. This type of message seems supported by moral law, denoting a mission on a grand scale, as disclosed by Pascarelli. President Videla also summoned everyone in his speeches to adhere to the essential national being. For example, to celebrate the first year of the coup, he gave a public speech in which he officially formulates his "unity" proposal. In his speech, he values the support of the armed forces, who "have accompanied their soldiers to a victory that is looming today and that belongs to the entire nation". Videla adds that the regime's aim is to "instate authentic, political and durable order, based on freedom, equality, justice and security".[42] Equality for Videla, however, is in fact rejection of diversity. The "authentic" order he foresees then, implies his one-sided truth, which is not necessarily shared by everyone. Therefore, more than a "proposal for unity", his speech was an *ultimatum*: those who were not aligned with the regime's national being would be considered subversive and, hence, dangerous enemies of the state.

The mass media, together with school textbooks and all study material, were especially careful in their dealing with history, the construction of the Argentine past, and, especially, the "national being". The military authorities seemed particularly interested in "drilling" their notion of national being and their Christian and moral values into the youth by using the radio and the press. For them, the impact potential of these media was superior to those of textbooks or books. Some history books were discontinued, whereas other books were distributed by Eudeba (Buenos Aires University Press) and promoted through special competitions and gifts such as a trip to Antarctica. Some of those competitions were directly connected to the Conquest of the Desert, Roca's infamous expedition in which indigenous people were massacred.[43] Eudeba published several dozen books by Argentine authors in which the Conquest of the Desert was presented as an event of national pride and where the fatherland had come about thanks to epic expeditions and brave warriors.

In 1979, to celebrate the fourth centenary of the founding of the City of Buenos Aires, the town hall entrusted a special task to Carlos María Gelly y Obes, Director of Museo Saavedra. The exhibition was called "The Pacification of the Pampas".[44] In it, the genocide of the indigenous population of Patagonia was ideologically legitimised. Interestingly, this happened at the same time the military forces were killing and disappearing thousands

---

41 *Clarín, suplemento especial* (Buenos Aires), 27 March 1977, p. 15.
42 Blaustein and Zubieta, *Decíamos ayer*, p. 179.
43 The Conquest of the Desert was a military campaign carried out by the government of Julio Argentino Roca, against the Mapuche, Tehuelche, and Ranquel nations, with the aim of obtaining territorial dominion of the Pampa and Eastern Patagonia, until then under indigenous control. It was one of the first genocides in the country.
44 Invernizzi and Gociol, *Un golpe*, p. 52.

of civilians, justifying themselves by means of a "dirty war" in which the enemy of the state had to be eliminated. It would be hard for contemporary Argentines not to draw a parallel between the massacre of the indigenous people in the nineteenth century and the new disappearances in the twentieth. Historically, the method used by some governments to solve conflicts was the genocide of those considered their enemies. Whereas in one century it was the so-called "Indians", in the next century it was government opponents. Though these historical instances were motivated by different purposes (land appropriation in one, eradication of communism in the other) and happened at different scales, the construction of an internal enemy and its disappearing was framed within an imposed ideology.

Another example worth mentioning is found in the speech President Videla gave during the celebration of the centenary of the Conquest of the Desert. He said: "It was an integration founded on respect for a brave lineage that thereby agreed to civilisation and citizen responsibility. How can we omit, in this sense, an emotional reference to the attitude of that little Indian who with his faith symbolised such virtue and purity?".[45]

In that quote, Videla speaks of "unity" again. For him, the "brave" attitude of a "little Indian" (a symbolic individualisation) connected him to civilisation. Here, the foundational binary "civilisation vs. barbarism", popularised by Domingo Sarmiento in 1845, emerges as a useful analytic tool. The diminutive form "little Indian" used by Videla may be interpreted as pejorative. We now know very well that the indigenous inhabitants of the land that today is called Argentina had no choice other than to surrender to the Spanish conquerors. If, as Videla says, these first inhabitants "symbolised virtue and purity", then how would he explain the thousands of Indians killed during the Conquest of the Desert? The "little Indian" had no choice. Either he adopted the white man's ideology and gave up his land or he was killed. Videla confuses facts with accepting "citizen responsibility".

Moreover, in Córdoba, for example, after the public burning of books by authors such as Marcel Proust, Gabriel García Márquez, Pablo Neruda, Mario Vargas Llosa, Eduardo Galeano, and Saint-Exupéry, among others, the III Cuerpo de Ejército published a comuniqué saying:

> To ensure that nothing remains of these books, brochures, magazines, etc., this resolution is made to bring an end to using these materials to deceive our youth about the genuine good represented by our national symbols, our family, our church and, finally, our most traditional spiritual heritage synthesised in God, Fatherland and Home.[46]

It is clear from the previous quote that the fusion of the national symbols of the family and the church formed the "one true" national being. This

---

45 Blaustein and Zubieta, *Decíamos ayer*, p. 292.
46 Blaustein and Zubieta, *Decíamos ayer*, p. 122.

definition left out any alternative religion, family structure, or political idea. In this way, the expected behaviour of each Argentine citizen is based on an imposed idea, externally manipulated by authority (political, legal, social, and ecclesiastical). The essence that unites the great Argentine family, or Argentine team, is an invariable and unique national being, Catholic and Western.

In sum, the "national being" imposed by the regime was unique, Catholic, based on Western and Christian values, and absolute, in that it did not admit any form of diversity or variation from those norms. Any challenge to this definition was considered subversive and deceitful.

The enemy

The metaphorical language used in official rhetoric was widely accepted, and different groups of the population heard this call to collaborate with the process of "healing" the fatherland. All Argentines were called to collaborate with the regime, reminding them of their duty to cooperate as citizens, denouncing subversion or simple suspicion of it. Therefore, a sense of insecurity and paranoia led people to distrust everything and each other. The "enemy" could be anywhere, and it was necessary to stay alert. Emphasising that the nation was in a state of war guaranteed the military Junta the right to defend the country from an attack on its sovereignty.

Indeed, in their speeches, the phrases "guerrilla" and "common enemy" were used and overused, often accompanied by photographs and stories of murdered police officers and narratives of armed clashes between the police and civilians. The message was imparted through loaded words and visual images. It is necessary to point out that the enemy is not seen as a human being, it has no name or surname, it is stripped of the fundamental values upheld by the Process, such as, for example, the family. It is seen under one label: "subversive". That generalisation of the enemy allows the creation of polarised roles that guarantee power: us and them. For example, an editorial in the Catholic magazine *Criterio*, cited by *La Opinión* on 5 February 1976, reads "a hundred dead are a hundred fewer enemies, and if there were more, the better, whatever the manner of their death".[47]

However, there is a certain personalisation of the enemy in cases in which, despite not having a name or a face, it could be identified. In the front-page headline of newspaper *La Razón* on 20 July 1976, the phrase "the guerrilla warfare is beheaded"[48] is used to report the death of a montonero leader. The term "beheaded/headless" makes metaphorical use of the enemy's body. It is a simplifying act, singling an individual out of the dissident crowd. In one of his public speeches, Admiral Massera addressed the individual:

---

[47] Blaustein and Zubieta, *Decíamos ayer*, p. 68.
[48] Blaustein and Zubieta, *Decíamos ayer*, p. 135.

"Your weapons are your eyes, your ears and your intuition".[49] Each person was summoned to take responsibility in the national cleansing crusade. The Process used such phrases to impose their ideology and manipulate society. Their speeches were designed to appeal through being consistent and stable, and to address each individual intimately, personally, as in communion with the government.

Some examples of how the message was "drilled" into the audience are found in the word games coined by the military itself or their advisors, such as the one that circulated during the visit of the Human Rights Commission: "Argentines are right, and human".[50] Through this play on words, with the double meaning of "right" (derechos) more akin to "lawful" in English, President Videla referred to the Commission's visit, possibly in an attempt to present it as an ally of the "enemy". The plural noun "human rights" was repurposed as plural adjectives by beginning the sentence with "Argentines are" and including the conjunction "and" between the words, splicing the idea into two separate concepts. The intention was to disqualify any report that the Commission could present. Stickers with this phrase written on the Argentine flag were distributed throughout the country. People stuck these stickers on their lapels, on the windshields of cars and in the windows of their houses. The intention was to instill in the populace the idea that the Commission acted on behalf of an international campaign organised by exiled subversives, who from abroad wanted to devalue Argentina. For this reason, it was necessary to be "alert" and "defend the country from the enemy's tricks".

Another example of the imposition of the "common enemy" figure is a booklet published in 1977 by the Ministry of Culture and Education and distributed in all schools with the title: "Subversion in the Field of Education: get to know our enemy". The booklet describes what military officials call subversive actions. It explains how ideas infiltrate through teachers sympathetic to the subversive cause and affect the minds of young students, who are led to "become enemies of the social organisation in which they live in peace, and friends of those responsible for the riots who turn them in favour of the triumph of another ideology foreign to the national being".[51]

The Junta's most important mission was to "defeat the enemy". In their own words, the main cultural enemy was Marxism.[52] The official rhetoric simplified their theory and reduced it to the figure of the "enemy". This subject had the ability to camouflage itself, to penetrate schools, universities, and the media in disguise, with the simple goal of confusing young people and guiding them down the wrong path. If this enemy was so skilled, then it required the intervention of a specialist force, highly trained in detecting such

---

49 Feitlowitz, *A Lexicon*, p. 38.
50 Blaustein and Zubieta, *Decíamos ayer*, p. 179.
51 Blaustein and Zubieta, *Decíamos ayer*, pp. 167–68.
52 "In short, everything that was Marxist was subversive but not everything subversive was Marxist": Invernizzi and Gociol, *Un golpe*, p. 51.

a threat.[53] The military intelligence team claimed that its members were the only ones trained for this "enemy identification" task. This ideology gave the military the foundations to claim the right to control education, culture, and the media, as they presented themselves as the only professionals trained to carry out this mission successfully.

The enemy could be anywhere. Therefore, the entire culture had to be scrutinised. Invernizzi lists a varied selection of material that was analysed: almanacs, calendars, posters, plays, novels, school texts, religious texts, foreign language teaching books, atlases, encyclopaedias, poetry, essays, newspaper articles, brochures, bestsellers, magazines, newspapers, and television programs, as well as all kinds of activities including circuses, literary contests, congresses of writers, foreign books—even those that were not translated into Spanish—film directors, films, radio programs, and photos.[54]

The speeches of military officers often singled out the enemy, reducing a multitude of forms of resistance to a single figure. This drastic simplification, rhetorically effective, manifests its Manichaeism in the tendency to use rigid binary distinctions that divide reality (good and evil, civilisation and barbarism) and in the categorisation of its political opposition as demonic, in keeping with an archaic Christian metaphysics.

The enemy often exists in a situation of war. In order to talk about an enemy, one had necessarily to talk about war. Monseñor Olimpo Santiago Maresma, Bishop of Mendoza, said in his homily on 9 July 1976:

> today our fatherland is threatened from inside and outside. That is why our work must be holistic: it must embrace body and spirit... It comforts us to see today the Captains of the Armed Forces demonstrating their faith in the protection offered by the Mother of God, faith that comes from many years ago, when San Martin gave us the first example... We are in a quasi-civil war that we have not declared but has been declared to us.[55]

The enemy was accused of having started a war, which Massera described as "a war between didactic materialism and idealistic humanism... a war between freedom and tyranny... between those who are in favour of death and those who are in favour of life. And this is prior to a policy or an ideology. This is a metaphysical attitude".[56] The description of war that Massera made with ample use of literary resources, trying to present the enemy, "whose objective is destruction in itself, although they are masked by social redeemers", as not open to dialogue, ended up being a description of the real-life attitude of the armed forces, which preemptively terminated any possibility of dialogue with civilians.

---

53 Invernizzi and Gociol, *Un golpe*, p. 49.
54 Invernizzi and Gociol, *Un golpe*, p. 51.
55 Blaustein and Zubieta, *Decíamos ayer*, p. 152.
56 Uriarte, *Almirante Cero*, p. 140.

In this war, General Acdel Eduardo Vilas publicly declared that he supported "even excesses of [his] men if the result is important for our objective", with reference to his actions during Operation Independence in the mountains of Tucumán.[57] A few months later, the magazine *Extra* published photos of several officials under the title "Heroes" (Vol. 139, January 1977) Note that the text of the article says that "memory has a great capacity for forgetting" to justify that, perhaps, in the selection of heroic characters "fundamental figures may have been omitted".[58]

There was also reference to an external enemy, extending the frontiers of war: "the anti-Argentine campaign abroad". The magazine *Para Ti*, in February 1979, published a series of postcards with photos of the soccer World Cup and the streets, which people could cut out and send to their friends or relatives who lived abroad. The postcards were titled: "Argentina: the whole truth". They also had phrases such as: "The war ended in Argentina. These flags are the symbol of a peace that we managed to attain. The Soccer World Cup was an exam that we had to sit and that we approved. You, very far from us, dared to judge us. You listened to the subversive delinquents and gave them a tribune". These postcards with apparently very eloquent photos used the idea of war and the enemy associated with football, as explored previously. They compare a friendly sports tournament with an "exam" and sports opponents with "subversive delinquents", who were given a "tribune", that is, a space on the "pitch" or the arena of the test. The flags to which the quotation refers are those of the accompanying image, in which a girl is seen on her father's shoulders, carrying an Argentine flag, during the celebrations of the national soccer team's triumph. The text identifies them with "flags of peace", as if the soccer pitch had been a battlefield.

The disappeared

The enemy, who, as already mentioned, was stripped of identity—in the forms of name and surname, face, or family information—nevertheless managed to obtain an important place in the history of Argentina. The military authorities, in describing the enemy as "disappeared", granted them a new identification. This new label brought unexpected effects for the de facto government. What they wanted to erase from existence and surround with an atmosphere of doubt and suspicion was turned against them. The suspicion and doubt fell, instead, on the military authorities themselves.

In the face of international accusations about thousands of disappearances in the country, General Harguindeguy called the figures "insane" and refused to provide a true figure based on a "military secret".[59] Regarding the

---

57 Blaustein and Zubieta, *Decíamos ayer*, p. 154.
58 Blaustein and Zubieta, *Decíamos ayer*, p. 172.
59 Horacio Verbitsky, *Malvinas: la última batalla de la Tercera Guerra Mundial* (Buenos Aires: Editorial Sudamericana, 2002), p. 170.

disappeared, General Videla spoke with foreign journalists and, as published on the first page of *La Opinión* on 13 December 1977, he said, bluntly, that there are four determining causes of the official ignorance of the whereabouts or the fate of many people:

- Clandestine passage to the ranks of subversion;
- Leaving the country with a change of name, after militance in extremist organisations;
- Impossibility of recognition of bodies mutilated by explosions, fire, or projectiles, as a result of wars between legal forces and terrorist elements;
- An excess in repression.

Videla himself attributed the term "disappeared" with the following meaning:

> the disappeared, as such, is unknown. If he reappeared, he would have an X treatment. But if the disappearance became certain, then his death would have another treatment. As long as he is disappeared, he cannot have special treatment, because he has no identity, he is neither dead nor alive…[60]

Initially, the military authorities denied and discredited the existence of the disappeared. Later, and because of the increasing reports, testimonies, and evidence, the military authorities adopted the role of victims of political persecution, celebrating masses and religious services in memory of those fallen in the war against subversion. A few months after the coup, on 2 November 1976, Massera delivered a speech titled "Those who Died for the Fatherland" ["Los muertos por la Patria"] from which his description of the enemy is worth quoting: "We are fighting against nihilists, against delirious destruction, whose objective is destruction itself, although they are masked by social redeemers".[61] Facing the evidence of the disappearances and public pressure, often of the church itself, it was suggested to forget: as stated by General Luciano Benjamín Menéndez, former Commander of III Cuerpo de Ejército de Córdoba, "There is a willingness to forget, it is best to forget now. The disappeared disappeared and nobody knows where they are".[62]

By the end of 1978, newspapers started to publish requests calling for the whereabouts of the disappeared, to which the government responded with silence. The Chief of the Federal Police, Juan Bautista Sasiaín, affirmed in statements to *Clarín* journalists that it caused him irritation that those who headed the lists of claims for the disappeared were writers, public leaders, who, having had the opportunity to occupy situations of power, had not taken the opportunity to alert the population about subversion and had even had

---

60 Blaustein and Zubieta, *Decíamos ayer*, p. 334.
61 Uriarte, *Almirante Cero*, p. 141.
62 Blaustein and Zubieta, *Decíamos ayer*, p. 452.

the luxury of playing with maternal feelings, "a cruel feeling, loaded with guilt and despair, because it prompts those who never knew who they had lost before they lost them to take up the search...".[63]

As for Videla's successor, General Viola, president of the Republic in 1980, said that:

> the Armed Forces will not allow a review of what has been done against terrorism. Ethically, *for us*, allowing those who have fought with honour and sacrifice to bring peace to the Argentines to be prosecuted would constitute a betrayal and a grievance to the memory of those who have fallen victim to acts of terrorism. No account is asked of a *glorious* army.[64]

The analysis of the rhetorical strategies of the military regime reveals the sinister power games that words can contain. There is a double meaning in military rhetoric. The "national being" refers to a common identity and calls for national unity through the images of the family, the role of women, the role of each member of the national team, and the joint struggle against the disease contracted thanks to the common enemy. The population was invited to unite and collaborate with the regime, to become its accomplice, be it by playing against its soccer opponent, by fighting against subversion—an internal enemy—and/or supporting the war against an overseas enemy, during the Malvinas/Falklands War. *Clarín*, 7 April 1977, published the following:

> Any indication that you observe and that may contribute to the joint forces about the presence of these social misfits will allow their faster arrest and prosecution. Do not hesitate to report any abnormality you detect, no matter how insignificant it may be. Thus you will also participate in the struggle in which the Argentine People are engaged. (From a statement issued by the V Command of Zone I of the Army, which warns of a "desperate campaign of destruction orchestrated by subversive elements".)[65]

In a *Clarín* advertisement of 17 April 1982, the population was invited to write letters to different world leaders on the Malvinas conflict, so that they would receive millions of Argentine voices on the issue. Again, the population was encouraged to participate in the war, to "unite" against the anti-Argentine campaign. The advertisement suggested that the reader add "a photo of himself or his family, any simple, human, everyday photo" and write what "his heart and reason dictated to him on the vocation of peace of the Argentines".[66]

At the same time, identity was altered in different ways: by imposing a single vision, many other alternative positions that did not necessarily belong

---

63 Blaustein and Zubieta, *Decíamos ayer*, p. 362.
64 Blaustein and Zubieta, *Decíamos ayer*, p. 346, my emphasis.
65 Blaustein and Zubieta, *Decíamos ayer*, p. 186.
66 Blaustein and Zubieta, *Decíamos ayer*, p. 486, underlined in original.

to the dangerous group or that threatened national security were left aside. In addition, a new identity was invented: the disappeared. The resulting irony is clear: it called attention to those whom the military regime wanted to strip of their identity. The lack of information, or the presence of manipulated information, gave rise to new discourses, true or not, that arose out of the need to grasp the scattered fragments of that fractured identity.

Yet a single story and a lack of identity do not go well with rock culture. The emerging countercultural rock movement kept growing during this period and saw this crisis as an opportunity to develop creative strategies to resist. The official manipulation of words may have been what inspired rock musicians to write lyrics with coded words, in a kind of boomerang effect of the regime's censorship and word-using techniques, until, little by little, word by word, the "subversives" as portrayed by the Process became the skilled songwriters in the story by wielding the military leaders' own weapon against them.

CHAPTER FIVE

Concealed Meaning

Codification of Dissident Messages in Songs

"Les contaste un cuento sabiéndolo contar"

—*Charly García*

In *The Human Condition,* Arendt articulated the idea of action, meaning the ordinary qualities that heroes possess.[1] For Arendt, "action" referred to a conception of politics based on an individual's capacity to do the unexpected. This capacity means that humans have the potential to change their lives in meaningful ways. In order to take action in this sense, humans must think independently from authority while thinking interdependently with others. Those who take action are seen as heroes, unlike normal, everyday citizens. In the case of Argentine rock in its early stages, during the PRN, this action is observable in a variety of forms. However, in this analysis, we are particularly compelled by action in the form of performed and broadcast words, text, the song itself. As Bicknell puts it,

> What is communicated or fails to be communicated through a song? I have already claimed that the presence of text sets song apart from other types of music. So it might seem obvious that what singers communicate is song lyrics. Yet while singers do communicate words, that is not all they do. There is much more to be said.[2]

The songs that were written during this period constitute a cryptic response to the guidelines with which the youth were bombarded from many angles, including political speeches, the media, the press, the church, and the education system. The foregoing chapter explored the main pillars of the official discourse and how the military leaders used language to erase any

---

1 Hannah Arendt, *The Human Condition* (Chicago: University of Chicago Press, 1998 [1958]).
2 Bicknell, *Philosophy,* p. 10.

alternative identity. The ideology of the regime was also upheld and disseminated by supportive publications. For example, some right-wing magazines that circulated at the time, such as *Cabildo*, had interesting ideas about rock. *Cabildo* published a series of articles titled "Rock and Subversion".[3] The author of those articles, Carlos Manfroni, explained how rock music was "the most subversive, anti-Christian, anti-metaphysical and countercultural movement that has ever existed. It turns young people into uncontrollable animals, like Pavlov's dog".[4]

A book from July 1977, by Alberto Boixadós, explained the effects of rock and pop music on young minds: "Dr. Joseph Crowe, Professor of Psychology at Pacific Western College, has expressed that 'The use of the rhythm of rock can produce hypnotic states. Young people listen to the same song hundreds of times…, repetition is the basis of hypnosis'". Analysing Woodstock Festival, Boixadós explains:

> These festivals sometimes last a long time. The New Port was extended to five days and, as someone observed, the attendees acquired conditioned reflexes, such as Pavlov's dog; when they heard a rock song they opened their hearts to the Vietcong flag and the total liberation of man; when they heard a pop song they wanted to kill a policeman. And all through its melodies.[5]

Oddly enough, in a society in which church youth groups and Boy Scout troops were not allowed to meet, and the punishment for speaking out against the government was quite literally death, rock concerts were permitted to continue. It is not surprising that concert attendance during the period surged, as performances became a meeting place for the youth, who had been negated by the official media and disappeared by the regime.

On the same day that the *Prima Rock* festival was held in 1981, the de facto president, Roberto Viola, addressed a message to the youth, broadcast on national radio and TV, in which he expressed his confidence in the existence of a new generation, able to correct "past mistakes".[6] He also highlighted the efforts made, in terms of public management, to establish a dialogue with the youth sectors:

> Initially the National Government has assumed obligations in this regard, placing the general aspects that concern the youth at the level of direct presidential advice; taking the first steps to articulate a system of action without the need to create new organisms; implementing a student survey

---

3 Marchini, *No toquen*, p. 243.
4 Cited in Marchini, *No toquen*, p. 243.
5 Alberto Boixadós, *Arte y subversión: arte, mistificación, política* (Buenos Aires: Areté, 1977), p. 48.
6 Lisa Di Cione, "Rock y dictadura en la Argentina: reflexiones sobre una relación contradictoria," *Revista afuera* 10 (15): 1–9, 2015, at p. 4.

plan and another one of housing for young couples, orchestrating the development of internal migrations with cultural and sports activities and seeking the concretion of an active participation of youth in all the aspects that have to do with the national task through a continuous dialogue.[7]

The mention of "direct presidential advice" refers to the work undertaken by journalist Alfredo Olivera, who, though he had rejected the position of press secretary of the government, accepted the position of presidential adviser on youth issues, working to consolidate a space for informal dialogue between the government and the figures considered as referent among young people. The official had an office in San Telmo where he was visited by several of the most relevant producers, journalists, and rock musicians. Sergio Pujol mentions that Charly García, David Lebón, Rodolfo García, León Gieco, Luis Alberto Spinetta, Nito Mestre, and Jorge Pistochi were among the people who attended this office.[8] Darío Marchini[9] adds all the members of Serú Girán and his representative Daniel Grinbank to the list of visitors.[10]

Drawing on Bicknell's conceptualisation of a fully adequate account of meaning in songs, which requires an understanding of meaning as social and as emerging in the interactions between a work, a performer, and an audience,[11] this chapter analyses the alternative dialogue that the youth managed to establish, despite the censorship conditions outlined in Chapter 3 and the manipulation of words described in Chapter 4. How to create youth identity in these pressing circumstances? How to communicate with others who share similar ideas? In order to explore these questions, this chapter first considers the space created by rock magazines in their "letters from the public" sections. Then, following on from Chapter 2, it explores Charly García's songs in his next two bands: La Máquina de Hacer Pájaros and Serú Girán, in which "action" took the shape of a new language in the lyrics of songs.

Communication via rock magazines: Dreams and imaginary trips

In 1976, shortly after the coup started, a new magazine was born: *Expreso Imaginario* (Imaginary Express). It was a life-changing project for many young people at the time, as the publication became a refuge where they could communicate and express themselves. This was not the first magazine that targeted a young and rock-loving audience, though. Other similar projects included *Pelo*, *Pinap*, *Cronopios*, *Rolanroc*, *Algún Día*, and *Mordisco*, among others. Even today, *El Expreso* is considered a countercultural icon.

---

7 "Viola's message to youth," *La Nación* (Buenos Aires), 21 September 1981, p. 11.
8 Pujol, *Rock y dictadura*, p. 187.
9 Marchini, *No toquen*, pp. 77–78.
10 Di Cione, "Rock y dictadura," p. 5.
11 Bicknell, *Philosophy*, p. 110.

Its main section was the readers' mail: a means of communication among the youth who, surrounded by death and silence, looked for ways to express themselves.[12] During its seven years of life, the magazine managed to evade censorship.

The editorials of *El Expreso* were also crucial texts for the readers, eager for alternative information and ideas. Most of those editorials used, according to Benedetti and Graziano, the idea of travel,[13] an essential metaphor of the counterculture: the magazine was a vehicle transporting readers to other places. It also made ample use of allegorical stories, written by Jorge Pistocchi. His allusions, coded in allegorical forms, echoed the collective manifestations of members of the Argentine counterculture, who would meet symbolically to share their ideas and find each other in similar mental and spiritual spaces.[14] Beyond the infinity of interpretations that those allegorical texts could invite, there was a purpose that remained almost sacred: not to suggest any type of ideological conviction, but to propose visions and ways. The magazine aimed at providing tools for readers to expand their knowledge, develop understanding towards the other, and, in this way, allow access to other forms of thought.[15] In their meticulous study of the magazine, Benedetti and Graziano write:

> *El Expreso Imaginario* was not only a fundamental means for the youth during the last dictatorship—obviously—but also—less obviously—a vehicle for the expression and relief of those same young people. In other words, in an increasingly suffocating context, where spaces for dialogue were in permanent retreat in the face of censorship, persecution, and even self-censorship, the magazine was a valve. In this theoretical artefact, the "Communication Triangle" designates the three sides of this communication phenomenon: the relationships between readers and magazine, magazine and readers, and some readers with others.[16]

El Expreso had a section called "El Rincón de los Fenicios" (The Phoenicians' Corner) that was more or less a classified advertisements area. However, besides advertisements for selling instruments or publicising merchandise, this section functioned as a meeting board where people could contact others to start personal and collective relationships. Some examples of those advertisements follow:

> Busco flacos y flacas de cualquier edad que se interesen en la música, libros, poemas o simplemente en la vida, para entablar amistad. Claudio

---

12 Sebastián Benedetti, and Martín Graziano, *Estación imposible. Periodismo y contracultura en los '70: la historia de Expreso Imaginario* (Buenos Aires: Marcelo Héctor Oliveri Editor, 2007), p. 29.
13 Benedetti and Graziano, *Estación imposible*, p. 95.
14 Benedetti and Graziano, *Estación imposible*, p. 98.
15 Benedetti and Graziano, *Estación imposible*, p. 99.
16 Benedetti and Graziano, *Estación imposible*, p. 104.

Cánepa (N. 14, IX – 1977) [I am looking for guys and gals of any age who are interested in music, books, poems, or simply in life, to make friends].

URGENTE: Necesitamos gente loca sin delirios en la mente para formar comunidad. Zapiola 4288 (N. 16, XI – 1977) [URGENT: We need crazy people who have no mental delusions to form community].

DESEO contactarme con jóvenes de mentalidad abierta, que sientan la alegría de vivir. Juan A. Alonso (N. 16, XI – 1977) [I WISH to contact open-minded young people who feel the joy of living].

Todos los que traten de ser "un ser humano completo" escríbanme, por favor. José María Fernández. Paraná, Entre Ríos (N. 20, III – 1978) [Everyone who tries to be "a complete human being" write to me, please].[17]

Strategically placed after the editorial letter, the readers' mail grew in size and importance. It became the "heart of *El Expreso*", a correspondence flow that, even though it was free and spontaneous, was stimulated and channeled by the magazine itself.[18] Several decades before the popularity of social-media platforms, *El Expreso* was effectively a social network. Benedetti and Graziano consider that if the idea of rock as a movement had not been so central in the magazine, it would have never managed to build the complicit bond it shared with its readers, who included rock musicians, amateur journalists from underground magazines, and artists from different disciplines, as well as a committed audience of rock fans.[19] The pages of the *Expreso* reverberated with life because, somehow, connected to that collective unconscious everyone was facing their own fear.

Though the *Expreso* is one of the main publications that provided a space for the youth to "meet" and express themselves, there were, as mentioned before, many others. There was, in Miguel Grinberg's words, "an impressive lateral information circuit".[20] This circuit included underground pamphlets, fanzines, magazines, anthologies, and all sorts of small publications in many different areas of the country.

Pelo was another of the best-known magazines, and had a section called "Correo de los Sueños" (Dreams Mail), where readers were invited to share their dreams as a way of stimulating the imagination. It did, that was, until the day the editor received a phone call from a military official who, without further ado, ordered him to get rid of that section of the magazine. He added that "Argentine youth were not to dream, they just had to stick to the reality of work and study for the growth of the Nation".[21]

---

17 Cited in Benedetti and Graziano, *Estación imposible*, pp. 111–12.
18 Benedetti and Graziano, *Estación imposible*, p. 114.
19 Benedetti and Graziano, *Estación imposible*, p. 184.
20 Grinberg, *Cómo vino*, pp. 115–16.
21 Juan Manuel Cibeira, *La biblia del rock. Historias de la revista Pelo* (Buenos Aires:

Pelo had been founded by Daniel Ripoll in 1970. He explained that he chose that name for the magazine because the word "hair" was probably the most incendiary and countercultural one at the time. To have long hair or an unconventional hair style was a form of resistance, a way to say NO.[22]

In other words, there an unstoppable counterculture was finding ways for its members to express themselves, and those members were steadily growing in numbers. Rock concerts were very small, fanzines and magazines reported what was happening in those concerts, and, little by little, the youth were finding ways to use their imaginations, though "they were not allowed to dream". Charly García, introduced in Chapter 2, is probably the contemporary Argentine popular musician who has had the most impact on the daily lives of people living in this country. His ideology, his way of seeing the world, as well as his decisions on where to position himself have attracted public attention like almost no other case.[23] It is no surprise, then, that having analysed his albums with his band Sui Generis, his two following bands have been chosen for this section. The first one is La Máquina de Hacer Pájaros, and the second one, his last band before going solo, is Serú Girán. Both created opportunities for the imagination, for dreams, and, certainly, for dissidence.

La Máquina de Hacer Pájaros

As we know, the dictatorship began in March 1976, and, two months later, García inaugurated his band La Máquina de Hacer Pájaros as an almost immediate response to the PRN. García had dissolved his band Sui Generis in 1975, after the many problems with censorship previously discussed. His new band, "The Bird-making Machine", produced two albums. The first one, also called *La máquina de hacer pájaros*,[24] musically was a response to models of English symphonic rock. However, the music of La Máquina possessed García's distinctive touch: his disconcerting lyrics. A critic even said that their songs were composed of "unintelligible lyrics by hermaphroditic voices".[25] These "unintelligible" lyrics were what would allow García to express his disagreement with the dictatorship without risking his life.

In a previous study, I demonstrated that García's main rhetorical strategy is the use of allegory.[26] In a previous chapter, we also saw that the regime's most-used trope was, similiarly, allegory. It almost seems that García, perhaps having identified this trope in the military discourse, decided to borrow it

Ediciones B, 2014), p. 97.
22 Provéndola, *Rockpolitik*, p. 78.
23 Di Pietro, *Esta noche*, p. 17.
24 La Máquina de Hacer Pájaros, *La máquina de hacer pájaros* (Microfón/Sony BMG, 1976).
25 Cibeira, *La biblia*, p. 97.
26 Favoretto, *Charly en el país*, pp. 11–15.

and put it to new uses, turning the dictatorship's discourse weapon of choice against them. One of La Máquina's strategies was to use Aesopian allegory. However, García's rhetorical technique declined to include the traditional moral that educated or preached to the reader, instead opening a space in which the reader/listener was the one who had to come up with a moral or conclusion. This is clear in the first allegory García produced under the dictatorship: a machine that produced songs as if they were birds. Birds are often associated with freedom; their wings represent the ability to fly. The only way to stop the free flight of a bird is to cage it—to put it behind bars—or cut off its wings. García and his machine invented birds that could be neither caged nor censored.[27]

The first album constitutes a pessimistic reflection on the state of the political–social situation generated by the regime. The enunciator conflicts with the reality that surrounds them. The themes of this album are organised around allegories of the senses, of perception, and of the oxidation process, as will be explained shortly. This lonely and pessimistic outlook[28] presented an alternative picture that showed the deception of the authorities and the impossibility of "seeing" for many. Specifically, the song "Cómo mata el viento norte" (Lethal North Wind) plays with the idea that sensory perception can be misleading: "a beggar shows jewels to the blindman on the corner". That line of the song evokes a popular axiom: "there is no worse blindman than the one who does not want to see". Deceit in the form of jewels (a metaphor of all things attractive, ostentatious, and brilliant) is offered by low-class officials (the beggar figure is a metaphor of low class in reference to the human class, not to the social class). Both the deceitfulness of the officials and the credulity or ignorance of the common citizen (the blindman on the corner: metaphor of conformism, interpreted in light of the popular refrain mentioned above) are emphasised. The song was a call to the audience to reflect: "con los ojos cerrados no vemos más que nuestra nariz" ("with closed eyes we cannot see further than our noses"). This same theme of seeing, being blind, or keeping one's eyes closed continued in "No puedo verme" (I Can't See Myself):

> I can't see myself.
> The guitar boy screamed:
> I need to turn black.
> I can't see myself.
> His mom cries and calls the doctor
> to save him from hell.
>
> No puedo verme
> el chico de la guitarra gritó

27 Mara Favoretto, "Charly García: alegoría y rock," *Musica popular em revista* 2 (1): 125–51, 2013, at pp. 107–08.
28 Conde, *Poéticas*, p. 227.

> necesito volverme negro.
> No puedo verme.
> su madre llora y llama al doctor
> para que lo salve del infierno.

In this song, the poetic voice—"the boy"—wants to turn black to be seen. Generally, black is what is not seen and needs to be illuminated by light to be made out. Contrary to this generalisation, "the boy" of the song needs to be camouflaged, hidden, turned black so as not to attract attention. It is only in going unnoticed that he will be able to "see" his true identity or ideology. His mother, apparently a victim of the great confusion generated by the official regime and its rhetoric, trapped in the medical jargon of the military Junta, calls the "doctor" in order to "[save him] from hell", in this way mixing the anatomical with the spiritual. In the face of this devastating reality, there seemed to be few viable options: confinement, exile, hiding, or closing one's eyes.

However, not everything is negative and pessimistic in the songs of La Máquina. García knew that the PRN would not last forever. Among the songs that reveal a message of hope associated with the temporality of the regime is, for example, "No te dejes desanimar" (Do Not Be Discouraged), in which García posits a different, more promising future:

> Do not be discouraged,
> do not allow them to kill you,
> so many more tomorrows are to come.
>
> No te dejes desanimar
> no te dejes matar
> quedan tantos mañanas por andar.

In contrast, "Rock and Roll" includes an invitation to the listener: "Desoxidémonos para crecer, crecer" ["Let's deoxidise to grow"]. The metaphor of deoxidisation is valid if we take into account that it is a process by which a substance loses some of its properties. When iron oxidises, it rusts. According to this interpretation, iron, a metaphor of the fixity of the conservative concepts of the military regime, wears out on contact with "natural agents" such as air or salt water, poetic symbols of freedom and pain. Inviting the listeners to "deoxidise" presupposes that they are already "rusty", that the rigidity of the imposed ideas cannot be preserved over time, but will rust. It is also a way to anticipate the facts, to foresee what would happen after having endured the military government, since the song was composed shortly before this period began. This metaphor is continued in "Por probar el vino y el agua salada" (Because of Tasting Wine and Salt Water), in which, when "forgetting to be king (sovereign) and happy", the town rusts (tests the salt water), time stops, in a kind of stand-by ("the cuckoos cry, the clocks suffer"), and the control of censorship over the press is underlined ("newspapers are never published").

In a word, in the first album of La Máquina, metaphors were combined in a larger allegorical structure. Sensory perception and the deoxidisation process symbolise that reality that was perceived through the senses but denied by the media ("we see no further than our nose"). García's songs expose the sense of deception and manifest a desire to persuade the audience to deoxidise and explore alternative options.

In 1977, the second album of La Máquina de Hacer Pájaros, *Películas* (Movies),[29] was released. The allegory in this case plays with references to fiction and censorship. Films could symbolise a hobby (passing time while waiting for the dictatorship to end and censorship to cease), or it could refer to the fiction invented by the state, what Argentine writer Ricardo Piglia calls "the narrating machine",[30] among other possibilities.[31]

The first track on that second album of La Máquina, "Obertura 777", was an instrumental, as if no words could be said. The symbolic inclusion of an instrumental track that opened the space for musical communication between García and his audience was elliptically empty of words. However, the interesting thing about this first track was its title, which might invite paranoid interpretation too. The number seven is symbolically associated with numerous biblical references. It is a number that denotes perfection ("seventy times seven") and spirituality; it recalls the creation of the world in seven days, the Sabbath being the seventh. The year of the album's release also ends in double seven. That is to say, the possibilities for the symbolic interpretation of the number are numerous and varied. Of course, by not having a written poetry that serves as evidence, the interpretation of the song could also bring the risk of paranoid reading. Yet it should be remembered that the possibility of multiple interpretations is one of the functions of allegory, as defined by Fletcher.[32]

The song "Qué se puede hacer salvo ver películas" (What to Do Except Watch Movies) again denounced the censor system and the absence of freedom of expression. This song was, for Pujol, "the most committed to the political and social reality of the country, although at that time it was not clearly understood".[33] The invitation to watch movies, a kind of consolation or distraction, was based on the triviality of the current entertainment films:

> My two cats fall asleep on the TV,
> I go out for a walk to kill time

29 La Máquina de Hacer Pájaros, *Películas* (Microfón/Sony BMG, 1977).
30 Piglia, *Crítica*, p. 106.
31 "Power is also sustained in fiction. The state is a make-believe machine... The information services use more novel and effective narrative techniques than most Argentine novelists. And they tend to be more imaginative": Piglia, *Crítica*, pp. 106–07, my translation.
32 Angus Fletcher, *Alegoría. Teoría de un modo simbólico*, translated by Vicente Carmona González (Madrid: Ediciones Akal, S.A., 2002), p. 77.
33 Pujol, *Las ideas*, p. 65.

>   Sobre la TV se duermen nis dos gatos
>   salgo a caminar para matar el rato.

At times it seemed that García amused himself by challenging the censors, since the title of the subject attracted attention (surely it was subversive) but the lyrics baffled the listener hoping to find direct dissidence. "What to Do Except Watch Movies" was an allusion to repression and censorship. If there was an alternative, it was not mentionable in 1977.

Serú Girán (1978)

In 1978, after spending some time in Brazil, García returned to Argentina with a new band: Serú Girán. The allegory in this new name moved around these apparently empty words, lacking identifiable semantics. The literary device explored in this album was nonsense. The name Serú Girán had no known meaning. These were invented words, chosen by García because of their musicality, which was suggestive: if there were words that were forbidden, why not invent new words for which we should search for a meaning. The nonsense that García used appeared as a subversion of language, a rebellion against imposed semantic codes, resulting in new texts that, far from presenting a unilateral interpretation, presented a new linguistic variety to be explored. García's creative tool, instead of using the "permitted words", invented new ones that not only questioned tradition but also challenged semantics. The name of the band, also the name of their first album, probably alluded to a future temporality. "Serú Girán" suggests verbs constructed in the future tense in the Spanish language. The linguistic game that opens is suggestive: "serán" ("will be") results from the combination of the first syllable of the first word and the last syllable of the last word. Curiously, it is the third person of the plural of the future of the verb "to be". This experiment allowed him to open windows to new areas of intensity in the language, so that poetry would take on new life, at the same time bringing some hope for the future of rock ("serán"/"will be"), once freedom of expression is restored.

Serú Girán's self-titled debut album[34] short circuits the problem of censorship with a unique new proposal: "invent a language".[35] The 1978 album literally forges a completely new language: "Cosmigonón, gisofanía, serú girán...". The nonsense lyrics of this first song, "Serú Girán", obviously challenge interpretation. The band Serú Girán was introduced to the public at Luna Park on 28 July 1978 and was for many years the most popular band of Argentine rock, to such an extent that its members were called "The Argentine Beatles". As stated by Conde, "given their permanent records in album sales and the high number of spectators that their concerts attracted, Serú made

---

34 Serú Girán, *Serú Girán*.
35 Dente, *Transgresores*, p. 86.

a contribution today considered crucial for rock music to become massive in Argentina".[36] The name of the band, which denoted a certain fracture in the language, was, as we mentioned, significant: although it was not possible to speak in the Argentina of the day, there was no provision, communication, or decree that prevented citizens from inventing new words. The audacity of an unintelligible text, as well as that of a text censored out of existence, could generate multiple interpretations. The first track on the first album, a love song that idealises the beloved woman, also has a phrase with no known meaning as its title: "Eiti Leda". In a poetic and fascinating way, the medical-saving language of the regime is retaken, although this time, the metaphor of the injection is subverted. It was not the "anti-subversion" vaccine that García refers to, but rather the song sounds like a desperate love request:

> ... along some highway,
> one with infinite signs
> that say nothing. ...
>
> Can't you see my blue cape,
> my shoulder length hair,
> the fatal light,
> the avenging sword.
> Can't you see how white I am, can you?
>
> ... sobre alguna autopista
> que tenga infinitos carteles
> que no digan nada...
>
> ¿No ves mi capa azul
> mi pelo hasta los hombros
> la luz fatal
> a espada vengadora?
> ¿No ves que blanco soy, no ves?

The "road signs that say nothing" are perhaps a reference to confusing publication criteria. Then, the song presents questions that allude to the naivety of some. The phrase "can't you see how *white* I am?" possibly has to do with purity, with what has not been stained or corrupted. Or it could also indicate a "target" ("blanco" can also mean "target" in Spanish). The variety of meanings and interpretations allows the audience to play with different allusions. Being a target would be a justification for the poetic voice to hold an avenging sword. The "fatal light" and the "avenging sword" allude to justice, which at some point would have to come, although in a distant "future", as indicated by the title of the album.

Continuing with the theme of nonsense titles, "Seminare" is a description of the youth of the moment, "those who drove fast bikes and evaded reality;

---

36 Conde, *Poéticas*, p. 251.

and followed the hippie worldview that rock retained for itself, of love".[37] The album ends with another song with indecipherable lyrics. "Cosmigonón" was another in a series of invented words, in this case resembling an augmentative, almost grotesque utterance, which could suggest a "cosmos", that is, a "great world", ridiculed. Like Lewis Carroll's "Jabberwocky", nonsense words were included that, through their grammatical approach, challenged the reader's imagination.

As has been observed, both the opening and the closing of Serú Girán's first album come by way of incoherent sentences, without semantic meaning, which, because of the impossibility of associating them with any ideological system, could not be censored.

An interesting song recorded by Serú Girán in 1979, on the album *La grasa de las capitales* (The Capitals' Grease),[38] is "San Francisco y el lobo" (Saint Francis and the Wolf). Already the title of the song seems to fulfil a double role: on the one hand, you can see the mixture of metaphors that allude to nature and the process of colonisation. San Francisco is undoubtedly an allusion to the Franciscan missionaries sent by the Catholic monarchs of Spain with the specific task of converting indigenous people to Catholicism. And on the other hand, he is the figure of a beloved monk, whose messages of peace and brotherhood transcended political and religious boundaries. Saint Francis of Assisi is widely known for his relationship with the animals he called "brothers". In one famous story, Saint Francis tames a wolf that used to attack the city of Gubbio, and devour animals and men. "San Francisco and the Wolf" is an interesting Aesopic allegory that, again, presents different possible interpretations. The most obvious, recalling the history of the wolf of Gubbio, identifies the wolf with the enemy of the people (or villain), and San Francisco with its "tamer" or saviour, which in a context such as that of the dictatorship in Argentina, represents the alliance of the church with military power.

"Noche de perros" (Dogs' Night) paints a dark picture: "you are lost among the streets that you used to walk, you are wounded like a bird in the sea. Blood". The present was devastating: ordinary citizens did not know where they were; they were lost in the same place where, before the dictatorship, they could walk around safely and with confidence. The word "blood" immediately after "sea" seems strategically placed. It could suggest a sea of blood as a symbol of violence and state terrorism. This supposed sea of blood anticipated the next song on the album: "Los Sobrevivientes" (The Survivors), in which the city is also described as a labyrinth that hides and oppresses those who continue to resist. García reflected on repression, imposed identity, the search for identification, and the need to belong to the country despite the overwhelming reality: "we will never have roots, we will

---

37 Pujol, *Las ideas*, p. 103.
38 Serú Girán, *La grasa de las capitales* (Music Hall, 1979).

never have a home, and yet, you see, we are from here". More devastating was "Friday 3AM", in which the poetic voice, the main character in the song, opts for suicide. After having changed "time and god, and music and ideas", the protagonist takes the "gun to the temple" and shoots three shots, which is an action that is physically impossible, though the onomatopoeia "bang, bang, bang" seems to confirm it.[39]

Probably the only way to encourage some optimism during the time of the Process was to conceive of its end. People had to think about the possibility of change, of movement, of closing a cycle and opening a new one. The title of the album *Bicicleta* was a metaphor that indicated movement. The bicycle is a means of transport that takes whoever uses it from one place to another. In this way, García offered, through his music, a medium, an option that mobilised, that was dynamic. The audience of Serú Girán, by then, had grown enormously and was waiting for the band's new musical proposal. In the year 1980 some expressions of annoyance against the regime and censorship amongst some journalists began to be noticed. On 6 June, Serú Girán presented *Bicicleta* at the Obras stadium. The tickets, which had started to be sold twenty days in advance, sold out quickly. This new album included one of the most outstanding works of García, in which he achieved, perhaps, his maximum capacity of allegorical abstraction, "Canción de Alicia en el país" (Song of Alice in the Land), presenting an extremely suggestive ellipsis. Obviously, the word "wonder" was censored from the title by its own author.

> Who knows, Alice, this country
> wasn't made just because.
> You're going to leave, you're going to go out
> but you stay,
> where else are you going to go?
> It's just that here, you know
> the tongue-twister twists your tongue
> the murderer murders you
> and it's too much for you.
> The game that made you happy is over.
> Don't tell what you saw in the gardens, the dream is over.
> There are no more walruses or turtles
> A river of heads crushed by the same foot
> play cricket under the moon
> We're in no man's land, but it's mine
> The innocent are the guilty, says his lordship,
> the king of spades.
> Don't tell what's behind that mirror,
> you won't have power
> nor lawyers, nor witnesses.

---

39 Favoretto, "Charly García: alegoria y rock," pp. 113–14.

Light the lanterns that the wizards
are thinking of returning
to cloud our path.
We are in everyone's land, in life.
Over the past and over the future,
ruins upon ruins,
dear Alice.
The game that made you happy is over.

Quién sabe Alicia este país
no estuvo hecho porque sí.
Te vas a ir, vas a salir
pero te quedas,
¿dónde más vas a ir?
es que aquí, sabes
el trabalenguas trabalenguas
el asesino te asesina
y es mucho para ti.
Se acabó ese juego que te hacía feliz.
No cuentes lo que viste en los jardines, el sueño acabó.
Ya no hay morsas ni tortugas
Un río de cabezas aplastadas por el mismo pie
juegan cricket bajo la luna
Estamos en la tierra de nadie, pero es mía
Los inocentes son los culpables, dice su señoría,
el rey de espadas.
No cuentes lo que hay detrás de aquel espejo,
no tendrás poder
ni abogados, ni testigos.
Enciende los candiles que los brujos
piensan en volver
a nublarnos el camino.
Estamos en la tierra de todos, en la vida.
Sobre el pasado y sobre el futuro,
ruinas sobre ruinas,
querida Alicia.
Se acabó ese juego que te hacía feliz.

It was an allegorical description of Argentina during the military dictatorship, but the interplay between the real and the imaginary was the opposite of Lewis Carroll's story. Instead of starting with logic to reach absurdity, in García's song, the process was reversed. For example, the phrase "a river of heads crushed by the same foot play cricket under the moon" alludes to repression and authoritarianism ("the same foot"), and the idea is reinforced by adding, "we are in no man's land. But it's mine. The innocent are the guilty, says his lordship, the king of spades". The assertion that the innocent are the guilty probably indicates that all Argentinians, to a greater or lesser extent, and depending on their awareness of reality or the information they had in 1980, already suspected or feared that the disappeared individuals were not all "subversive criminals".

The song played with the animals from the story and the pseudonyms of some politicians of the time. The witches, walruses, and turtles led the audience to associate them with the nicknames of López Rega, Onganía, and Illia, politicians who were frequently mentioned during those times. It could also be associated with María Estela Martínez de Perón, the president ousted by the military coup, as well as the figure of Alice, displaced by "the king of spades". Furthermore, it advised, "don't tell what you saw in the gardens", emulating a precise and very typical instruction in popular speech, comparable to the Argentine phrase "no te metás" ["don't get involved"]. It's notable that the message was emphasised by the phrase "you won't have power, nor lawyers, nor witnesses". The common citizen (represented by the figure of Alice) had no one to turn to. Personal security only lay in hiding, ignorance, or anonymity. Like the country it inhabited, the allegory of Alice conveyed fear and uncertainty.

The song can be divided into two parts: the first presents the situation, while in the second, the advice is not to tell what has been seen, and the melody changes, creating an atmosphere of stillness and confinement with a bass drum, clearly alluding to a military march. The contrast between these two parts is almost tragic. The game became frustrating and eerie: "You won't have power".

The encoding of Alicia's allegory was so sophisticated that the same musicians of the band Serú Girán did not notice the message at the time. One of them, Pedro Aznar, in an interview televised via Argentine TV channel Volver, explained that

> The subject of the lyrics was crucial, it was the time of blacklists, broadcasting lists, what could and could not be played. The band obviously was like a platform where things were being said, but they had to be said carefully and the message had to be cunningly coded without it being too noticeable. I myself understood what Alicia really meant years later.[40]

The choked fury with which García sang the end of the song in the live concert reflected the fear, uncertainty, and anguish of the time in a way that perhaps no other musical work could. Its artistic and emotional qualities were remarkable. Listening to the song live on video recordings from the time, García's defiant look at the camera, the passion with which he performs it, along with the drama that the drums add in the background with a

---

40 Pedro Aznar, speaking about "Canción de Alicia en el país" as part of an interview now excerpted via the subscription TV channel Volver (which broadcasts from Argentine cinema and television archives), 28 October 2007, http://www.youtube.com/watch?v=j3NUybAPvpg.

"military" rhythm, draw in the listener, who is accustomed to another type of performance from this musician, never loaded with such seriousness and drama. The end of the song is abrupt, like a new "blow" that is built little by little: "It's over, That's over, That game is over, that game that made you happy was over". Note how the final phrase is constructed: unlike the modus operandi used by censorship, where words are eliminated and texts are thus shortened, the line grows, instead, little by little, until it reaches the end by handing down a final sentence for the regime.

Negotiations between the three armed forces to choose Jorge Videla's successor were quite closed, so General Roberto Viola took command in March 1981 without the same consensus his predecessor Reynaldo Bignone had enjoyed. This fact would mark his fate, since before the end of the year he was displaced by Leopoldo Galtieri, commander in chief of the army. As Viola's youth adviser, journalist Alfredo Olivera began to meet with the rockers of the time. Although agreements were not reached and the promises made in these meetings were not fulfilled, rock and power met for the first time in Argentine history. Would they ever negotiate terms of mutual support? Was that even thinkable in the rock world? Those encounters were indeed an interesting approach, opening a chapter that would continue the following year with the Malvinas/Falklands War.[41]

---

[41] Provéndola, *Rockpolitik*, p. 120.

CHAPTER SIX

War of the Words
The Day a War Became an Opportunity

"No bombardeen Buenos Aires"

—*Charly García*

"El kamikaze comprendió su error: Allí, morir así es en vano"

—*Luis Alberto Spinetta*, Kamikaze

When it was no longer so easy to refer to subversives as "enemies", the military Junta needed to find another entity on which it could pin the term. By 1981, the dictatorship's popularity was in decay, and it seemed that the military forces wanted to have their own war. As the regime declined, attention fell on the possibility of claiming the recovery of the Islas Malvinas/Falkland Islands, which were (and still are) under UK rule. The leader of this new war would be General Leopoldo Galtieri, Viola's successor in the presidency of the nation.

By 1982, the Junta's influence was fading due to a combination of factors: the deepening economic crisis, the considerable decline in power of the military Junta, skyrocketing inflation, and the increase in the general population's discontent. For this reason, the Junta decided to act on Argentina's claim to the Malvinas/Falkland Islands, reclaiming the British Overseas Territory on 2 April in a bid to curry favour with constituents through stirring patriotic fervor. The media announced the landing of Argentine troops on the islands and the recovery of their sovereignty. Yet at the time, there were those who distrusted this new military strategy.

The dispute over the sovereignty of the islands was historical, and the Argentine regime decided to take military offensive action in 1982. There were three key elements that played a decisive role in this decision. First, the decline of the dictatorship; second, the increasing reports about violations of human rights in Argentina and the consequent international pressure; and third, a very costly miscalculation. The Argentinean government thought that it could count on other nations' support and that Ronald Reagan was going to be, if not supportive, then neutral. However, the US privileged its alliance with the UK, siding with its old ally. On 14 June, after the sinking of the Argentine ship ARA *General Belgrano* by the British, which cost more than 300 lives, Argentina surrendered unconditionally.[1]

War of the words

Whereas the early 1960s saw the birth of Argentine rock, it was in 1982, during the Malvinas/Falklands War, that the genre reached its peak. This may come as a surprise, especially when considering the military dictatorship's anti-youth and anti-artist stance. Yet the effect that the dictatorship had on Argentine rock was such that it is now possible to talk about pre- and post-dictatorship variants.

Just over one month after the landing of the troops, with the tempo of operations increasing after a United Nations (UN) attempt to mediate was rejected, on 16 May the regime sponsored the "Festival of Latin American Solidarity", a massive rock concert intended as a show of support for the Malvinas/Falklands War. Added to this, General Galtieri issued a decree prohibiting music sung in English from being broadcast on radio and television, given it was now the "language of the enemy".

Just as the outcome of the Malvinas/Falklands War would hasten the military government's downfall, the misguided attempt to coopt youth culture by way of the Festival of Latin American Solidarity backfired. Throughout the event, concert-goers chanted anti-regime slogans, foiling the Junta's efforts to project an image of unconditional devotion to the generals' project. Added to this show of discontent by audience members, many artists came out in opposition to the official stance; Luis Alberto Spinetta, for example, made the following statement: "[a]s free musicians in our country, we are totally convinced that the war offensive must end".[2] Perhaps the moment that was most illustrative of this resistance came when León Gieco sang "Solo le pido a Dios".[3] The audience response, as captured in recordings of the event and as attested in concert-goer testimonials, suggests that the song became a focal point for anti-war sentiment; not only was there a roar of audience approval at its conclusion, but an uncharacteristic hush descended as Gieco intoned:

1 Mara Favoretto, "Brothers in Rock: Argentine and British Rock Music during the Malvinas/Falklands Conflict," in *The Bloomsbury Handbook of Popular Music and Social Class*, edited by Ian Peddie, 291–311 (New York: Bloomsbury, 2020), p. 292.
2 Quoted in Vila and Cammack, "Rock Nacional and Dictatorship in Argentina," p. 146.
3 León Gieco, *IV LP* (Music Hall, 1978).

> I only ask God
> that I am not indifferent to war
> A huge monster that stomps
> All over people's naivety...
>
> Solo le pido a Dios
> que la guerra no me sea indiferente
> es un monstruo grande y pisa fuerte
> toda la pobre inocencia de la gente...

The word "war" had different connotations during the dictatorship, depending on who was wielding it, and to what purpose. In the early days of the coup, the Junta declared a "war against subversion", the officials' term for what from the beginning was a deliberate and sustained persecution of leftist ideology. As explored in Chapter 4, war terminology abounded in the Junta's rhetoric, especially in the way that rhetoric constructed an enemy that it was imperative for the Junta and the Argentine people to fight. This enemy was especially threatening and devious because, unlike typical enemies, it was an internal one. The fact that the 1974–83 period of state terrorism in Argentina is often referred to as the "Dirty War"—a term that has been rejected by several historians because it was not technically a "war", but a term the military discourse utilised to justify or legitimise the number of victims—is itself a product of this official, bellicose discourse.

The claim for the sovereignty of the Malvinas/Falkland Islands in 1982 meant that the use of the term "war" expanded, in that it was no longer something to be wielded solely against internal proponents of leftist ideology. Instead, it was something waged on the battlefield in the Southern Islands against an external enemy, the British soldiers. And it was also a battle against all British citizens, including their language and their music, which of course had been, until that moment, played on Argentine airwaves.

In a bid to enlist support from young Argentines, instead of condemning rock music, the Junta decided to promote the same rock musicians they had previously persecuted by encouraging them to rally around a common cause. They hoped the space created by the Festival of Latin American Solidarity would encourage youth collaboration with the regime. Yet event co-organiser and rock producer Daniel Grinbank's meeting with government representatives to agree on the terms of the festival was widely criticised.[4] Further, in direct contrast to the festival's purpose, which was to raise funds for the Defence and Military Commands Ministry of Argentina campaign, both the musicians who performed at it and those who turned down the invitation expressed vehement disavowal of the war, onstage and off. Most of the musicians who chose to appear at the festival performed anti-war songs, and

---

4 Provéndola, *Rockpolitik*, pp. 126–27.

the audience supported this stance. The message was clear: young people wanted peace.

Following the decline in support for the regime, by the end of 1981, opposition groups joined forces in the form of Multipartidaria, which was able more effectively to challenge the regime. On 30 March, 40,000 people took to the streets to demand an end to military rule, only to be met with violent repression from the regime. Just three days later, on 2 April, Argentine forces stepped ashore on the Malvinas/Falkland Islands, coinciding with a public consensus about the war, as well as a nationalistic campaign to win support for what many were coming to believe was a military crusade.

Since Europeans visited the islands in the sixteenth century, the dispute over the islands' sovereignty has been ongoing. They were first controlled by Britain, latterly by Spain. Four years after Argentina gained independence in 1816 it laid claim to the islands, but, since it did not establish a stable colony there, in 1833 the British took control of the islands once more. The naval base they established at Port Stanley encouraged a small settlement to grow up around it and meant that Argentine calls for the territory to be decolonised were mostly opposed by the British-descended inhabitants. The British government conceded to an eventual transfer of power to the Argentines in a memorandum of understanding signed in 1966, but the islanders cited Argentina's economic instability, military dictatorships, and cultural difference as disincentives for becoming part of Argentina, with tension steadily escalating over the years. In 1982, this tension came to a head when Junta-backed President Galtieri ordered a military intervention. Argentine troops landed on the islands on 2 April, claiming sovereignty. The British response was delayed due to the islands' distance from Britain, but when its task force arrived a few weeks later it quickly defeated the Argentines, leading to Argentina's surrender on 14 June.

Media access to the islands was non-existent for the duration of the short war. The only first-hand reports came from official news agency Telam,[5] which meant the regime could carefully control and manipulate any information conveyed to the population. This dynamic created fertile grounds for triumph talk, mocking of the British and calls for a nationalistic union. Yet several news outlets distrusted the military strategy, including local magazine *Humor*, which in its April 1982 editorial says "This is not a magical event. We are the first to perceive it and hope not to be the only ones". It is a comment that clearly signals the distortion of reality achieved by the sudden nationalism conveyed by the media and Galtieri's messianic tone, both signs of the make-believe spin being peddled as news.

An exhaustive investigation into the regime's presentation of events through media outlets was undertaken by Argentine investigative journalist Horacio

---

5 Nick Caistor, "Whose War Is It Anyway? The Argentine Press during the South Atlantic Conflict," in *Framing the Falklands War: Nationhood, Culture and Identity*, edited by James Aulich, 50–57 (Milton Keynes: Open University Press, 1992), p. 56.

Verbitsky.[6] This investigation scrutinised the news reports published during the war, providing a meticulous analysis of the falsehoods utilised in order to sway public opinion. Headlines highlighted by the study include, for example, "Strong losses of the enemy in combat fought yesterday"[7] and "Argentina's counter attack was deadly",[8] while an official advertising campaign declared "We are already winning".[9] Some of the messages, when taken together, were of a contradictory nature, which the Argentine population came to identify as suspect. For example, during Pope John Paul II's visit, the newspaper *Crónica* published his photograph on its front page on 11 June 1982 with the title "Holy Father, Peace Be with You", immediately followed by an article headed "English Disaster", which included the statement "bombarded by air and by land, the invaders move away from Mount Kent".[10] Two days later, news of the defeat of Argentine troops hit the press. Ironically, Admiral Massera's determination to preserve the honour of military institutions saw him issue a statement in which he said, "Thank God, today we continue to think that the supreme good is justice and not peace, because there is no lasting peace without justice".[11]

In addition to these mixed messages, appeals were made via TV and radio to raise funds and supplies for the Argentine soldiers fighting on the islands. Again, reality did not hold up to the farce. A month after people donated money, wedding rings, chocolate, cigarettes, and much more besides, questions began to be sent in to editorial offices. On 15 July 1982, for example, the following was published in *Gente*: "How could it happen that a chocolate with a letter sent by a 7-year-old boy to our soldiers fighting in the war was sold days ago at a kiosk in Comodoro Rivadavia?".[12] Such questioning points to the public's growing awareness that many of the boxes donated for the soldiers never reached their destination, and the resulting furor that such revelations stoked, leading to elections being called and democracy restored in 1983.

Between April and June 1982, the censors banned TV and radio stations from broadcasting any music sung in English. In this new climate, the media had to fill the space vacated by international artists with national ones. Radio hosts and television producers risked losing their audience if they substituted folklore or tango for rock, and so Argentine rock suddenly had an unprecedented amount of airtime, which gave it ample opportunity and space to grow. This despite the Secretary of the Culture of the Nation previously

---

6 Verbitsky, *Malvinas*.
7 On the cover of *La Nación*, on 22 May 1982.
8 *Crónica*, on 10 May 1982.
9 Blaustein and Zubieta, *Decíamos ayer*, p. 477.
10 Blaustein and Zubieta, *Decíamos ayer*, p. 489.
11 Uriarte, *Almirante Cero*, p. 200.
12 Blaustein and Zubieta, *Decíamos ayer*, p. 500.

having described said music as "false culture".[13] It seems that, from the regime's perspective, "false culture" was the lesser evil when compared to the "music of the external enemy". Argentine rock soared in popularity. Its production levels increased significantly and did not decline with the fall of the regime.

Ironically, then, this redirected censorship became a positive force for creativity and cultural expression locally. In other words, censorship had the unintended effect of encouraging the development of rock as a resistance movement. Previously, local rock had been considered a threat to national Western and Christian values, yet now Argentine rock was renamed *rock nacional*, and the censoring of the foreign "language of the enemy" meant it could thrive. "Suddenly, rock was Western and Christian, and the Comité federal de Radio diffusion (COMFER) endorsed it energetically".[14] Very quickly, the TV screen and the radio airwaves were filled with *rock nacional* shows, such as *Rock R.A.* (Canal 13), *Música prohibida para mayores* (ATC), and *Tribuna 21* (Canal 9).[15]

The effect was perhaps not what the censors had intended. Their sudden pivot towards considering rock nationalist when previously they had persecuted it, coupled with the increased space that such a stance gave it, meant that many more people were exposed to the lyrics, which included political dissidence in messages encrypted to evade the censors. Added to this, rock followers were less likely to identify English with the "enemy" as per military rhetoric, because rock ideology was based on pacificism. Most Argentine musicians admired many British musicians, including the pacifist John Lennon, making the rhetoric about all British citizens being "the enemy" an argument much less likely to be accepted and adopted.

Perhaps the regime's decision in 1982 to endorse a music that previously it had condemned as "subversive" was grounded in the fact that many of the soldiers who fought in the islands were under thirty years of age. The government made a demagogic decision to attract the support of the youth in the war against Britain, suddenly legitimising a music form that until then had been repressed. If anyone could rouse the youth's support, it was rock musicians. Rock producer Daniel Grinbank met with the authorities to discuss the terms of the resulting Festival of Latin American Solidarity, at which time it was decided that rock would be the only music genre represented.[16]

The Festival of Latin American Solidarity was thus held on 16 May 1982 in explicit support of the Malvinas cause. It was attended by 60,000 people, with thousands of others watching a live broadcast on TV or listening to it on the radio. Its dual purpose was to reflect the desire for peace that animated many a rocker and to raise funds for the soldiers faced with the

---

13 Pujol, *Rock y dictadura*, p. 219.
14 Pujol, *Rock y dictadura*, p. 219.
15 Provéndola, *Rockpolitik*, p. 126.
16 Provéndola, *Rockpolitik*, p. 127.

harsh climatic conditions of the islands while they defended the sovereignty of their country. Yet the participating rockers, once they took to the stage, criticised those who had invited them to sing, and performed their political dissidence. This dissidence was reflected in the audience reaction: anti-war lyrics by the rockers were met with the audience's "cantitos" (chants), which made it clear to the authorities that the youth supported neither the war nor the regime. For example, one chant was, "the wall, the wall, for all the soldiers who sold the nation", which suggested an inversion of the official killing method: "the wall" referred to the execution wall, and thus the chant suggested a role reversal in which the regime-backed gunmen, not the political dissidents, were shot. In other words, the regime's attempt to unite the youth and participate in their crusade had the opposite effect, giving a loudspeaker to those who were virulently against it. Some bands, such as Virus, decided not to participate in the festival organised by the regime. Their song "El Banquete" (from their 1982 album *Recrudece*)[17] refers to that particular moment in Argentine history.[18]

> We have been invited to a great banquet.
> There will be ice cream,
> They will give us sorbets.
> Young calves have been slaughtered
> To prepare an official dinner.
> A lot of money has been authorised,
> they promise a masterful menu.

> Nos han invitado
> a un gran banquete
> habrá postre helado
> nos darán sorbetes.
> Han sacrificado jóvenes terneros
> para preparar una cena oficial.
> Se ha autorizado un montón de dinero
> pero prometen un menú magistral.

The song contains several elements of criticism: the young calves stand for the young soldiers sent to war without the appropriate training or equipment; the "masterful menu" refers to the elaborate press coverage manipulated by the regime. And the "sorbets" that the musicians will be given during the banquet will only extract what has already been processed, blended, so that there are no identifiable arguments or sides but one, unrefutable melted "truth" to suck up.

---

17 Virus, *Recrudece* (DG Discos, 1982).
18 Daniela Lucena, and Gisela Laboreau, "El rol del cuerpo-vestido en la ruptura estética de Virus durante los últimos años de la dictadura militar," *Música hodie* 15 (2): 192–202, 2015, at p. 195.

Songs of peace

The musicians' desire for peace during the Process was expressed through several overlapping strategies that exemplified the anti-war and anti-regime sentiments. Four artists whose Process-era work stands out for its artistic merit, and for the variety of creative ways that it incorporated an anti-war stance while simultaneously managing to evade the censors, are Luis Alberto Spinetta, Charly García, Raúl Porchetto, and León Gieco. Spinetta released *Kamikaze*,[19] a concept album that explored the atrocities of war while studiously avoiding mention of the islands in question; García released *Yendo de la cama al living*,[20] in which he expressed the feelings of a generation and predicted the end of the military Junta's hold over the country; and Raúl Porchetto's *Reina Madre*[21] drew parallels with English citizens, reminding his Argentine audience that they were as much victims of the Margaret Thatcher government as the Argentine soldiers were victims of Galtieri's rule. Meanwhile, León Gieco's aforementioned song "Solo le pido a Dios" became an international anti-war anthem.

Launched in the same year as the Malvinas/Falklands War, Spinetta's concept album *Kamikaze* was a blazing manifesto, and included a statement printed on the inner envelope of the cover in which the musician declared his opposition to violent confrontation and his respect for any who self-immolate in the name of an ideal. The red cover art of the album includes the blurry, over-exposed image of a face lying on one side, with all the passion implied by dying for one's beliefs, if Spinetta's own words are anything to go by: "We value things based on the levels of our ignorance. That is why I deeply admire the decision of those young Kamikazes, regardless of the abomination of war". Several layers of meaning are encoded in this message. On one level, it denounces the nationalistic stances that suddenly supported the dictatorship's military mission, as well as the media's complicity in disseminating far-from-objective information, its ridiculing of the "enemy", and it confidence that the war would be won. Added to this, the message underscores the audience's "ignorance"—its belief in the regime's version of events promulgated by the media. Finally, Spinetta puts paid to the idea that a war could have any winner, reminding us that it is an "abomination" while simultaneously expressing deep respect for the soldiers, whom he calls "kamikazes", a term with heroic and passionate connotations that generalises the concept, avoiding a purely Argentine reference. In this way, Spinetta's audience is encouraged to think beyond the local; he gestures to a universal concept that spans centuries and continents.

19 Luis Alberto Spinetta, *Kamikaze* (Ratón Finta, 1982).
20 Charly García, *Pubis angelical / Yendo de la cama al living* (DG Discos/Interdisc/Universal Music, 1982).
21 Raúl Porchetto, *Reina Madre* (Interdisc, 1983).

In fact, the titular and opening song, "Kamikaze", describes the kamikaze warrior as someone who is "crazy", who then "understood his mistake: to die like so is to die in vain" ("comprendió su error: morir así es en vano"). "Águila de trueno" (Thunder Eagle) alludes to Tupac Amaru II (Jose Gabriel Condorcanqui Noguera), the Andean leader sentenced to death by dismemberment in 1781 for having raised an army to improve the rights of indigenous Peruvians suffering under Spanish Bourbon reforms ("they will have sent to ask Gabriel to join with his body" ["habrán mandado a pedirle a Gabriel que se junte con su cuerpo"]). "Águila de trueno II" (Thunder Eagle II) speaks of "a man who cries in the street" ["hombre que llora en la calle"] possibly grieving the death of his son ("after a brief torment your gaze settled on the temple where a son calls" ["luego de un breve tormento tu mirada se posó en el templo donde un hijo llama"]). In this way, the idea of the kamikaze—the warrior who gives his life for a cause, but in vain—is universalised. The pain, the crying, the anguish, and the impotence seem to increase in "Ah! Basta de pensar" (Ah! Stop Thinking), where allusion to the powerful is made in terms of "donkeys and forgiveness, such cruel omnipotence" ["los asnos y el perdón, qué omnipotencia cruel"]. "La aventura de la abeja reina" (The Adventures of the Queen Bee) narrates a nightmare in which death is a cave, described as "total silence, lower world" ["silencio total, mundo inferior"]. The war veteran stars in "Y tu amor es una vieja medalla" (And Your Love Is an Old Medal), a tough song that describes how "gold and death changed your will, they changed your laugh into fear" ["El oro y la muerte cambiaron tu querer Trocaron tu risa por temor"]. War affects everyone, even the victors, who are left wearing a comparatively meaningless medal after they have lost everything, even the capacity to love.

This conceptual album tackles important themes and suggests that we are responsible for our own destiny; we must create a world of love and peace. The song "Quedándote o yéndote" (Staying or Leaving) uses commandments reminiscent of those in the Bible ("you will create the peaceful land you wish to see" ["deberás crear si quieres ver a tu tierra en paz"]). This is a key song that sums up life as a natural cycle where love prevails:

> The rain erases evil
> And washes all the wounds of your soul
> This water carries
> The force of fire...
>
> la lluvia borra la maldad
> y lava todas las heridas de tu alma
> este agua lleva en sí
> la fuerza del fuego...

Water washes, erases, and carries away, and is signaled, here, as a fundamental aspect of the circle of life, showing that we all form part of something greater. This broadening of perspective and interconnectedness of all things reflects the kamikaze motive of self-sacrifice, being guided by "the light" ("Casas marcadas" [Marked Houses]), a message that in 1982 was welcomed by most Argentines.

Indeed, 1982 was a key year for Argentina, with the Malvinas War and the paranoia it unleashed marking the end of the dictatorship and making audiences more receptive to societal critique. This tendency was encapsulated by Charly García in the title of his most political album: *Yendo de la cama al living* (Going from the Bed to the Living Room),[22] which can be interpreted as metaphorically describing the process of "waking up" to reality, especially in light of the album content.

The widespread feelings of confusion and numbness that the historical moment caused can be seen in many of the album's lyrics, for example: "Although you live in fictional worlds there are no signs of anything alive in me". Many of the songs are multilayered and emotive, including "Yo no quiero volverme tan loco" (I Don't Want to Become So Crazy) and "Inconsciente colectivo" (Collective Unconscious). The album's denouement comes in the ironic number "No bombardeen Buenos Aires" (Don't Bomb Buenos Aires), in which British exports such as the BBC, the Clash, whiskey, and the Beatles are namechecked. Here, the references to what happens in times of war are undeniably direct: ("the Gurkhas continue advancing, the old guys are still on TV, the soldiers' bosses drink whisky with the wealthy"). A compelling semantic fusion occurs in the line, "I hear a tango and a rock and I feel that's who I am", which brings together references to the two music genres that were instrumental in identity formation among young Argentines at the time: the Argentine tango and English rock. In this way, the media's nationalism during the war was undermined, with the audience forced to confront the hypocrisy inherent in such displays of insularity and parochialism.

> We all can lose, we all can win
> Among circus ropes and evil trenches
> ... My mind had doubts and I pretended not to see them
> ... Things are not what they seem to you
>
> Todos podemmos perder, todos podemos ganar
> entre las sogas del circo y las trincheras del mal
> ... mi mente tuvo dudas y fingí que no las vi
> ... las cosas ya no son como las ves.

The title of the song ("...every now and then" ["canción de dos por tres"]) references the coups d'etat that took power in Argentina during the previous decades. All regimes that were committed to the eradication of communism from the country's political landscape. The "circus" alludes to the make-believe stories staged by the regime and supported by the press,

---

22 Charly García, *Pubis angelical / Yendo de la cama al living.*

while the "trenches" are a clear reference to the war. There is a sort of *mea culpa* in this song: "my mind had doubts and I pretended not to see them" ["mi mente tuvo dudas y fingí que no las vi"] speaks about the confusion generated by the Festival of Latin American Solidarity. In fact, several musicians who participated in the festival later expressed their regret, as it may have looked like they were supporting the war and the regime.[23] García acknowledges in those two lines that he, along with many others, for an instant fell into the traps of a patriotic fervor, though he woke up to the truth soon enough ("things are not what they seem"). When asked about his song "No bombardeen Buenos Aires" and how he came up with that idea, García replied:

> I was sick of listening to my friends or other people who believed the government's stories. I remember that I was recording in the studio and it seemed to me that there was an unreality that was getting stronger than reality. There was an underlying reality that was our tremendous inferiority.[24]

The unreality referenced here—the idea that Argentina could win a war against a world power—was what inspired the song, and also led to his mocking the military government's theatricalisation of war, because he felt that the topic could be discussed no other way. Unlike in earlier albums, the lyrics of "No bombardeen Buenos Aires" are relatively transparent, their messages not encrypted. One of its most suggestive messages is the mention of the Clash's *Sandinista!*, not only because the band was English, but also because that 1980 album was the band's most politically controversial. The album made use of nonsense, just as did García in the albums he recorded with his band Serú Girán at the same time that *Sandinista!* was released.

Meanwhile, Raúl Porchetto released his album *Reina Madre* (Queen Mother) in 1983, the eponymous song of which offers another perspective on the war.[25] Far from mocking the English or viewing them as enemies, the song portrays a soldier who questions his government, highlighting the way the English were also told lies by their politicians. The fact that it is told from the perspective of an English soldier in the first person encourages the audience to identify with this "enemy":

> Mother, what's going on here?
> They are like me
> And they love this land, so far away from home
> I can't even remember its name
> Why am I fighting?
> Why am I killing?

---

23 Provéndola, *Rockpolitik*, p. 127.
24 Chirom and García, *Charly García*, p. 116.
25 Raúl Porchetto, *Reina Madre*.

104   CODED LYRICS

> Pero, madre, ¿qué está pasando acá?
> Son igual a mí
> y aman este lugar tan lejos de casa
> que ni el nombre me acuerdo
> ¿Por qué estoy luchando?
> ¿Por qué estoy matando?

The song continues to show that the English government is no better than the Argentine one in regard to telling stories on the large screen. It highlights the distance between the reality of war and the safe life of those in power:

> Today the Queen walks around her gardens
> While the sun kisses her roses, life is good,
> The Parliament makes sure everything runs as usual
> And that nothing disturbs her calm day
>
> Then she will attend a famous director's film premier
> A story about the scourges of war and men
> And she will be moved and will applaud the powerful ending…
>
> Hoy, la Reina, pasea en los jardines
> el sol besa sus rosas, la vida le sonríe
> el Parlamento cuida que todo siga igual
> que nada perturbe su calma.
>
> Luego tendrá una premier de cine de un director famoso
> que cuenta los flagelos de la guerra y los hombres
> y se emocionará y aplaudirá su buen final…

León Gieco's "Solo le pido a Dios"[26] is the most popular song associated with the Malvinas/Falklands War, even though it was written many years before the war began. (Interestingly, *Kamikaze* included songs that Spinetta likewise wrote much earlier, though he hadn't recorded them.) It is widely considered a peace anthem, with translations into many languages and interpretations by Bruce Springsteen, Mercedes Sosa, U2, Joan Manuel Serrat, and Shakira. At first glance the song appears to be nationalistic, yet its hymn-like tones are in fact an inversion of the official discourse on war: "I only ask of God that I not be indifferent to war, a huge monster that stomps all over people's naivety" ["Sólo le pido a Dios que la guerra no me sea indiferente, es un monstruo grande y pisa fuertetoda la pobre inocencia de la gente"].

Post *Falkvinas*

Once the Malvinas/Falkland Islands War was over, President Galtieri resigned and the new president, Reynaldo Bignone, led the transition to democracy.

---

26 León Gieco, *IV LP*.

The dictatorship's support for rock music was incredibly profitable for local producers long after that support had waned, for it caused national rock to grow as a genre proper and its reception to expand. Many Argentine rock songs of later years hark back to this period in Argentine history, revisiting the war in an attempt to come to terms with what was for many a confusing and painful time—so much so that, nowadays, the term "Argentine rock" has replaced "national rock" in an attempt to disassociate the genre from the confusing historical moment.

Massera's reaction against the military defeat in the Malvinas/Falklands War was to preserve the honour of the military institutions. He issued a statement, faithful to his sophisticated rhetorical style, in which he said: "Thanks be to God, today we continue to think that the supreme good is justice and not peace, because there is no lasting peace without justice".[27]

When they returned from the war, the soldiers were hidden from the public, no honour or reception was organised for them, and some ended up selling items to the public on public transport to survive because they struggled to find work. During the war, 649 Argentine soldiers died, but after the war the number of dead rose to 1,300. They thought they would enjoy a reception as heroes and, instead, their reception resembled that of a losing team after a soccer game. Fito Paez's song "La canción del soldado y Rosita Pazos" (The Song of the Soldier and Rosita Pazos)[28] refers to those 1,300 and to the trauma experienced by the survivors. The soldier in the song is received by a loving woman who tries her best to comfort him, but he ends up committing suicide ("the war kills us" ["la guerra nos asesina"]). There were many other songs dedicated to this war trauma, such as "Héroes de Malvinas" (Malvinas Heroes) by Ciro y los persas;[29] "La isla de la buena memoria" (The Island of Good Memory) by Alejandro Lerner;[30] "Gente del sur" (People of the South) by Rata Blanca;[31] and "Algo de paz" (Some Peace) by Raúl Porchetto,[32] just to mention a few.

The war implied a major nationalist project, since national honour and national dignity were at stake. The government made use of the war to mask internal troubles, divert attention towards "bigger problems" than the economy, repression, or the disappeared, and to raise nationalist feelings and thus unite public opinion against a common external enemy. Yet there was a major internal victory for the rock musicians who had been suffering the persecutions of the regime. In this way, the strategy of the military authorities was reversed. By banning music in English, which only a certain audience understood, songs in Spanish, especially national rock, filled the broadcasting

27 Uriarte, *Almirante Cero*, p. 200.
28 Fito Páez, *Yo te amo* (Sony Music, 2013).
29 Ciro y los persas, *Espejos* (300 Producciones, 2010).
30 Alejandro Lerner, *Todo a pulmón* (Raviol Records/Interdisc, 1983).
31 Rata Blanca, *Rata Blanca* (Universal, 1988).
32 Raúl Porchetto, *Metegol* (Music Hall, 1980).

spaces in a language that, although sometimes encrypted, was much more readily comprehensible. The irony of the situation was that one censorship was replaced with another. The "music of the enemy" could not be broadcast, as if it might influence the development of war to the south.[33]

The result of the dictatorship was incredibly profitable for music. Argentine rock grew as a genre proper, its reception expanded, and, contrary to what the military had expected, it refused to support the war.

---

33 Favoretto, *Alegoría*, p. 276.

CHAPTER SEVEN

Words Set Free

Speech and Thought in Post-Dictatorship Songs

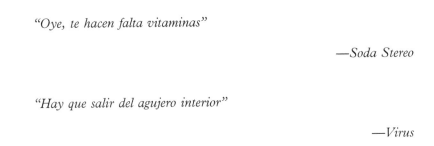

"*Oye, te hacen falta vitaminas*"

—*Soda Stereo*

"*Hay que salir del agujero interior*"

—*Virus*

After the war, the production and sale of rock albums increased, until Argentine rock became a highly profitable product. In fact, Argentine rock was one of the few national products to experience an upturn between 1983 and 1987.

In 1981, thirty-seven LPs were produced, a significant step given the sixteen recorded in 1979. In 1982 there were sixty-three, in 1983 there were seventy-seven, and in 1984 there were eighty-one.[1] This success paved the way for new bands and musicians who labelled their music "Rock Nacional".[2] Changes in the political arena—democracy—brought changes in cultural production. With the lifting of censorship, freedom of speech was a reinstated right to be enjoyed. This is obvious in the lyrics of new bands' songs, as we will discuss in this chapter. First, though, let us look at the socio-political context in which these songs emerged.

On 30 October 1983, after a decade of state terrorism, a democratic election took place in which Radicalism won against the hitherto undefeated

---

[1] Alabarces, *Entre gatos y violadores*, p. 85.
[2] Cristian Secul Giusti, and Federico Rodríguez Lemos, "Si tienes voz, tienes palabras: análisis discursivo de las líricas del rock argentino en la 'primavera democrática (1983–1986)'," dissertation (Buenos Aires: Universidad Nacional de La Plata, 2011), p. 49.

Peronism. The new president was Raúl Alfonsín, who made the exemplary decision, of historical value and international impact, to bring the military juntas to trial for the human rights violations committed. In order to give strong support to the investigation of human rights violations during the dictatorship, a commission of notable citizens was created, called the National Commission on the Disappearance of Persons (CONADEP). The commission's final report was delivered to the president in 1984 under the title *Nunca más* (Never Again). The report detailed the confirmed disappearance of about 9,000 people and a total of 1,086 cases reported to justice, and documented the repressive role played by the dictatorship between 1976 and 1983. It also exposed the existence of clandestine concentration camps throughout the country, such as the School of Mechanics of the Navy (ESMA, in Buenos Aires), La Perla (in Córdoba), and the School of Faimall (in Tucumán).

On 9 January 1984, the new democratic government annulled all existing broadcasting blacklists. The Ministry of Culture of the Municipality of the City of Buenos Aires began to organise free popular music concerts in summer. Although many rockers were inclined to demonstrate politically, democracy brought in a new generation of young people. They were not inspired by or interested in conventional politics, even in democracy. Many bands at the time were interested in experimenting with new sounds, new aesthetics, dance, and body performances just for fun and entertainment. The municipalities in different parts of the country supported many concerts and Argentine rock became widely popular.

Thus, the decade of the 1980s was when rock became a permanent fixture in Argentina as a mass cultural phenomenon. However, as explained by Provéndola, the cracks in the relationship between politics and rock in the post-dictatorship period began to appear in 1987. The new cultural secretary of Buenos Aires, historian Félix Luna, eliminated rock from the traditional free events of the Buenos Aires summer, arguing that rock shows often caused acts of violence.[3]

Until the Malvinas conflict, Argentine rock had been fundamentally non-danceable, since the concerts were conceived as a "mass ritual": concertgoers, contained by the external repression, listened sitting down and in reverence.[4] In fact, as we have explored in the previous chapter, during and after the Falklands War, local rock went on to occupy places that were previously considered "enemy" spaces: radios, television, and discotheques. Suddenly Argentine rock could be danced at discos, something unthinkable before 1981, although the music was gradually mirroring what was happening throughout the world.[5]

---

3 Provéndola, *Rockpolitik*, p. 151.
4 Eduardo Berti, *Rockología, documentos de los '80* (Buenos Aires: Beas Ediciones, 1994), p. 34.
5 Secul Giusti and Rodríguez Lemos, "Si tienes voz," p. 111.

In these new democratic times Argentine rock lyrics became characterised by their self-referentiality, unlike previous decades when they were defined in terms of the collective feelings and in utopias of change that involved everyone. Indeed, in the 1980s Argentine rock became eclectic and varied, and both bands and audiences were now interested in dancing, pleasure, and body movements. Argentine rock adopted the world-wide physical trends of the '80s, but at the same time it had content that was specific to this country and constituted a significant contribution to Argentine culture.[6] There was, as Secul Giusti observes, an aesthetic turn that took place inside Argentine rock under democracy, when rock went from being a vehicle of marginal expression to being another element of the cultural industry.[7]

This chapter explores three aspects of rock song production during the democratic 1980s. First, the transition songs that still alluded to the dictatorship and could now critically engage with politics in a more overt way since the end of censorship. Secondly, the transition songs that embraced freedom and were, in fact, explorations and innovation in the genre, a move forward without much political reference but using a self-referent poetic voice which is mainly hedonistic and playful. The third group of songs comprises those that paved the road for the styles in the 1990s and the emergence of what was called "rock chabón".

Transition songs

From 1981, while censorship eased and the dictatorship mellowed in many ways, Argentine rock began to generate its own marginal spaces where new creative aesthetics flourished. Those underground spaces witnessed the development of the punk, post-punk, and pop genres. This cultural explosion also brought significant changes to the lyrics of the songs in these genres, which started to incorporate irony, sarcasm, and playful images. Some of these also spoke about the self as an individual, leaving behind the social and communal messages of rock songs, and highlighted hedonism, pleasure, sexual encounters, and fun times. Though apparently superficial, these songs marked a rupture with the past and endeavoured to attract those young people who had ceased to engage with the political aspects of Argentine rock, or had never engaged with those aspects to begin with.

Thus, the underground stream of pre-democratic Argentine rock became an alternative that distanced itself from the near past and provided a new space where people could simply relax and have fun. This was the time when now very popular Argentine bands developed, such as Virus, Soda Stereo, Patricio Rey y sus Redonditos de Ricota, Sumo, GIT, Zas, Los Twist, and

---

6 Cristian Secul Giusti, "Rompiendo el silencio: la construcción discursiva de la libertad en las líricas de rock-pop argentino durante el período 1982–1989," doctoral dissertation (Buenos Aires: Universidad Nacional de La Plata, 2017), p. 227.
7 Secul Giusti, "Rompiendo," p. 178.

Los Abuelos de la Nada (second band formation, different from that of the 1960s).[8]

While all this innovation and exploration was happening in underground circles, 1982 was a crucial year for the more popular bands. As we have seen, the paranoia of the war and the English-language ban presented an unprecedented opportunity for local rock musicians. Rock festivals made a comeback, including the popular BA Rock (Buenos Aires Rock). Elections were announced, political parties' campaigns started to dominate the media, and rock music broadened its audience. That same year Charly García launched his masterpiece *Yendo de la cama al living* (Going from the Bed to the Livingroom, 1982) and travelled to New York, where he recorded his album *Clics modernos* (Modern Clics),[9] produced by Joe Blaney. This album, today a classic, marked a fundamental change in the work of this artist, a turning point that distinguished a before from an after. He became much sharper in his criticisms and no longer needed to encrypt his rebellion, as there was now no reason to fear censorship. For example, the "confinement" denoted by the metaphor of the song "Yendo de la cama al living" (Going from the Bed to the Living Room) had to do with censorship and the political situation, but perhaps it had even more to do with that blind nationalism that could be seen on the streets at the time of the war. Indeed, many of those who had suffered the consequences of a repressive government supported that government during the war, moved by a clear manipulation of popular emotion by the military and the media. Already living under democracy and enjoying the greater freedom of expression it entailed, not only did Charly manage to get out of confinement, but he also opened the door to a wider context: he left the country to explore the world of music and the new technologies applied to its production in New York, recording his new album *Clics modernos* (1983) there. The cover of this album, in black and white, shows a different Charly, with a modern look, serious, smoking, leaning on a wall graffitied with a black silhouette, perhaps a reference to the disappeared, on which a white heart has been placed and eyes and a smile have been drawn. The allusion to the disappeared on the cover of the album was a way to remind those who had suddenly been carried away by nationalism and supported the government's Malvinas crusade that they were forgetting that the same government was responsible for the disappearances of thousands of people. *Clics modernos*, in a way, marked the end of the dictatorship and the reinstatement of democracy.

Yet Charly García was not the only one to release a transition album. Several other bands released ironic songs, some of which included mockery of the transition period, a sign of disbelief. "Pensé que se trataba de cieguitos" (I thought They Were Blind)[10] by Los Twist mocks the death squads, while

---

8 Secul Giusti, "Rompiendo," pp. 68–69.
9 Charly García, *Clics modernos* (DG Discos/Interdisc/Universal Music, 1983).
10 Los Twist, *La dicha en movimiento* (SG Discos/Interdisc, 1983).

Celeste Carballo sings "Now I can relax" on her 1983 album *Mi voz renacerá* (My Voice Will Revive),[11] a playful, ironic song that ridicules the current state of affairs:

> Now I am calmer,
> Since everything's all fixed...
>
> Ahora me quedo más tranquila
> como todo está arreglado...

The same year, 1983, saw the release of a variety of songs that referred to the transition in different ways. Dúo Fantasía included a song called "Argentina, otra operación" (Argentina, Another Surgery) on their album *El futuro es nuestro* (The Future Is Ours).[12] The song made use of the same rhetorical strategies that had been employed by the dictatorial regime and suggested another "treatment" based on love and happiness. The band Virus launched their third album, *Agujero interior* (Internal Hole),[13] with song lyrics that encouraged the audience to enjoy a life of pleasure and imagination. Miguel Cantilo titled his new album *Unidad* (Unity)[14] and gave some advice about the elections: "Let's not antagonise because we have to vote". Los Abuelos de la Nada sang about "hope born over a rainbow" and that "youth without unity was not true" ("No se desesperen" [Do not get desperate], on *Vasos y besos* [Glasses and Kisses]).[15]

To return to Charly García, his follow-up album, *Piano bar*,[16] began with the song "Demoliendo hoteles" (Demolishing Hotels), which over the years would become a common phrase among Argentines. The song's opening line, "I was born with Videla", could be interpreted as the birth of his fame under the dictatorship, the separation of the private self from the public self-character. In this way, "Born with Videla" marks a key moment: Charly had known fame with Sui Generis but it was not until the dictatorship that he transcended generations and genres to become a national celebrity. The text clarifies that "we all grew up without understanding and I still feel abnormal" ("Demoliendo hoteles"). That was one of the main characteristics of the transition: the lack of understanding of what had happened and the strange, "abnormal" feeling that pervaded the youth. The confusion came from the denial of the disappearances and then the report by the CONADEP contradicting those claims; the lies in the press during the war; the cases of corruption; and, moreover, the confusion promulgated by the use of language.

---

11 Celeste Carballo, *Mi voz renacerá* (Interdisc, 1983).
12 Dúo Fantasía, *El futuro es nuestro* (Sazam Records, 1983).
13 Virus, *Agujero interior* (CBS, 1983).
14 Miguel Cantilo, *Unidad* (Sazam Records, 1983).
15 Los Abuelos de la Nada, *Vasos y besos* (Interdisc, 1983).
16 Charly García, *Piano bar* (DG Discos/Interdisc/Universal Music, 1984).

Those that claimed to be governing guided by love, God, and Western and Christian values were caught out as torturers, killers, and liars.

After stating that he was still feeling "abnormal", Charly set the temperature of the post-dictatorship society: "Everyone has a trip in their minds, it is difficult for us to come to an agreement" ("Promesas sobre el bidet" [Promises over the Bidet]). The song points to a divided society in which "weird new hairstyles" sounds like a manifesto. The song "Cerca de la Revolución" (Close to Revolution) speaks of this same confusion with greater drama—"the analysts will not be able to understand... people bay for blood, I am singing this song that once was hunger"—and adds a phrase that, far from any mockery, is loaded with emotion: "if these words could give you faith, if this harmony could help you grow, I would be so happy". Exile continues to be a constant theme in some songs, such as "Tuve tu amor" (I Had Your Love) and "Rap del exilio" (Exile Rap), in which he mocks the flexibility of some political ideas, names key political figures such as Perón and Che, but ends up drowning everything in a more popular/populist idea: "Let's go dance". In other words, in just a few lines Charly references the left, Peronism, exile, and the political class that dilutes reality with populist entertainment in the form of a great national and popular dance. The album closes with "Interferencia total" (Total Interference), a song that announces that we are all wrong and that "we violate everything we love just to live".

Regarding human rights, many Argentines were looking forward to the juntas being put on trial in 1985. This judicial process meant that Alfonsín's presidency became an exemplar among all the recovered democracies of Latin America, given that Argentina became the only country in the region to condemn the leaders of a dictatorial regime. Throughout the trial, 700 people testified and 450 officers were prosecuted.[17] Indeed, trialing the juntas constituted a moment of historical change and the major symbol of the transition to democracy. The trial also updated a version of the so-called theory of "the two Demons". Two forms of extreme intolerance were constructed then and continue today: on the one hand, the so-called "terrorism" of the ultra-left and, on the other, the state violence of the ultra-right. This conceptualisation meant victimising society, as society was portrayed as a spectator of what happened, deceived and harmed by a war between the military on one side and the guerrillas on the other.[18] These representations ensured that members of society were cast as innocent victims during a war, inuring them against feelings of guilt for having allowed a coup to convince them it was the best option, for having supported the regime during the first years, and for believing the lies broadcast by the state-managed media.

---

17 Secul Giusti, "Rompiendo," p. 86.
18 Gonzalo De Amézola, "La última dictadura militar en la escuela Argentina: entre la historia reciente y la memoria colectiva," *Revista de teoría y didáctica de las ciencias sociales* (17): 29–56, 2011, at p. 33.

At the time, two of the most significant songs were probably "Mejor no hablar de ciertas cosas" (Best Avoid Certain Topics)[19] by Sumo and "La muralla verde" (The Green Wall)[20] by Los Enanitos Verdes. The former spoke about a tornado which "swept through my city and my primitive garden. A tornado swept through your city and your primitive garden. But no, best avoid certain topics". The tornado in the song can stand for the military regime and the "primitive" garden can be a reference to the naivety of a high proportion of the population. Though censorship was not operational at the time that this song was released, the choice not to talk about "certain topics" can be a mockery of a divided society that was still at odds with the political events, probably foreshadowing what was coming next. Los Enanitos Verdes went a bit further and were less optimistic:

> I'm standing on the wall that divides
> all that was from what will be
> I'm looking how those old illusions
> after the wall they become real
> …
> They will disappear again
> Disappear
> …
> I'm looking at how my wounds have closed
> And how a new heart bleeds
>
> Estoy parado sobre la muralla que divide
> todo lo que fué de lo que será
> estoy mirando cómo esas viejas ilusiones
> pasando la muralla se hacen realidad
> …
> Vuelve a desaparecer
> desaparecer
> …
> Estoy mirando cómo mis heridas se cerraron
> y cómo se desangra un nuevo corazón

In sum, the poetic voice in the song has a pessimistic view of the status quo, despite the "wall" dividing dictatorship from democracy. Disappearances, according to the song, seem to be cyclic and new sorrows are just around the corner.

These songs seemed to be a clear foreshadowing of Alfonsín's gesture—trialling the juntas—which would then be diminished when the radical government yielded to the pressures of the military, business, and political power factors.

---

19 Sumo, *Divididos por la felicidad* (CBS, 1985).
20 Los Enanitos Verdes, *Simulacro de tensión* (Sony Music, 1986).

At the start of 1987, during the period known as "Holy Week" or "Easter", a new crisis challenged democracy. Alfonsín needed to act quickly to reassert his authority and to calm down the very angry military officials. The resulting two laws, "Punto Final" (Full Stop) and "Obediencia Debida" (Due Obedience), limited and prevented justice, infuriating the general population. These two laws limited the extent to which war crimes would be tried.

The Due Obedience Law (1987) absolved all lower- and middle-ranked military officials from their participation in the kidnapping, torturing, and killing of prisoners, on the basis that they had been following orders. The Full Stop Law (1986) stated that after the trial of the Junta, by which some high-ranked military officials were convicted and sentenced, there was no longer a need for the investigation or prosecution of suspects. The law also determined a deadline (February 1987) for any formal complaints about crimes committed by the security forces during the military dictatorship.

These two laws were in clear tension with the government's message of seeking justice for the human rights violations that took place during the dictatorship. Furthermore, the economic crisis was deepening. In order to control economic difficulties, the radical government launched a new economic program: the Austral Plan. Though successful at the start, as it managed to lower the very high inflation, the state's debt became unmanageable and default was inevitable.

Inflation skyrocketed, provoking civil unrest. President Alfonsín had to resign before his due date and hand the leadership to the newly elected Peronist Carlos Sául Menem. To make things worse, President Menem (1989–99) granted pardons to all military officials. It was only after 2003, under Néstor Kirchner's presidency (2003–07), that these decrees and laws were reversed and declared unconstitutional.

Perhaps the highlight of the body of songs produced in this period might be "Yo no me sentaría en tu mesa" (I Would Not Sit at Your Table) by Los Fabulosos Cadillacs.[21] The song references the altercation that the band had with officials of Alfonsín's political party, UCR, after the event "UCR Youth Goes with You". In this regard, the singer of the band, "Vicentico" Fernández Capello, distanced himself from Alfonsín's sympathisers and remained critical of the government, refusing to share space with the national deputy Jesús Rodríguez, arguing that he would not sit at the table of a person who signs the Due Obedience Law.[22]

Singing songs of freedom

In democratic times, Argentine rock started to lose the supporting role for youth identity that it had held during the dictatorship. This was in part

[21] Los Fabulosos Cadillacs, *Yo te avisé* (CBS, 1987).
[22] Provéndola, *Rockpolitik*, p. 152.

because now there were political parties, human rights movements, and unions. Argentine rock is part of a process of transformation and of construction of meaning and, as such, it modified stylistic variants and generated a greater diversity of narratives from a notion of freedom.[23] In this way, local rock started to give room to a greater diversity of narratives and youth values. The fact that there was now complete freedom of expression is celebrated in "Yo soy tu bandera" (I'm Your Flag) by the band Los Abuelos de la Nada:[24]

> Freedom,
> sister to my friends
> Freedom
> nothing ties me and I'm alive
> never die, Freedom…
>
> Libertad
> hermana de los amigos
> Libertad
> nada me ata y estoy vivo
> no te mueras nunca, Libertad…

An interesting movement in the 1980s was La Trova Rosarina, a term used to identify the generation of musicians in the city of Rosario, which emerged at the beginning of 1980. The movement was characterised by linking rock, tango, and folklore, poetry, and narratives with purely literary intentions. Among its most prominent musicians were Fito Páez, Juan Carlos Baglietto, Jorge Fandermole, Silvina Garré, Adrián Abonizio, Fabián Gallardo, Rubén Goldin, Lalo de los Santos, and Ethel Koffman, just to mention a few. One of the main frontmen and leaders of the movement was Juan Carlos Baglietto, who also organised a show and its compiled album called *Por qué cantamos* (Why We Sing) in 1985.[25] The title was taken from the poem/song written by Uruguayan Mario Benedetti and Argentine Alberto Favero, performed by several artists.[26] The song was extremely successful as a powerful hymn:

> Life is nothing but a moving target
> You will ask why we sing?
> …
> We sing because cruelty has no name
> and instead destiny has a name
> …
> We sing because survivors
> and our dead want us to sing.

---

23 Secul Giusti, "Rompiendo," p. 167.
24 Los Abuelos de la Nada, *Vasos y besos*.
25 Various Artists, *Por qué cantamos* (EMI, 1985).
26 Marcelo Fernández Bitar, *50 años de rock en Argentina* (Buenos Aires: Sudamericana, 2015), p. 150.

> La vida es nada más que un blanco móvil
> usted preguntará ¿por qué cantamos?
> ...
> Cantamos porque el cruel no tiene nombre
> y en cambio tiene nombre su destino
> ...
> Cantamos porque los sobrevivientes
> y nuestros muertos quieren que cantemos.

Juan Carlos Baglietto was not a composer but a singer, and his choice of repertoire was impeccable. The winning mix of poetic songs and an engaging performance meant his music became hugely popular across the whole country. For example, his song "Tratando de crecer" (Trying to Grow Up)[27] made it clear that "growing up" did not mean "settling" and insisted on looking towards a positive future: "I still want to change something, I still want to, thank God" ["todavía tengo en menta cambiar algo, todavía y a Dios gracias todavía"].

In September 1984, twenty-one-year-old Fito Páez, the composer of many of Baglietto's songs, including "Tratando de crecer", launched his first album. Having just left Baglietto's band, and becoming, as keyboard player, the newest addition to Charly García's, Fito composed a handful of songs that showed an outstanding talent. His first solo album, *Del 63* (Born in 1963),[28] is a remarkable representation of the transition feelings of that generation. For example, the titular "Del 63" is an autobiographical song which tells the story of his short life and the context in which he grew up. He calls on everyone to participate in the new democratic period: "we are all guilty and we have to solve this mess". The album also includes an outstanding political song, "Cuervos en la casa" (Crows in the House), in which La Casa Rosada or the Pink House—the government house in Buenos Aires—is bluntly criticised, something that would have been inconceivable just a few months before:

> Crows in the Pink House, crows in the Pink House
> Raising crows, at the Pink House
> A trumpeter caught a cold, they are sucking his blood
> I wonder what I'm doing here, they're sucking my blood
> This is the status quo; the fans were turned on
> My General, how good you look! it seems that you have eaten traitors today
> Fire!
>
> Cuervos en Casa Rosada, cuervos en Casa Rosada
> Cría cuervos, la Casa Rosada
> Un trompetista se resfrió, están chupándole la sangre

---

27 Juan Carlos Baglietto, *Baglietto* (EMI, 1983).
28 Fito Páez, *Del 63* (EMI, 1983).

> Yo me pregunto que hago aquí, están chupándome la sangre
> Este es el cuadro de situación, prendieron los ventiladores
> Mi general, qué bien se lo ve, parece que hoy comió traidores
> ¡Fuego!

Besides the new freedom of expression, the idea of "singing" as expressing oneself is a concept repeated in many songs in the 1980s. An idea inaugurated and developed during the dictatorship was that one possible means of expression in the midst of repression was a song. Fito Páez includes this idea in several songs on the same album, for example in "Un rosarino en Budapest" (A guy from Rosario in Budapest) he sings:

> I will bark, I will bark, until the rage is exhausted
> I will sing, I will sing, that's my only weapon.
>
> Ladraré, ladraré, hasta que agote la rabia
> Cantaré, cantaré, esa es mi única arma.

Paéz's interesting choice of words, "singing is my only weapon", is clearly a feeling carried on from the very recent political period. His song "Rojo como un corazón" (Red as a Heart) reiterates the same concept:

> I want to cross the line before they come back
> …
> And I realise that this song
> Is not the same song as yesterday
> and it's not a matter of chords or rhythms
> there are no return passages…
>
> Quiero cruzar la línea antes que vuelvan
> …
> Y me doy cuenta que esta canción
> no es la misma canción de ayer
> y no es cuestión de acordes ni de ritmos
> es que ya no hay pasajes de regreso…

The lyrics of this song show a clear break from the past ("there are no return passages") and hope for a new future. The line "before they come back" speaks about the fear of the idea of a new coup. As we have seen, dictatorships until then had been cyclical in Argentina, so the chances of a new one must have seemed quite high. In "Nunca podrán sacarme mi amor" (They Will Never Take My Love Out of Me), Fito Páez makes a clear statement in defence of love: the freedom to love shows the possibility of change and even of "stubbornness".[29] Thus, the song links freedom to different forms of love: love to do, to create, to believe, and to live in society:

---

29 Secul Giusti, "Rompiendo," p. 169.

> They can sell a country
> And be on God's side
> But they can never take my love out of me...
>
> Pueden vender un país
> y estar del lado de Dios
> pero nunca podrán sacarme mi amor...

Páez was not the only musician who sang of freedom. There were many others. Secul Giusti's study dissects songs that present a search for freedom, songs that themselves act as an attempt to rebuild such freedom after the catastrophe that was the latest dictatorship. This vision presented democracy as a utopia of freedom and a transition towards equality. For Secul Giusti, "freedom was operated as a central position in the public agenda of the transition and worked to guarantee the construction of hope".[30]

Secul Giusti identifies three major transition albums: *Soda Stereo* by Soda Stereo,[31] *Locura* (Madness) by Virus,[32] and *Oktubre* by Patricio Rey y sus Redonditos de Ricota.[33] *Soda Stereo* (1984) was highly influential during the transition and introduced a new sound in Argentine rock. The band became popular in most countries in Latin America, with new aesthetics and lyrics that talked about liberation, fun, the body, and hedonistic pleasures. In "Te hacen falta vitaminas" (You Need Vitamins) the poetic voice asks, "What are you waiting for to free yourself? To dare? Or are you waiting for someone to come and wake you up?" ["¿Y qué esperas para soltarte? ¿Para animarte? ¿O supones que alguien viene a despertarte? Oye, te hacen falta vitaminas"]. In a way, the question is not rhetorical; the singing voice is expecting a response from the audience.

The 1985 explosion saw record labels and publishers launching new albums, special magazine editions, and program concerts commemorating the twenty years of Argentine rock, reconfiguring, again and again, the new and old stories of the movement.[34] Record sales, both studio and live recordings, were riding high. Argentine rock was in a moment of supreme success in the universe of the national spectacle and continued to grow into new ideas. In its early days, this genre had not been intended as music to dance to. As we have seen, the main interests were the political message and the lyrics. Yet in this new democratic period, bands such as Virus and Soda Stereo changed that. Their songs defied the original structures by adding a dancing dimension to the other features. This twist represented a new aesthetics that still preserved the poetic and ambiguous lyrics. Though dancing had been considered a trivial activity, far from the serious political statements pursued

---

30 Secul Giusti, "Rompiendo," p. 165.
31 Soda Stereo, *Soda Stereo* (CBS, 1984).
32 Virus, *Locura* (Music Hall, 1985).
33 Patricio Rey y sus Redonditos de Ricota, *Oktubre* (Del Cielito Records, 1986).
34 Secul Giusti, "Rompiendo," p. 102.

by Argentine rock, in this new democratic period it was viewed as a liberating and stimulating practice.

In 1986, Patricio Rey y sus Redonditos de Ricota launch their album *Oktubre*, possibly one of their most political. The images on the album cover reference communist iconography. The songs visit themes such as the Cold War, the Malvinas/Falklands War, consumerism, and postmodernism. This band would later become a very interesting stand-alone case in Argentine rock, with several books published about the particular rituals and mass events that their concerts became. Los Redondos (a name by which the band has been known for decades) are an independent band who prioritise direct communication with their audience during concerts. Carlos "Indio" Solari, the leader and composer of most of their songs with cryptic lyrics, insisted that "the only way to understand [their] music, was to participate in it".[35] Indeed, the audience plays a pivotal role at The Redondos' concerts, in a sort of communion with the band.

The 1990s and early 2000s: Songs of resentment

As already mentioned, Alfonsín resigned in the midst of a huge crisis, hyperinflation, looting, and social chaos, six months before completing his term. His successor was the charismatic Menem, who would soon transform his rural look into a celebrity one.

This was the first time since 1928 that Argentina had had two successive democratically elected governments. In the absence of government plans, and convinced that it was necessary to act favourably towards the international economic and financial powers in facing the great inherited crisis, Menem submitted to the instructions of the Washington consensus. According to a decalogue presented by the American economist John Williamson, Latin American countries should accept the total opening of customs borders, the deregulation of prices and salaries, the sale of public companies, and submission to the control of international organisations, especially the International Monetary Fund. Menem was one of the Latin American presidents, together with Collor de Melo in Brazil, Fujimori in Peru, Sánchez de Lozada in Bolivia, and Salinas de Gortari in Mexico, among others, who accepted the neoliberal catechism, even with the known and unfortunate consequences of unemployment, indebtedness, and political and economic crises.[36]

Menem's political discourse was plagued by Messianic phrases such as "Argentina, stand up and walk" or "Follow me, I won't disappoint you". Yet he would soon sign the pardon of the military Junta by decree, warranting them total impunity. Menem also introduced the neoliberal economic model,

---

35 Marcelo Gobello, *Banderas en tu corazón. Apuntes sobre el mito de los redondos* (Buenos Aires: Ediciones Corregidor, 2014), p. 18.
36 Pacho O'Donnell, *Breve historia argentina. De la Conquista a los Kirchner* (Buenos Aires: Aguilar, 2014), pp. 315–29.

which would bring devastating consequences for industries, business, and jobs. Under the motto "productive revolution", his government privatised state-owned companies at ridiculous prices, favouring corruption at scales never seen in Argentina.

Two main changes affected Argentine society, hand in hand: while privatisation meant people lost their jobs, hospital budgets shrank, and more people became poor, on the other hand politics became showbiz and politicians were depicted in the media as celebrities. TV shows portrayed a charming, laid-back president, the image of a "typical macho", always surrounded by beautiful women and driving expensive cars. Menem cultivated the image of a "winner", drove a Ferrari Testarossa, underwent plastic surgery to look younger, played sports, and danced tango and Arabic dance on TV shows. He also lied to the point that he promised, speaking to an entire primary school, that Argentina would build a super-modern space station where spaceships would be able to travel to Japan in one hour.[37] His "Argentine macho" profile was, to all appearances, successful, as he was re-elected.

This period has been dubbed "the neoliberal genocide of the 1990s" by two medical doctors, Dr Miguel Leguizamón and Dr Angel Gonzalez, who worked at the time in a hospital in the province of Tucumán, in the north of the country. Before Menem's administration, eighteen per cent of children admitted to the hospital were malnourished. After the implementation of neoliberal policies, this increased to eighty per cent. These children, they wrote, were not only malnourished and severely ill, but also undocumented. They did not officially exist according to the census. These were the new "disappeared". If there was no registration of their existence, there was no way to prove the devastating reality that was causing them to die at such a young age. By 2003, according to the statistics, about a hundred people died from starvation in Argentina per day, and half of them were children.

Menem's successor was Fernando de la Rúa, whose profile was the polar opposite. He was austere, shy, and less popular, and was soon categorised as "boring". His "boring" low profile was soon associated with weakness, and the unfortunate financial measures taken by his treasurer, Domingo Cavallo, contributed to worsening his popularity. The police repressed massive protests, looting, and violence in the streets with more violence. Amid social chaos, de la Rúa had to flee the Pink House in a helicopter, leaving the country without a president.

The following week was unique in Argentine history. There were five different presidents in just a few days. Among those changes, Adolfo Rodríguez Sáa emerged as an enigmatic administrator whose innovative policies were applauded and welcomed by the public. Yet his colleagues did not agree with him and withdrew their support. Rodríguez Sáa resigned and

---

37 La Nación, "A la Estratósfera," 30 September 2017, https://fb.watch/jwIybadvwg/ (accessed 27 March 2023).

fled to San Luis, his province. Rumours in San Luis tell a different story about Rodríguez Sáa's resignation: apparently, his children's lives had been threatened. In 2002, Eduardo Duhalde became the president of the transition period towards the new elections. Néstor Kirchner won in 2003, inaugurating what would later be called "the K era" or "Kirchnerism".

In the 1990s, rock incorporated a new social base to verbalise resentment and disagreement with political discourses. The consequences of impoverishment and changes in the social pyramid also caused an intellectual impoverishment of rock, which many called "rock chabón", where the fans of the bands are likened to football fans.[38]

What defines rock chabón, Provéndola explains, is the implementation of a remarkable number of dynamics that are typical of soccer culture, completely redirecting the countercultural nature of rock. It goes from a culture of resistance to a culture of endurance (called "aguante" in Argentine slang), a tension that is no longer external—towards everything that rock is opposed to—but internal.[39] "Endurance", explains Provéndola, means to tolerate self-imposed obstacles in order to enjoy music in an epic way (despite ramshackle concert venues, lengthy peregrinations to a show venue, and police sieges). In this context, fans see themselves as "enduring" rock culture in order to enjoy its music.[40] The ultimate goal of this endurance, or new resistance, is not to reach an ideal, improve a way of life, or modify the system itself, but simply to start a celebratory event that is shared in all corners of the country, a sort of carnival as a form of celebration and enjoyment as an alternative modality to that established by a system that is perceived as hypocritical.

The "carnival" emerges in a context of chaos, impunity, social abandonment, and obscenity. It is no surprise then to find there are many songs that speak about the disappeared, impunity, and the need for justice. However, the band that arguably made an impact in this decade was Bersuit Vergarabat. Especially between 1989 and 2007, their songs were characterised by grotesque realism, hybridity, wordiness, abject aesthetics, and rituals of "perpetual party" that denounced and protested the devastating reality. At the same time, they looked for new ways of connecting with the audience, incorporating the marginal, madness, the sexualised body, and a strong sense of the present moment. An eclectic rock band, Bersuit Vergarabat outgrew its underground origins not only to become highly popular in Argentina, but also to tour several countries in Latin America. It achieved several platinum records and won an award for Best Band of the Year.[41] The aesthetics of

---

38 Provéndola, *Rockpolitik*, p. 170.
39 Provéndola, *Rockpolitik*, p. 170.
40 Provéndola, *Rockpolitik*, p. 171.
41 Silvia Citro, "El rock como un ritual adolescente. Trasgresión y realismo grotesco en los recitales de Bersuit," *Trans. Revista transcultural de música* 12: n. p., 2008.

its production have been described as "a peculiar grotesque realism" and its concerts categorised as "rituals of transgression".[42]

To the apparent "party" and "celebrity-like" lifestyle of some representatives of the government, Bersuit Vergarabat juxtaposes another "party", where the celebrity is the marginal. This "party" is like a "perpetual carnival" that redefines Argentineness and creates a new dissident space. This space emerges as a form of linguistic alienation that distances the band and its followers not only from the political elite and the more affluent classes, but also from the poetics and culture of Argentine rock, which had reached its peak in the two previous decades.

Bersuit Vergarabat initiated a moment of rupture: though they are categorised as an Argentine rock band, their lyrics, aesthetics, and cultural practices distanced them enormously from their predecessors and invited their followers to incorporate sounds, words, and practices that had been inhabiting the margins for decades. Their profane representations seem to give their audience a sense of our own vulnerability and permeability, a permeability that connects us with the subaltern citizens whose experiences we often marginalise or ignore.

"De ahí soy yo" (That's Where I'm From)[43] is a song that describes, according to Bersuit, the spiritual misery that negates a sense of self while at the same time finding pride in that misery.

> Everything that comes from outside stinks
>
> It sticks inside me, I'm a septic tank waiting to be opened, there's no way out as my soul is like a huge trumpet blocked by mucus and phlegm...
>
> In this enormous hive with bees that produce intestinal problems, honey becomes diarrhea and my destiny is shit... my mouth evacuates my being.
>
> To anyone who asks where I live: imagine that Argentina is the asshole of the world and that asshole has two cheeks: one is Buenos Aires and the other one is Montevideo. The sphincter of that same ass receives all the shit, rivers of shit
>
> Generous companies generating misery,
>
> Spreading gangrene, poisoning my veins, silent murderers designing a radioactive landscape: so much shit. Everybody remembers the city of Avellaneda because of its strong smell of shit: that's where I am from (and I am another type of shit). That's me, and that's my land.

---

42 Citro, "El rock."
43 Bersuit Vergarabat, *Bersuit* (Universal Music, 2006).

There's nothing more anti-ecological than an unhappy person:
a stupid one, liar, trafficker, peddler of tons of pain, a real
powerhouse, a sick parasite orchid that sucks on light and life, it
has no love and it constipates with grotesque failure... it blindly
goes on... Shitty Pride! Shitty arrogance... my future is a shitty
project.

My shit, your shit, our shit, their shit, shitty unconscious, shitty
psychopaths... that's how my beloved shit is... it's mine, deeply
mine, profound, human... suffering sick souls. That's where I am
from.

We will build a huge paper mill to clean our mouths, to clean our
asses...

There's nothing more anti-ecological than an unhappy person.

Todo lo que entra desde afuera es mal olor
y se me pega en mi interior, que es pozo ciego por abrir
y no hay manera, con mi alma asordinada
como una enorme corneta, tapiada por los mocos
y las flemas que se inflaman, y las flores que se queman
en esta enorme colmena de abejas que fabrican más problemas, intestinos
y la miel se hace diarrea y es un culo mi destino
y por la boca solo espero una inmensa verborrea

evacuando el ser
verborrea vertiéndose

y cualquiera que pregunte a dónde vivo
imaginen que Argentina sea el culo de la tierra
y que ese culo tenga un culo y Buenos Aires sea una nalga
y la otra nalga, la hermana montevideana
y el esfínter mismo de ese inmenso culo
reciba toda la mierda, ¡ríos de mierda!

empresa generosa cultivando miseria
regando con gangrena y mis venas se envenenan
asesinos silenciosos diseñando el paisaje radiactivo, ¡una mierda!
la ciudad de Avellaneda
todo el mundo la recuerda por su fuerte olor a mierda
de ahí soy yo, otra mierda
ése soy yo, esa es mi tierra.

No hay nada más antiecológico que un infeliz, que un infeliz

Un infeliz que es fabricante, traficante
portador, vendedor de toneladas de dolor

> una verdadera usina, una raquítica orquídea parásita
> que chupa luz, que chupa vida
> no tiene amores y se constipa de grotescos fracasos y avanza ciego
> y se embelesa por ser parte de una vez de esta maldita mierda
>
> ¡Qué orgullo de mierda! ¡Soberbia de mierda! ¡Proyecto de mierda!
>
> El futuro que me espera, sensaciones de mierda
> poesía burda, mierda muerta, mierda tuya, mierda de ellos
> mierda mía, mierda nuestra, nuestra mierda
>
> ¡Inconciencia de mierda! ¡Psicópatas de mierda!
> Así es mi mierda querida
> mía, bien de adentro, profunda, humana
> penosas almas, ay
> mal heridas, de ahí soy yo y
>
> no hay nada más antiecológico que un infeliz, que un infeliz
>
> y construiremos una enorme papelera
> para limpiarnos la boca, para limpiarnos el orto...

The lyrics of the song are shocking indeed, and they become even more powerful when performed live, given the band frontman, Gustavo Cordera, appears dressed as a tango singer, a genre shared by Montevideo and Buenos Aires, an identity marker for both cities. "La Argentinidad al palo" (Argentineness with a Hard-on) is another song that recounts some of Argentina's historical facts, in a concoction that lists famous inventions, major sports achievements, some of its main celebrities, many cases of political corruption, cases of violence against women, and the claim of having the most beautiful women in the world, whose admirers' main religion seems to be worshipping their perfect backsides.

"Sr Cobranza", a song composed by another band, Las Manos de Filippi, became popular after Bersuit recorded their own rendition, possibly because of the videoclip that promoted the song. In it, the lead singer, Gustavo Cordera, becomes more and more furious as the song progresses, and uses a considerable amount of insults and cursing towards the politicians of the time. The song goes from anger to madness and then revenge, predicting that those in power will lose it in violent circumstances. Because of the potency of the insults, the song has been partially censored many times.

The success of this band probably points to the fact that these songs may have acted as a means of connecting listeners to others and to situations; united people from diverse social groups; and enabled the audience to articulate their resentment. In the Argentina of the 1990s and early 2000s, a new sense of togetherness was brought about by the communal lambasting of those in power. By means of rituals (in the concert space), language (in the lyrics of the songs), and humour (in the performance and content of the songs), Bersuit Vergarabat's cultural production seems to have acted as a bridge between inarticulate resentment and articulate protest.

In sum, the neoliberal politics of the 1990s in Argentina contributed to the collapse of the economic system and social devastation, amid a climate of corruption, impunity, and social abandonment. While some politicians had celebrity-like, luxurious lifestyles, there was a considerable increase in poverty, unemployment, and injustice. The growing contrast between those in power and the people who had voted for them provoked the rage of the Argentines.

The lyrics of the songs of Bersuit Vergarabat display anger, dissent, and hopelessness in the face of a devastating reality. By incorporating aesthetics of grotesque realism, the abject, the marginal sectors of the social fabric, and the sexualised body, these songs reside at a distance from the sophisticated lyrics of the Argentine rock of the 1970s and 1980s and open new spaces of inclusion and dissent for the youth. Thus, violence, cursing, insult, and mockery become central frictions within the narrative in the songs, amid a festive atmosphere of excesses and hopeless *laissez faire*.

Despite the many musicians and bands that emerged during and after the dictatorship, and their popularity and success, there is an undisputed general consent when it comes to pointing at the main Argentine rock representatives and pioneers. Those are Charly García and Luis Alberto Spinetta, whose lyrics have been dissected throughout this book's chapters. Both musicians display particular qualities, given their resistance during the iron years, and undoubtedly share the throne of Argentine rock idols. However, as we will expand upon in the next two chapters, each of them seems to be sitting at either end of a pendulum, whereas all other Argentine rockers are eternally moving back and forth, in the hope of one day finding some balance.

CHAPTER EIGHT

Words Made Eternal
Charly García and the Parody of a Rock Star

"No tengo fin"

—*Charly García*

Charly García once quipped, "There were no rock stars here. There were only rock musicians, until I came along. I invented the concept".[1] His "invention" was, in truth, a parody of the rock star. He had a clear vision of the popularity Argentine rock would achieve over the years. He was an artist who knew how to gain a place on the throne of Argentina's popular idols. Furthermore, when faced with the music industry's attempts to manufacture his public image and manipulate him as an artist, Charly García seems to have been one step ahead of the strategies of the capitalist machinery. He took the reins of his own fame, not without adding a personal, megalomaniac touch. "I'm thinking of creating a tax on Charly García", he said once, "what do you expect, that I exist for free?".[2] This remark hints at the labour involved in the parodic construction of the rock star. The ways in which this construction was shaped are the topic of this chapter.

When did Charly "invent" his rock stardom? He clearly did not decide to become a rock star the first time he sat at his piano. It was a long, slow process that was carefully constructed, and it can be observed, in addition to his interactions with the press and his performances, in the lyrics of his songs right from the beginning. Before García began his solo career, before creating his "rock star" persona, Charly was already writing phrases that underlined how different he was from his colleagues: "while I watch the new waves, I

---

1 AA.VV, *Grandes entrevistas de Rolling Stone. Íconos del rock nacional* (Buenos Aires: Publirevistas, 2006), p. 59.
2 Nora Sanchez, "García Y2K," 11 January 2000, https://www.clarin.com/espectaculos/garcia-y2k_0_r1vgdJ2gCYx.html (accessed 17 October 2018).

am already part of the sea" ["Cuando miro las nuevas olas"[3]]. According to rock critic Simon Frith, a "star" is also a performance:

> The seductive voice mediates between nature (the real person about whom we fantasise) and culture (the performing person we get); it draws attention both to the social construction of our desire, to its artificiality, and to our obdurately subjective reading of it.[4]

Indeed, in December 2013, García was awarded the title of Doctor Honoris Causa by the University of San Martín for his contribution to Argentine music and culture. On this occasion, when he was receiving his diploma from UNSAM, García said: "Now I am a doctor, and you are my patients". This joke and wordplay are just one example of the many elements that contribute to the parody of the rock star he created and continues to keep alive. One cannot avoid seeing the connection to the Junta's medical discourse. In 2013, Charly borrows the same metaphor to indicate he is "in power" (he is a doctor). When García says "I invented it", he is referring to that construction, which, in his case, has local peculiarities. While this careful construct is perhaps less apparent in the chaos, scandals, and humour that have characterised many of his public appearances, both on and off the stage, in the lyrics of his songs it is clearly evident.

Sociologists such as Simon Frith[5] and George Lewis,[6] among others, focus on rock and roll as a product of the popular culture industry in capitalist societies. From the 1950s, rock and roll was increasingly controlled by the entertainment industry and the stardom system. Often, rock and roll musicians had to reinvent themselves to avoid falling into the trap of consumerism, a move that was not always met with success. Lawrence Grossberg suggests that "cooptation" is the model by which rock and roll reinvents itself, rejecting the moments of its past and present in order to more powerfully inscribe its own limit.[7] He explains that the notion of cooptation has allowed us to see the existence of rock and roll at the intersection between youth culture and hegemony.[8] Expanding further upon this subject, he writes:

> According to most histories of rock and roll, this process has been going on since the late fifties, and at each stage, rock and roll loses its power and becomes a commodity which can be produced, marketed and consumed. But it is also apparently true that each time it has happened, rock and roll breaks out of that coopted stance and reaffirms its affective power, creating

---

3 Serú Girán, *Serú Girán*.
4 Frith, *Performing Rites*, p. 215.
5 Frith, *Sound Effects*.
6 George H. Lewis, "The Meanings in the Music and the Music's in Me: Popular Music as Symbolic Communication," *Theory, Culture & Society* 1 (3): 133–41, 1983.
7 Grossberg, "Another Boring Day," p. 255.
8 Grossberg, "Another Boring Day," p. 254.

new sounds and new political stances. The result is that the history of rock and roll is read as a cycle of cooptation and renaissance in which rock and roll constantly protests against its own cooptation.[9]

Yet Grossberg's studies are mainly based on Anglo-Saxon rock and roll. In the Argentine case, the process described by Grossberg as a cooptation takes an interesting turn in Charly García's musical and artistic production. In fact, as has been mentioned, García took control of the affective relationship he shared with his audience. His original form of coopting is a parody construction of himself as a rock star that began to develop at a very early stage of his career and is most eloquent in his last two decades of production. If he had to become a star and a consumable cultural product, he would be the one to manage some of the dynamics involved in the process. Very cunningly, instead of being devoured by the stardom system, he puts it at his disposal.

Abnormality exploited

The key moment when this status as a rock star was consolidated is evident in his album *Piano bar* (1984),[10] which is also his first album under democracy. The lyrics of the songs on this album definitively underline the construction of the "I" character. Some of the lyrics on that album have already been analysed in Chapter 7. We mentioned how, in "Demoliendo hoteles" (Demolishing Hotels), the text clarifies that "we all grew up without understanding and I still feel like I'm abnormal" ["Todos crecimos sin entender y todavía me siento un anormal"], a phrase in which the self is portrayed as different from the norm. There was great opportunity behind this: the "abnormal" being would prove a fertile concept, many iterations of which would proliferate across his oeuvre. From now on, the idea would be exploited at every available opportunity, and it would grow to place Charly on the plane of the deities. In the second song of this album, "Promesas sobre el bidet" (Promises over the Bidet), abnormality is insisted on once more:

> Do you know that I have not learnt how to live?
> Sometimes I'm so fine, I'm so down
> Cramps in the soul.
> Everyone has a trip in their heads
> difficult for us to come to an agreement.
>
> ¿Sabes que no aprendí a vivir?
> a veces estoy tan bien, estoy tan down
> calambres en el alma
> cada cual tiene un trip en el bocho
> difícil que lleguemos a ponernos de acuerdo.

---

9 Grossberg, "Another Boring Day," p. 252.
10 Charly García, *Piano bar*.

Abnormality is always accompanied by pain and lack of sympathy, and it is a topic that will always enjoy full focus in his texts. For example, other songs on the same album highlight that "the sanest person is the most delirious" ("Raros peinados nuevos" [Weird New Hairstyles]) and that "analysts will not be able to understand" ("Cerca de la revolución" [Close to Revolution]). The lyrics underline the singer's difference from the rest of humanity with questioning phrases: "Why do you stay on Death Road? I do not know why you go to that place where everyone has derailed" ["¿Por qué te quedás en Vía Muerta? No sé por qué vas a ese lugar donde todos han descarrilado"] ("No te animás a despegar" [Don't Dare to Take Off]). In sum, *Piano bar* contains the main elements that will be explored from hereon in, all of which contribute to the construction of what would traditionally be called a hero, and, in rock culture, a star.

Unlike what happens with traditional rock stars, Charly is acutely aware of his unique quality precisely because he is the one responsible for creating, developing, and exploiting it. He provokes and challenges his audience, questioning whether his art is received in the way he intends: "How can you think I'm crazy when I can give you a morning sun?" ("In the city that never sleeps").[11] (The lyrics of this song are in English; hence no translation is needed.)

There are multiple anecdotes and stories about Charly's prodigy childhood—the "perfect pitch" that was discovered in the child Carlitos,[12] and his piano concerts as a child.[13] Some of his challenges entail his personal health and battle against alcohol and drugs, including his multiple rehab hospitalisations and problems with excesses and addictions, interspersed with periods of re-emergence and creative productivity.

The large-scale reproduction of the idol's image—iconography as propaganda—has existed since classical antiquity. The first to use this strategy was Alexander, who had an image of his face reproduced on coins and medals. Most heroes, leaders of importance, and historical figures have their busts and statues made and their portraits painted. The creation and display of these iconic images have to do with a claiming of territory, leadership, and sovereignty. In the case of Argentine rock, Charly made sure to stake his territory, become a leader, and consolidate the elements that would sustain his status as an idol and a pioneer. To be remembered for generations he needed a logo that identifies him quickly and separates him from the rest. Charly García created SNM (Say No More), an idea inspired by a line he heard in one of the Beatles' films. His logo was thus built on a European foundation, just like in the nineteenth century, in times of nation-building, when Argentine leaders looked to Europe as an ideal to imitate. We know that the Beatles were the ones who inspired young García to dedicate himself to

---

11 Charly García, *Kill gil* (Sony Music/Del Ángel FEG, 2010).
12 Di Pietro, *Esta noche*, p. 29.
13 Di Pietro, *Esta noche*, pp. 20–24.

composing rock music, and he never stopped admiring them. Therefore, his logo is, in turn, a reference to his own idols.

As he has shown in many of his songs, Charly is deeply aware of how the Argentine being works. And he probably knows how nationalism works through music. Maybe that is why he decided to make his own version of the Argentine national anthem and record it on his 1990 album *Filosofía barata y zapatos de goma* (Cheap Philosophy and Rubber Shoes).[14] Esteban Buch, in his study of the Argentine national anthem *O Juremos con gloria morir*, dedicates an entire chapter to an analysis of Charly's version of the hymn, a version that he considers especially subjective and expressive. It also highlights a considerable novelty: Charly sings it alone.[15] García himself explains his interpretation of the hymn's lyrics as follows:

> There are parts of the lyrics that are very disturbing and very theatrical as well. That "freedom, freedom, freedom" bit—you can say the word a different way each time: it might sound like a protest or a request and at the same time I am it, and it is freedom. Is it understood? I want to say that of the three freedoms, one is me. Do not exclude me from liberties anymore. I am part of a generation that is freedom, a freedom well earned. So do not tell me how to sing the Anthem. I earned my place here: they put me in a box three times a week, for nothing. I know what freedom is and I know what it is to lose it. That is why I believe that the Anthem, despite the controversies, unites more than what is disunited…[16]

Buch says that, when a journalist asked Charly if he believed his claims about freedom, he replied: "I can create a good make believe… I can make you believe".[17] If we agree that a national symbol such as the anthem represents the whole nation, then all the nation's components must be represented through it. Therefore, national union materialises every time a citizen hears or sings the part of the anthem that he feels represents him. It is here that Charly's genius comes to light: as Buch points out, he understands something crucial about a key line in this solemn song, which is "freedom, freedom, freedom". He performs each utterance of the same word in a different manner, in this way constructing multiple bridges to reach all Argentines, allowing them to cross at least one. It is only then, says Charly, that the anthem can bring people together.

In his lucid and brilliant analysis of the controversy unleashed from the time the rock version of Charly's national anthem became known—through

---

14 Charly García, *Filosofía barata y zapatos de goma* (Sony BMG, 1990).
15 Esteban Buch, *O juremos con gloria morir: una historia del himno nacional argentino, desde la Asamblea del año XIII hasta Charly García* (Buenos Aires: Eterna Cadencia, 2013), p. 223.
16 Eduardo Berti, "El Himno para todo público," *Página 12* (Buenos Aires), 28 October 1990.
17 Buch, *O juremos*, p. 225.

the subsequent denunciations and its prohibition, to its legal authorisation—Buch speaks of Charly as a contemporary hero. For him, "after the Falklands war, in Argentina the war heroes are tired, but there are the substitute heroes with a microphone in their hands".[18] Without a doubt, García seems to have grasped the essence of the national being, the dynamics of Argentina as a community, based on individualism and a history of polarities that went from civilisation and barbarism—oppositional ideologies in the nineteenth century—to the divisions of our days. He even presents these polarities as part of Argentines' spirituality: "everything is built and destroyed so quickly [...] it is part of our religion" ("Parte de la religión" [Part of our Religion]).[19] Such an essence is characterised as not only present at times of conflict or dictatorship, but as part of the Argentine being:

> He feels guilt, he lives tortured
> he's not that smart.
> He never moves forward, he walks sideways
> he is afraid of his own mind,
> It is part of our religion.
>
> Él siente culpa, él vive torturado
> él no es tan inteligente
> él nunca avanza, camina de costado
> él tiene miedo a su mente
> es parte de la religión...

The phrase "never moves forward, walks sideways" is striking. In a country where natural resources abound, with many wondering why Argentina is not among the first-world nations, Charly takes care of diagnosing the national problem: some guilt, not much intelligence, and a lack of ability to advance as consequences of religion. The "decent man" of the song fails ("he lives tortured") because of his religion.

In addition to Charly's version of the anthem, his logo SNM, and his own synthesis of the Argentine being, a life-sized statue of Charly already exists, as if he were a Roman emperor. Erected in the city of Mar del Plata in 2013, next to that of Nito Mestre and in honour of the legendary band Sui Generis, the bronze statue is today a tourist attraction. A photograph published by *Clarín* on 6 February 2013, on the occasion of the tribute statue's inauguration, shows the local authorities standing next to real-life Charly. In that photo, Charly's hand is covering the front zip of his pants, in a suggestive and provocative way. During the opening ceremony, while he was being honoured by the municipality of the city, he gave a short speech in which, among other humorous things, he said: "I am a statue. Now I can do anything ... Talk to my statue!"

---

18 Buch, *O juremos*, p. 234.
19 Charly García, *Parte de la religión*.

Eternity in music

Without a doubt, Charly's mission is to live forever through his music. Sometimes, the mission seems to be the recognition of his individuality and his determination to claim his unique talent ("I am already part of the sea" [ya soy parte del mar]); at other times, it seems a complaint: "You could understand that I came here on a mission: I want to heal but my hands only play" ("Podrías entender").[20] Quite rightly, Jorge Monteleone explains that García has constructed an image of himself that is located between the real and the fantastic:

> his compositions have always oscillated between anarchic individualism and confrontation with the institutional. On the one hand, he offered a gesture of mania and extravagance that could end in madness or suicide.[21]

Yet there is no doubt that he will transcend his own death through his music. He reminds us of the fact, just in case it was not clear enough: "I live through an illusion [...] through a song" ("Casa vacía").[22]

> I live through
> an illusion
> I live in a lost cause
> I live through
> a song
> every day that's how it is
> ...
> I live in a house
> I live in a house that's empty...
>
> Vivo a través de una ilusión
> Vivo en una causa perdida
> Vivo a través de una canción
> Así es todos los días
> ...
> Vivo en una casa,
> Vivo en una casa vacía...

The "empty house" may well be the illusion of fame and popularity. Indeed, Charly's fan base, who buy his albums and attend his concerts, legitimise his exceptionality, a power that he expresses in various songs. In perhaps the most

---

20 Charly García, *Say no more* (Sony BMG, 1996).
21 Jorge Monteleone, "Figuras de la pasión rocker. Ensayo sobre rock argentino," *Everba* 1 (Summer), 2002, http://everba.eter.org/summer02/figuras_jorge.htm.
22 Charly García, *Say no more*.

effective, he alludes to the eternity of his art: "I will open your heart again, even if a thousand years pass, I will give you my love" ("Transformation").[23]

His exceptionality as a spokesperson for the youth and as a rock star who transcends the ordinary is expressed in other ways as well. He claims misunderstanding on several occasions and he also makes it clear that it is he who is in control, despite the apparent chaos: "This song will last forever because I made it so" ("Chipi Chipi").[24] The idyllic space he created is free of temporary markers and mundane structures: "I come from another war, from another sun, I go around and where I am going and where I am from there is no time" ("Love is Love").[25] The distance from the rest of humanity is what solidifies his authority. His journey is often portrayed as a deep spiritual and artistic need. The rock star, who "climbs a ladder, accomplishes a mission" ("Chipi Chipi"), is responsible for clarifying that the place where he comes from is intangible:

> I only have this poor antenna
> that transmits what to say
> a song, my illusion, my sorrows,
> and this souvenir.
> I climb the ladder
> I accomplish a mission...
>
> Yo solo tengo esta pobre antena
> que me transmite lo que decir
> una canción, mi ilusión, mis penas
> y este souvenir
> Yo subo la escalera,
> yo cumplo una misión...

Charly constantly tries to awaken his audience and push them to take off, to break free from the norm, to experience new alternatives:

> Why are you staying in Dead Street?
> Why are you staying at the door?
> I don't know why you're headed to that place
> where everyone has derailed.
> Why don't you dare to take off?
>
> ¿Por qué te quedás en Vía muerta?
> ¿Por qué te quedás en Vía muerta?
> No sé porqué vas hacia ese lugar
> donde todos han descarrilado
> ¿Por qué no te animás a despegar?[26]

---

23 Charly García, *Kill gil*.
24 Charly García, *La hija de la lágrima* (Sony BMG, 1994).
25 Charly García, *La hija de la lágrima*.
26 Charly García, "No te animás a despegar," *Piano bar*.

Sometimes he is involved in dangerous situations, scandals, and controversial actions, but it seems that this is not always understood the way it was intended: "Look, kid, I jumped for you" ["Mirá pendejo, me tiré por vos"] ("Me tiré por vos"):[27]

> I was very bored
> in deadly Mendoza.
> I said: What am I missing now? ...
> just learning to fly!
> I jumped for you.
>
> Estaba muy aburrido
> en mi Mendoza fatal
> Dije, ¿qué me falta ahora?
> Sólo aprender a volar
> Mirá, pendejo, me tiré por vos.

Undoubtedly, these lyrics refer to a widely reported incident when Charly threw himself into the pool of the hotel where he was staying—from the ninth floor. Whatever the reason for such a death-defying jump, Charly knew how to exploit the public attention the stunt earned him, and, as he did on other occasions, he captured the moment in a song. "I jumped for you" suggests a complete surrender that was not interpreted as such. In truth, like that famous jump into the pool, often his art resembled a megalomaniac delirium, self-defined as "one more vice" ("Tu vicio"):[28]

> I am one more vice.
> In your mind I am just another vice.
> You can't leave me because I'm just a vice.
> Your vice.
>
> Yo soy un vicio más
> en tu vida soy un vicio más
> por qué no me dejás
> si tan sólo soy un vicio
> tu vicio.

A vice, something that usually involves pleasure as well as guilt or pain, is part of everyday life. It is sometimes needed to reach the end of each day. In addition to defining himself as a vice, this rock star sometimes highlights, somewhat contradictorily, the distance between himself and everyone else, his belonging to a lonely and painful place in another dimension where he is utterly alone and his desperation for attention sounds heartbreakingly seductive:

---

27 Sui Generis, *Sinfonías para adolescentes* (Universal Music, 2000).
28 Charly García, *Influencia* (EMI, 2002).

> I know that I am unbearable
> I know that I made you laugh
> I know, I am unbearable
> but... someone in the world thinks of me.
>
> Yo sé que soy imbancable
> yo sé que te hice reír
> yo sé soy insoportable
> pero alguien en el mundo piensa en mi.²⁹

In fact, in "Say No More", Charly claims "you failed, you did not see who I am" ["Fallaste, no viste quién soy"], as if it were an essential task for his "allies" to really capture the essence of their idol. In addition, after a while away from the public eye, recovering from his alcohol and drug addictions and excesses, García made a triumphant return that was highlighted with a new interrogation of his audience:

> Che, if you really take me seriously
> You should know why
> Deep down it's not a mystery
> You should know why
> ...
> Che, if you put the shirt on
> You should know why...
>
> Che, si en verdad me tomás en serio
> deberías saber por qué
> En el fondo no es un misterio
> deberías saber por qué
> ...
> Che, si te ponés la camiseta
> Deberías saber porqué...³⁰

In this song, once again, García alludes to symbols of great popularity, such as a football shirt as an identity marker. In this case, the shirt is a symbol of the communion between the artist and his audience, an attribute that implies a movement in the spectators towards their idol. The first word of the song is the unmistakable "che", associated with everyday Argentine speech. In this song, like years ago in "No te animás a despegar" (You Don't Dare to Take Off), Charly seems to separate himself again from the norm and claim to be misunderstood: "todos van hasta ahi nomás"—"everybody is so beige".

---

29 Charly García, "Alguien en el mundo piensa en mí," *Say no more*.
30 Sebastián Ortega, director, Charly García, "Deberías saber por qué," videoclip (Buenos Aires: 2009), https://www.youtube.com/watch?v=sArDRGzBAmE (accessed 27 March 2023).

It is important to note that Charly addresses his followers as "allies", not as "subjects" or "fanatics" who gaze upon their idol as someone superior. Being allies, they are called to join the hero in their life journey, as equals, at the same level. Despite positioning himself parodically as a rock star in a discourse targeted at the mainstream, when he addresses his audience, he does so from a more intimate position: we are "allies" because "we are together in prison" ["estamos juntos en la prisión"] ("No importa").[31]

The construction of the character named "Charly García" is a parody that points to that perverse system that invents popular idols and uses them at its discretion: "nobody sells newspapers for the love of it" ("Transformación").[32] Before the system can use him, Charly does so himself. If it is an inevitable process, he prefers to be the one in control. When he was attacked by the press as a musician and as an individual in the wake of excesses in his private life, at first Charly reacted with discomfort. Soon, however, he began using that same public space and attention to reverse the situation and use it as a self-promotion platform: "I'm tired: they should accept that I am fabulous or that they go f*** themselves, I know what I am doing...".[33]

A self-built throne

Charly García's fusion of illusion and reality in the creation of the "rock star" character is clearly observable as we move forward in the chronological analysis of his artistic production; for example, it is most notorious on the albums *Demasiado ego* (1999), *Rock and roll yo* (2003), and *Kill gil* (2010).[34]

Already the title *Demasiado ego*, with "demasiado" meaning "too much", is a playful allusion to that parodic construction that we have analysed thus far. The images that illustrate the internal booklet of the album are newspaper clippings that clearly show the place that the musician occupies in the collective Argentine imagination, evident in headlines such as: "The Light is Back", "All Buenos Aires at Charly's Feet", and others that recall some of the debates and scandals in which he was involved, such as "No Dolls, No Helicopters, but Charly García Delivered". This refers to the concert during which Charly wanted to throw fictitious bodies into the river, emulating the "death flights".[35] After talks with the Mothers of the Plaza de Mayo, he

31 Charly García, *Kill gil*.
32 Charly García, *Kill gil*.
33 Martín Ciccioli, *Rockeado: la historia detrás de las canciones de tu vida* (Buenos Aires: Emecé, 2010), p. 30.
34 Charly García, *Demasiado ego* (Universal, 1999); Charly García, *Rock and roll yo* (EMI, 2003); Charly García, *Kill gil*.
35 "Death flights" ["vuelos de la muerte"] was the name given to the assassination of people carried out by the military dictatorship. Prisoners would be taken in a helicopter, naked and drugged, and then, after receiving a priest's final farewell, were thrown into the Río de la Plata. This story is clearly documented and explained in

decided not to go ahead with his idea. Episodes like this one are abundant in Charly's career and they are examples of the scandals and provocations that were a constant in his public life for many years. The most remembered are probably the day he pulled his pants down in public on stage (1987) and when he jumped into the pool of his hotel from the ninth floor (2000). The scandals in Charly's life abound and are capitalised as elements that feed the construction of the character: rock star.

Rock and roll yo presents a cover with drawings by Charly and includes "VSD" (Vos sos dios), a song composed with Joaquín Sabina, followed by a second version of the same song—same lyrics, different music—called "Tango". In these songs, the state of the hero is explicit—"You're God, you're Gardel,[36] you're the best"—and both musical versions of the same lyrics seem to condense the fusion between rock, tango, and the idolised image of García. The title of the album also alludes to the fusion between rock and roll as a genre and Charly as music: they are inseparable. The throne of Argentine rock has a name engraved on it, according to this construction, and it is "Charly García". A large part of the audience and the public seem to agree with this. For example, in 2002, when the "Gardel de Oro" award was granted to García, the speaker of the event presented Charly with the following words: "Everyone stand up as God is about to enter this room".

On *Kill gil* (2010) the song "Transformation" stands out. It seems to point to the system that invents and promotes fame for purely commercial purposes ("nobody sells newspapers for the love of it"), and speaks of fame's uniqueness, its freedom, its eternity, the press, and their commitment to heal through their music:

> Don't insist on putting locks on me
> I am free and I will not give up
> when I want to go out, I don't mind dying
> I am eternal
> I am eternal
> Every time you try to kill
> maybe you are killing somebody who treats you well
> every time you want to dress up
> all those costumes will tear your skin.
> ...
> I will open your heart again
> even after a thousand years I will give you my love
> I will open your heart again
> even if the transformation obliterates me.

Horacio Verbitsky, *Confessions of an Argentine Dirty Warrior: A Firsthand Account of Atrocity* (New York: New Press, 2005).

36 Carlos Gardel (1890–1935) is the most prominent figure in the history of tango.

No insistan en ponerme cerraduras
soy libre y no pienso desistir
cuando quiero salir, no me importa morir
¡no tengo fin!
¡no tengo fin!
Cada vez que trates de matar
quizás estés matando a quien te trata bien
cada vez que quieras disfrazar
todos esos disfraces abrirán tu piel.
...
Volveré a abrir tu corazón
aunque pasen mil años te daré mi amor
volveré a abrir tu corazón
aunque me desintegre la transformación.

This song is significant because it sounds like a testament, like a legacy, a harrowing expression of love and pain and, at the same time, it is visionary. It talks about the importance of being true to oneself ("all those disguises will tear your skin open"). It also points out the transformation that Charly himself would suffer in the coming years, in which he would leave the public stage and concentrate on recovering his health. Somehow, Charly foreshadows his transformation, which "obliterates him". At the same time, this "transformation" alludes to the physical death and decay of the human body and the eternal permanence of art.

A quick look at the many blogging and social-networking sites immediately shows that many phrases have been taken from Charly's songs to be reused in different contexts. The same thing that happened with tango in Argentine culture—phrases that began as tango lyrics are now used in everyday language—has happened with the lyrics of Charly's songs. Like popular tango expressions, many phrases from García's songs have become part of the everyday language of Argentines. It is not uncommon to see headlines, blog titles, and names of radio or TV programs that use those phrases without need of any reference to Charly. This is why "Tribulaciones, lamentos u ocaso...", "Demoliendo...", "trip en el bocho", "bienvenidos al tren", and many other phrases appear daily in Argentine culture. Without doubt, Charly's lyrics are already "part of [Argentine's] religion".

In fact, his album *Demasiado ego* comes with a script that contains many of the phrases that he uses as his maxims. These principles or teachings have been recorded in three different songs—"Veinte trajes de lágrimas I", "Veinte trajes de lágrimas II", and "Veinte trajes de lágrimas III" ("Twenty suits made of tears")—all included on his album *60x60*.[37] They seem to be the compilation of "the commandments" of that popular god, which remind

---

37 Charly García & The Prostitution, *60x60* (EMI Music/DSX Films, 2012).

us of the essence of his philosophy and his life teachings, all of them taken from the lines of his songs across several decades of artistic production.

Gender and freedom

In Charly's work, the representation of gender, conveyed by way of characters in unconventional and often magical situations, is part of a complex structure that questions traditional and religious roles imposed by conservative ideas. In none of Charly's songs are women demonised. On the contrary, they are often goddesses, heroines, saviours, beautiful, angelic, and utterly free. In contrast, they also appear as hostages, trapped, killers, and killed. During the time of authoritarian governments, metaphors of the former category abound, as if Charly were constructing an idyllic space where women could be housed and protected from the context of the dictatorship. Metaphors of the latter category appear later, in democratic times, marking a semantic shift that highlights and criticises the sexist vision of women. Unlike many of his peers, Charly is not comfortable, at least in his work, with the idea of women being "possessed" by men, nor do signs of homophobia appear. We also know that Charly has openly supported the Mothers of the Plaza de Mayo and expressed his admiration for them repeatedly because, according to him, "they made revolution and art at the same time and showed the way to those who were not yet awake".[38]

In Argentina, masculinity codes were established on the basis of a tough, virile, and heterosexual image. In Argentine literature, foundational literary works such as *Facundo* (1868)[39] and *Martín Fierro* (1872)[40] lack significant female characters. Tango began as a dance for men alone. Undoubtedly influenced by the Beatles, "the most famous 'men' of the 1960s",[41] who Charly named again and again in his interviews, Charly broke free from traditional views of masculinity and imbued his songs with a flexibility of ideas. The post-imperialist context in which the Beatles emerged coincided with the emergence of alternative versions of masculinity, both in the real and in the representative plane. Of course, the England of the sixties was far from the Argentina in which Charly listened to the Beatles' songs. Yet it is important to bear in mind that the age at which Charly was dazzled by

---

38 Charly says this before performing his song "Los dinosaurios" on the occasion of his concert at Plaza de Mayo during the celebrations for the twenty-nine years of recovery of democracy, at the Great Patriotic Popular Party on Democracy and Human Rights Day. Public TV, 9 December 2012, https://www.youtube.com/watch?v=mkOAQvurxJE&t=2s (accessed 27 March 2023).
39 Domingo Sarmiento, *Facundo: civilización y barbarie* (Santiago: El Progreso de Chile: 1845).
40 José Hernández, *El gaucho Martín Fierro* (Buenos Aires: Imprenta de La Pampa, 1872).
41 Martin King, *Men, Masculinities and the Beatles* (Farnham: Ashgate, 2013), p. 1.

the band was precisely his adolescence, when his ideological thoughts began to coalesce.

At the time of the Beatles, pop music was, according to Cohen[42] and Bannister,[43] a territory dominated by men, where gender roles were clearly defined. In the rock music scene, men had the main roles as musicians, producers, managers, and organisers, while women were the majority in the roles of groupies and spectators. The Beatles challenged gender constructions in different ways, and that spread to the rest of the world. They popularised a new image of masculinity in their slender and refined bodies and their neat, careful clothing and hairstyles. Their long hair was one of the strongest symbols, and suggested an intellectual, intelligent, and romantic masculinity. On the *Institutions* album, which, as has been explained, actually saw the light as *Pequeñas anécdotas sobre las instituciones*, Charly was forced to change the lyrics of the song "Instituciones": "I am a man who doesn't want to ask for permission to cry" had to become "When the sun comes to take my dreams to a fair place".[44] Although such a change satisfied censorship control, the "fair place" does not cease to be a dark reference. It is likely that it refers to a place in which men can mourn without questioning their masculinity. While the censors seemed to subscribe to the archaic idea that "men don't cry", they did not seem to notice that "dreaming of a fair place" alluded to a society in which those ideas no longer existed and men were allowed to express their feelings freely.

Eduardo Archetti, in his study on Argentine masculinities, agrees with Connell that masculinity cannot be understood as something fixed or universal.[45] According to Archetti, soccer, polo, and tango have historically functioned as models and "mirrors" of Argentine identity.[46] For Roberto Pitluk, author of *The Argentine Macho: Reflections on Impoverished Masculinity*, "the Argentine macho continues to act in the shadows and to contaminate social life, bringing consequences".[47] The male figure appears everywhere, profoundly affecting the socio-cultural construction of masculinities. According to the author, his identity is constituted especially by contrast with what "denies him the most, opposes him, contradicts him, hinders him,

---

42 Sara Cohen, "Men Making a Scene: Rock Music and the Production of Gender," in *Sexing the Groove: Popular Music and Gender*, edited by Sheila Whiteley, 17–36 (New York: Routledge, 1997).
43 Matthew Bannister, "Ladies and Gentlemen, The Beatelles! The Influence of Sixties Girl Groups on the Beatles," *Beatlestudies 3: Proceedings of the Beatles 2000 Conference*, edited by Yrjö Heinonen, et al., 169–79 (Finland: University of Jyväskylä: 2000).
44 Marchini, *No toquen*, p. 60.
45 Eduardo P. Archetti, *Masculinities: Football, Polo and the Tango in Argentina* (Oxford: Berg, 1999), p. 13.
46 Archetti, *Masculinities*, p. 116.
47 Roberto Pitluk, *El macho argentino: reflexiones sobre masculinidad empobrecida* (Buenos Aires: Ediciones Pausa para la reflexión, 2007), p. 16.

challenges or contradicts him, frustrates him, excludes him, strips him or strips him of his identity, that is to say, male identity is constructed above all by contrast with the feminine, the infantile, the senile and the gay".[48] In short, Archetti's and Pitluk's studies on Argentine masculinity point to the same thing: a machismo rooted in society that is clearly and explicitly evident in most cultural expressions.

Fortunately, nothing lasts forever. In recent years, Argentina has led change—at least in the legal field—regarding gender freedoms, passing the same-sex marriage law in 2010 (law 26618) and the gender identity law in 2012 (law 26743). However, the parliamentary debates that took place during the review process, prior to the formulation of these laws, reveal the same fracture in society that the laws are trying to improve. While the gender identity law was unanimously approved (*La Nación*, 9 May 2012), the same-sex marriage law was approved with a majority of only thirty-three votes in favour, twenty-seven against, and three abstentions (*La Nación*, 15 July 2010). These results suggest that, although on the surface Argentine society seems to have taken great steps in terms of gender, there is still a long way to go and there is still resistance to diversity. In 2020, reproductive laws were also updated, allowing a woman to terminate her pregnancy in the first fourteen weeks.

The representation of a version of masculinity that resisted traditional norms and played with gender roles through visual images, performance, and words positioned rock as a "dangerous" genre when it was met with the embarrassed gaze of some conservatives. For instance, consider the following texts by Carlos Manfroni, published in *Cabildo* magazine in 1983: "When a man renounces his status as such, he can only become an animal or a fag. Rock has the virtue of offering both possibilities". For Manfroni, rock, due to its "wild rhythm, exacerbates passions against the spirit", and rock music "creates conditioned reflexes similar to those experienced by Pavlov's dog". Manfroni was not alone. In this regard, more texts circulated assuring readers that rock was dangerous, such as this one by Alberto Boixadós:

> musical polyrhythm, typical of progressive music, accentuates the penetration of the message—be it subliminal or not—increasing the intensity of the subject's response. This is one of the peculiarities of new music: a changing frequency of three by four and five by four, similar to Pavlov's experiments. Dr. Joseph Crow, professor of psychology at Pacific Western College, has expressed that the use of rock rhythm can produce hypnotic states. Young people listen to the same song hundreds of times […] repetition is the basis of hypnosis. This increases the degree to which the listener is suggestible, generating future actions of an unpredictable type.[49]

---

48 Pitluk, *El macho argentino*, p. 37.
49 Boixadós, *Arte y subversión*, p. 48.

Manfroni was worried that the young rockers would become "Pavlov's dogs or sweet fags, in fact in neither case are they what our beloved homeland needs, today so thirsty for men".[50] The concerns of Manfroni, Boixadós, and other conservatives of the time were based, among other things, on the lyrics of Charly's songs, in which men were "strange".

Another song, "Blues del levante" (Pick up Blues), recorded on his live album *Adiós Sui Generis* (1975),[51] is a parody of the playboy, and contains a suggestive verse:

> Take off your clothes, be good
> It's the most natural thing
> Even my sister does it
> and my mom did it too…
>
> Desvestite no seas mala
> si eso es lo más natural
> Si lo hace hasta mi hermana
> y lo hizo mi mamá…

If one of the characteristics of Argentine machismo is to defend "to the death" one's mother and sister as if they were asexual beings impossible to imagine in intimate situations, Charly challenges it: "It's the most natural thing".

Charly's views on women appear quite early in his career production. In pre-dictatorship times, with his band Sui Generis, he had already composed songs such as "Fabricante de mentiras" (Fabricator), which at the time could not be recorded in the studio, but which was sung in live concerts to the ovation of those present. The story told in "Fabricante de mentiras" begins by simulating one of those romantic novels or soap operas in which in the first stanza the male figure is presented as a "fabricator" who invents "tin fables" ["fábulas de lata"] and whose "lies can bring pain" ["sus mentiras pueden traer dolor"]. The second stanza presents the "typical innocent girl" ["una típica inocente"] who "had never had love on her skin" ["nunca tuvo en su piel amor"] and who "believed what she was told" ["lo que le dijeron lo creyó"]. Up to this point, the story sounds familiar: a young virgin falls in love with a man who does her wrong. The result of this meeting, according to the song, is what "some may imagine: the girl… lost her chastity" ["Algunos lo podrán imaginar: la niña que, sin pena y sin gloria, perdió sus medias y su castidad"]. The song tells the story of a schoolgirl who has fallen in love and lost her virginity; however, instead of feeling ashamed, as her traditional education would have dictated, the girl in the story is happy: "But there is something you cannot explain: why the girl laughs instead of crying" ["Pero hay algo que no se puede explicar ¿Por qué la niña ríe, en vez de llorar?"].

---

50 Manfroni, as quoted in Marchini, *No toquen*, p. 246.
51 Sui Generis, *Adiós Sui Generis II*; Sui Generis, *Adiós Sui Generis III*.

In Charly's songs, as in Dante's work, women are able to transcend the poetic voice and, as in Shakespeare, the thematic exploration in the lyrics of his songs prevents the audience from drawing a uniform semantic map regarding the gender.

Throughout Charly's work, gender roles are fluid and elastic, and challenge social conventions. An interesting song that illustrates this idea is "Shisyastawuman",[52] included in the 1989 studio album *Cómo conseguir chicas* (How to Pick up Girls); "Shisyastawuman" is written entirely in English. The song seems to play with two ideas: "She is just a woman", nothing more than that, as if she were a minor being, or that she fulfilled a merely biological function; or quite the contrary, she is a deity, since the poetic voice assures the listener that "he sees her face everywhere he goes".

Cómo conseguir chicas also includes the song "Ella es bailarina" (She Is a Dancer), at the end of which a marriage of three people is celebrated: "He is a priest and he always fulfils his holy duty: in a dirty nightclub he married the three of them" ["Es un sacerdote y siempre cumple con su santo deber: en un club nocturno reventado los casó a los tres"]. The "three" characters are a dancer, a police officer, and a teacher, all representatives of gender stereotypes. The woman wears "a mink scarf and a golden bra" ["la estola de bisón y el soutien dorado"], the teacher "knows everything he should know" ["sabe todo lo que debe saber"], and the policeman "always does his duty fairly" ["siempre cumple con su justo deber"]. However, the priest, representative of divine power, guarantees them access to marriage, a sacrament at the time reserved for heterosexual couples. Marriage here does not come from the law of men but from the power of God through his mediator on Earth.

Homosexuality appears several times in Charly's songs, always naturally, without being highlighted as something special or different. For example, in "No soy un extraño" (I Am Not a Stranger),[53] "Two guys in a bar hold hands, turn on a tape recorder and dance a real tango" ["Dos tipos en un bar se toman las manos, prenden un grabador y bailan un tango, de verdad"]. Later on, the same song launches a prophetic message, "unprejudiced people will come", like a sort of thermometer that measures the temperature of a society that was beginning to temper the homophobic ideas that had been amply fuelled for years. As Grinberg originally published in 1975: "The cultural expression of a music-focused generation has cycles fully linked to the environment where musicians (its vehicles) tune in to sensory processes and translate them into harmonies or dissonances". In this case, it was more than sensory processes, since ideological changes were beginning to be noticed.

Undoubtedly, many rock stars have become commercial products. Once representatives of counterculture and resistance movements, rock musicians have in many cases been absorbed by the system as a profitable product. In

---

52 Charly García, *Cómo conseguir chicas* (Sony BMG, 1989).
53 Charly García, *Clics modernos*.

Argentina, Charly García subverted this process and put it to new ends: he created a parody of the rock star using his own stardom and popularity. In fact, García seems to have taken control of the mechanisms by which popular icons are created. He has a logo, a mission, and a set of principles that work as pillars on which to rest his stardom and his legacy. By controlling his popularity and his stardom, Charly García seems to have gained control over the process of becoming a popular rock star, to the point that he has also ensured immortality through his music and language: "I live through an illusion ... alive through a song" ("Casa vacía").[54] His "transformation" (his own death) is achieved through his creation of music as an "eternal song", an immortal production of Argentine rock and roll. Everything fits perfectly into the whole—even the logo "Say No More" can be seen as an aspect of this construction. Each element fulfills a perhaps accidental, perhaps purposeful function, but one that is, undoubtedly, essential. "Cosmos" in Greek means "order". In the chaotic cosmos of Charly García, everything has a reason to be, everything fits perfectly like pieces of a great puzzle, and the rock star "climbs a ladder and fulfills a mission".

León Gieco once said that "the day Charly García is absent, Buenos Aires will be black and white".[55] Without a doubt it was Charly who added "show" to national rock performance. But he also added a throne, and he sat on it. In fact, on the album *Demasiado ego*, recorded live, in the song "Hablando a tu corazón", you can hear him shouting: "I'm going to be the king of Argentina and you won't ... the highest level of power". And yet, in December 2014, when the Argentine senators and deputies met at the House of Congress to legislate the National Day of Musicians, they did not choose Charly García's birth date. Instead, they chose 23 January, the date of birth of Luis Alberto Spinetta, whom they describe as a "talented musical composer and performer". What made them choose him? What makes Spinetta so special as to have streets and squares named after him all over the country, his songs used in some schools' curricula, his memory so strong and respected in Argentine society? The next chapter will aim to answer those questions by analysing one of his albums, released under censorship conditions.

While Charly García revels in his rock-star persona, playfully constructing and parodying the image of a typical rock star, Luis Alberto Spinetta stands in stark contrast as an artist with an exceptionally low profile, deliberately avoiding the spotlight of media attention. Spinetta's lyrical compositions are notably intricate, often veiled in layers of symbolism and metaphor. In the forthcoming section, we will delve into his 1976 album, *El Jardín de los Presentes* (The Garden of Those Present), where he employs a poetic strategy that weaves chaos akin to the cosmos into his work, all while imbuing it with profound meaning "replete with reality", creating a truly captivating artistic experience.

---

54 Charly García, *Say no more*.
55 Discovery Communications, "El Karma de Vivir al Sur," *People & Arts* (2002).

CHAPTER NINE

A Cosmos of Words
Luis Alberto Spinetta's Poetry

"Un columpio fabuloso en el espacio"

—*Luis Alberto Spinetta*

Luis Alberto Spinetta, one of the founders and pioneers of the genre, an undisputed pillar of Argentine rock, also stood out for other things. His peculiar vision of the time the country was going through, and his eccentricity, along with an impeccable work ethic, set him apart from the rest of his colleagues. In his case, far from focusing on the political moment and denouncing the facts, he was concerned with what few did, activating our transcendent memory and reminding us that we belong to an immense universe. His lyrics attempt to appease the existential anguish of the audience,[1] which, in addition to the socio-political context, is generated by the separation of man from the cosmos.[2]

Spinetta's image and personality are constantly pondered by those who were his colleagues and friends. One way he is remembered is as follows:

> Steadfast in his vanguardism, Spinetta did not give in, did not make concessions, did not try to adapt himself to the world around him. When in the 80s pop ended up engulfing the energy of rock, he was somewhat isolated, in his irreducible world. In a way, this most stubborn of Argentine rockers never left the yellow bridges [a reference to one of his songs]. That was his true manifesto. He never stopped looking for inspiration outside of rock to later disclose his findings—some revealing literature, almost always—into new songs.[3]

---

1 Favoretto, *Luis Alberto Spinetta*, p. 10.
2 Claude Lévi-Strauss, *Myth and Meaning* (London: Routledge and Kegan Paul, 1978).
3 Sergio Pujol, *Canciones argentinas (1910–2010)* (Buenos Aires: Emecé, 2010), p. 284.

When faced with a man of the kind of integrity that Spinetta possessed, the existentialist able to accept with serenity his insignificance in the universe, we are as intrigued as we are attracted to him. Spinetta, as his followers know, was determined to keep his profile low, and to highlight the issues he considered transcendent and important, always beyond himself.

In the specific context of Argentina, particularly in the neighbourhoods of Buenos Aires where a young Spinetta developed his creativity, there was a need for expression and freedom that perhaps was only possible through art. The dictatorships and the political and social repression of the 1960s, 1970s, and part of the 1980s created a favourable context for the protest song, for dissident art and for the development of coded strategies to evade censorship. Yet Spinetta went further. His art transcended the here and now to connect with universal existential issues.

Spinetta's main art form, having also dabbled in poetry and the visual arts, is songwriting. Following Bob Dylan's 2016 Nobel Prize in Literature, the discussion about the value of song lyrics as literature has once again gained prominence in literary circles and in the field of popular music studies. It is worth recalling that in 1913 Rabindranath Tagore received the same award and, in addition to literature, also wrote songs. Many musicians, such as Spinetta, also write poetry in addition to songs. Thus, is it necessary to maintain a boundary that separates these two types of writing? Do categorical definitions of types of text still hold validity? Contemporary literature plays with genres, blurs boundaries, and challenges readers from within the texts that are written, which, as Argentine critic Josefina Ludmer explains, constitute what she calls "post-autonomous literature", that is, literature or "the literary" that has now lost its autonomy: "Today, relatively autonomous fields (or delimiting spheres of thought) of the political, economic, and cultural are becoming increasingly blurred".[4]

Spinetta challenges his audience through his post-autonomous literary form, which is the song–poem, and in this sense, it may constitute the corpus of material observed by Ludmer to develop her concept. Speaking about Spinetta, writer Eduardo Berti dared to state that "he has already transcended rock, he is an Argentine cultural myth".[5] Such is his relevance to Argentine culture that in 2014, the National Institute of Music (INAMU) proposed declaring Spinetta's birthday as National Music Day, which produced different reactions. It was applauded by his followers but criticised by others, such as musician Juan Falú and music critic Federico Monjeau, as political opportunism by the government.[6] However, the objections were directed

---

4 Josefina Ludmer, *Aquí América Latina. Una especulación* (Buenos Aires: Eterna Cadencia, 2010), p. 153.
5 Ignacio Portela, "Spinetta trascendió el rock. Entrevista a Eduardo Berti," Todos estos años de Spinetta, *Revista Sudestada de colección*, número 11, pp. 18–21.
6 "Carta abierta de Juan Falú a Diego Boris por el día nacional del músico," It10digital, 1 January 2015, http://www.lt10digital.com.ar/noticia/idnot/220995/

towards the appropriation of Spinetta's figure and memory by the government at the time or towards the choice of a rock musician instead of other genres considered by some as more traditional, such as tango or folklore, and not towards the musician or his work, which continue to be praised even in the severe criticism mentioned. In 2015, at the initiative of INAMU and the Ministry of Education of the Nation, it was decided to distribute around 5,000 copies of a songbook with twenty-six of his songs to more than 500 educational institutions, thus demonstrating that the dissemination of his work is, for many, an integral part of Argentine culture and education.[7]

Memory studies scholar Avishek Parui states that culture emerges as a game between memory and representation, through contagious and affective experiences, as well as through material markers.[8] If culture can be seen as a form of contagion that produces affective markers that are transmitted through memory and materiality, the lyrics of songs popularised at crucial moments in history emerge as an excellent language device on that relationship between the songs, what they represented at the time of their first release, and what they represent today, when they are revisited, reconstructing the memory and recollection of that historical moment. While the analysis conducted in this chapter of an album by Luis Alberto Spinetta released in 1976, with his band Invisible, explores the meaning we could give to those songs today, it is also clear that the deep connection felt then—and still felt nowadays—by the audience that listened to these songs has to do with the great ability of the musician to visualise a much wider space than the present.

Indeed, Spinetta managed to connect whoever listened to him with beauty, light, love, and freedom. In his own way, he reminded us that they exist. In fact, when listening to his songs, a mystical element stands out, which takes us away from the here and now and transports us to a strange place, as sad as it is beautiful, where we remember the immensity of the cosmos of which we are a part. In that transcendent poetry, despite the horror of the present, Spinetta connects us with a timeless whole, and we remember, even if only for a while, the meaning of the life and history of not only mankind but the whole cosmos.

That is probably why it is difficult to grasp the ideas encapsulated within Spinetta's songs, as most of them do not belong to the present, being free

---

cartaabiertadejuanfaluadiegoborisporeldianacionaldelmusico.html (accessed 2 January 2015); F. Momjeau, "El día de la idiotez," *Clarín*, 14 December 2014, http://www.clarin.com/extrashow/Dia_Nacional_del_Musico-Diego_Boris-Juan_Falu_0_1265873724.html# (accessed 2 January 2015).

7 Ministerio de Educación, Presidencia de la Nación, 24 September 2015, "Las canciones de Spinetta llegan a las escuelas artísticas de todo el país," http://portal.educacion.gov.ar/prensa/gacetillas-y-comunicados/las-canciones-de-spinetta-llegan-a-las-escuelas-artisticas-de-todo-el-pais/.

8 Avishek Parui, *Culture and the Literary: Matter, Metaphor, Memory* (London, New York: Rowman & Littlefield, 2022), p. 7.

from spatial–temporal constraints. The songs from his universe come from a place that is not limited by geography, history, or philosophy. In them, everything converges: French literature, Latin American indigenous stories, surrealistic art, the reality of Buenos Aires, and the sound of his guitar. The "fiber ship made in Haedo" on which Captain Beto travels through the cosmos, in a song we will analyse shortly, is the perfect metaphor to begin to understand the place from which Spinetta's songs speak to us, a magical place. But at the same time, it is made up of images that come from very close, very "Argentinean" places, free from prejudices and restrictions, as the musician himself explains:

> I approach music as a nutshell approaches the edge of an endless ocean. With it, I express myself and feel that I am just a speaker. Music is something that is beyond our capacity. There is much more music that exists than what we can play. That is to say, both the music of being and the music of the universe exist, as well as the pages of music that we have created with our intellect. For me, everything is connected.[9]

The endless ocean is the entirety, the universe in its totality. The "walnut shells" are the songs that take us sailing on that ocean. They are creations that use basic metaphors, mythical images, and language to encode a mechanism through which the chaos of the universe is stabilised before our eyes. These myths structure our society and function as creative perceptions that give us security and comfort amid chaos. Far from dividing, the myth unites, reaching those indecipherable spaces and connecting them, forging the idea of a whole.[10]

This is why Spinetta's artistic production brings together varied aesthetics, eclectic styles, little-known or invented words, heterogeneous readings, and surrealistic poetry. The aesthetic framework of his work is the cosmos, vast, eternal, unlimited. In conversation with Argentine journalist and poet Miguel Grinberg in 1973, during an interview on his radio show *El son progresivo*, Spinetta says that in general, "the consciousness of society does not have free access, given the repression, to have [a certain] type of information, which is not information from another planet. It is precisely information based on the observation of the purest reality".[11] The dialogue continues, debating the type of repression that is not external but "invisible" and omnipresent. It is a kind of repression that we impose on ourselves—they say—and that the human being continually needs to invent ways to escape from. In sum, in the rock culture of the time, there was this general idea that it was necessary to

---

9 Luis Alberto Spinetta in Diez, *Martropía*, p. 158.
10 For a detailed study of the function of myth in Spinetta's songs, see Favoretto, *Luis Alberto Spinetta: Mito y Mitología*.
11 Miguel Grinberg, and Hoby De Fino, *Apasionados por el rock* (Buenos Aires: Editorial Atlántida, 2010), pp. 54–55.

escape from every type of repression, and many rock songs sought to achieve this task.

The Garden of Those Present

Recorded with Spinetta's band Invisible, *El jardín de los presentes* (The Garden of Those Present) was released in 1976, the year of the coup. In his transcendent poetry, despite the horror of the present, Spinetta connected whoever listened to his music with beauty, with light, with love and freedom. In his own way, he reminded us that they existed. Indeed, when listening to his songs, that mystical element stands out, takes us away from the here and now, and transports us to a strange place, as sad as it is beautiful, where once again we are invited to remember the immensity of the cosmos of which we are part, and to put our lives into perspective. The song, as a literary text, through a diversity of possibilities, can be seen as a form of representation in which matter becomes a metaphor that enters memory with its materiality and affectivity.[12] If memory is a form of representation, like literature, it also offers a perspective of absence as an open order of production that is subject to interpretation.[13]

In 1976, when the Argentine nation began to talk about the "disappeared", Spinetta released *El jardín de los presentes* with his band Invisible. Although the songs on this album were composed before the coup of 1976 and before the word "disappeared" entered the everyday lexicon, when revisiting the time, the fact of his contrasting the term "present" with the term "disappeared" that same year is quite significant. It even seems that the album invited us to remember and name those who were no longer "present" and create a garden for them to settle in the memory of the country. The album brought beauty, poetry, and transcendence, perhaps in a kind of vision, because the Triple A death squads had already ensured that many were no longer "present".[14]

On the album's cover, there are some sort of background spots that are far from resembling flowers in this garden—which is not a minor detail—and there is a face of a young man with makeup, looking down, perhaps representing an artist who is present but at the same time far away, his gaze lost, marked by deep sadness. He has a cap that covers his head, as if he were protecting his mind from something, and a little crown made of artificial flowers. In a moment of deep sadness and restlessness, only music would bring a little life to the garden of those who were still present, where the flowers seemed false, or lifeless.

---

12 Parui, *Culture and the Literary*, p. 3
13 Parui, *Culture and the Literary*, p. 8.
14 "Triple A" was the name by which the Argentine Anticommunist Alliance was known. It was an ultra-right-wing police and armed forces terrorist group that was responsible for the disappearance of thousands of people.

The first song on the album, "El anillo del capitán Beto" (Captain Beto's Ring), thematises exile, although hyperbolised, since the character has left not just his country but the planet (fifteen years ago, and thus probably in one of the dictatorships prior to that of 1976). The references to the surrounding context are striking: "If this goes on like this, not a sad shadow will remain" ["si esto sigue así como así, ni una triste sombra quedará"]. In fact, there were several coups and dictatorships that hit the country in the twentieth century. Beto, described as "the wanderer" ["el errante"], is a bus driver who sets off to fly through space. In his extreme solitude, he longs for the simplest things in life: shared maté (a typical Argentinean drink), tango, his mother, his friends, the noises and smells of the city ("Where would there be a city in which someone whistles a tango? Where are they, where are the garbage trucks, my mother, and the café?" ["¿Dónde habrá una ciudad en la que alguien silbe un tango? ¿Dónde están, dónde están los camiones de basura, mi vieja y el café?"]). Among his beloved objects, as symbolic representatives of his affections are a photo of popular tango legend Carlos Gardel, a River Plate soccer-team pennant, and a saint's stamp. Beto goes into exile "without a compass and without a radio" ["sin brújula y sin radio"] and will never be able to return to Earth. The landscape represented in this first song in which Spinetta speaks to his audience could not be more desolate. Yet the character yearns for everyday life (maté, tango, geraniums, stamp) and affections (my mother, the café).

Just as the album title spoke of the "present", the second song, "Los libros de la buena memoria" (The Books of Good Memory), contains in its title two key concepts for revisiting this time: books (if we think about censorship, blacklists, and burnings) and "good memory" (in times that cannot and should not be forgotten). Making the distinction "good memory" would imply that there is its opposite, a bad memory, or at least an alternative memory. Before those who stay listening "like a blind man facing the sea" ["como un ciego frente al mar"] when reading those books, who never heard "the crackling leaves" ["la hojarasca crepitar"], the poetic voice promises to bring them back to reality where they can react to so much confusion ("everything went dark, I don't know if the sea will rest anymore" ["todo se oscureció, ya no sé si el mar descansará"]) and return to "succeed in [their] soul" ["triunfar en tu alma"]. Faced with the destruction of millions of books, and the disappearance of objects and people, the "good memory" is a book that cannot be burned or prohibited. We can find here a reference to a much broader memory, which connects the present with the history of humanity and the modus operandi of authoritarian regimes. Just as in Germany and Alexandria, there would be book burnings in Argentina. It is a song full of pain and sadness, but with a halo of hope ("A stalk will have grown on the walnut tree" ["habrá crecido un tallo en el nogal"]).

The third song on the album is an instrumental, "Alarma entre los ángeles" (Alarm among the Angels). The text ellipsis is significant: the subject lacks words because the alarm signal is so horrendous that it cannot be verbalised. Who are the angels? Those who are no longer there, the dead, the disappeared, the innocent, the custodians of the garden of those present? The fourth song on the album emphasises that there are those who manage to continue dreaming, and "your dreams are so many that you can see the sky while you dance" ["son tantos tus sueños que ves el cielo mientras te veo bailar"] ("Que ves el cielo" [That You Can See the Sky]). "Ruido de magia" (Magic Noise) is another love song, like many in Spinetta's repertoire, romantic and nostalgic. The noise of "magic" is the roar that sounds before what "disappears" as if by magic. In this case, it is the end of love, although for the recipient who wants to see political references it is not difficult to establish the connection between the title and the status quo.

The next song, "Doscientos años" (Two Hundred Years), asks for "words, words" ["palabras, palabras"] at a time when censorship had eliminated words in bulk from all cultural products, and questions "what was the point of having swum across the sea?" ["¿De qué sirvió haber cruzado a nado la mar?"]. What use are physical achievements when, almost 200 years after the founding of the nation, words and thoughts are still truncated? Once again, history is seen in perspective, and we are reminded that it is not the first time that Argentine history has been stained with genocide.

If there is something that characterises Spinetta's work, it is his constant experimentation. Undoubtedly, the artist arouses emotions in his audience and teaches us by stimulating our senses through the use of complex poetry, loaded with often surrealistic images, such as "cappelletti that withstood the flood" ["un cappelletti que se bancó el diluvio"] ("Ventiscas de marzo")[15] and "the garlands will tremble all the goats next to the echo" ["las guirnaldas temblarán todas las cabras junto al eco"] ("Viajero naciendo"),[16] among many others. By using surrealistic images, the musician challenges and surprises his audience, prompting them to open new imaginary paths. In an interview with Gloria Guerrero, he explains his intention in using this type of triggering language: "what I do in these lyrics is think about how to give the best possibility to people. Look at the sky, call out and you will see how a new day arises. There are several concepts in which, in some way, I am talking to someone whom I want to protect and give light".[17] This is where Spinetta's constant desire for experimentation works to achieve the resonance of that desire in his audience: "what I want is for people to wake up, nothing more. But not to proscribe anything... Wake up just for the sake of it, that's it".[18] Perhaps the only way to emerge from the self-destruction process in which most of the world's population is immersed is through the

---

15 *Privé*, 1986.
16 Pescado Rabioso, *Pescado II* (Talent, 1973).
17 Gloria Guerrero, "'El gordo Spinetta.' Entrevista a Luis Alberto Spinetta. *Rolling Stone* 4, julio 1998," in *Las mejores entrevistas de Rolling Stone. Iconos del rock nacional 1967-2007* (Buenos Aires: Publirevistas, 2006), p. 134.
18 Spinetta in Guerrero, "El gordo Spinetta," p. 135.

exploration of alternatives in every sense, a true revolution that challenges our patterns of thinking and forces us to broaden our vision of the cosmos and our connection with everything that exists. Spinetta was convinced that through his work, he could induce people to see these creative worlds and be able to escape from self-destruction, from excessive drug use, from destroying our environment, through creative music: "music is a language that will always generate spirituality. The more loving and perceptive it is, the better it will take care of the sense of affection, of loving oneself".[19] How does he seek to achieve this? We will next see an example of a song that is like a lesson in itself.

The great feeling of guilt inherited from the indigenous genocides and the historical burden of the massacres can be imagined in "Perdonado (niño condenado)" (Pardoned [Condemned Child]) where "the masters do not rest, they no longer exist" ["los amos no descansan, ya no existen"] and the "white dog" ["perro blanco"] is a "condemned child" ["niño condenado"] (note the double symbol of innocence: white and child), who receives forgiveness and at the same time frees the soul that condemns him. Without a doubt, it is an act of unconditional love: forgiving is difficult and sometimes even impossible. However, seeing the criminal as a child is an act of greatness, it is talking about his smallness, his immaturity, and his inability to discern, for which, despite condemning him, he could be forgiven. Forgiving frees the soul from a negative feeling, but it does not mean avoiding justice, which is why in the title of the song it is clarified, between brackets, that the child is condemned. Forgiven, for being immature, small, dependent, but sentenced. The idea presented by this song is extremely challenging: could we forgive crimes against humanity?

In addition to referring to eternity and breaking temporal limits, Spinetta's poetry also breaks spatial borders. He explains it in the following terms:

> love becomes eternal and is put in harmony and synchronization just like the materials of the universe. There is great love and care to avoid something that is in the hands of God from falling apart. Man recognizes his profundity based on the notion of the density of the universe that he appreciates with his eyes since he looks at the sky. Now that we can travel on a plane and observe the world from above, we can see its vastness. Or with spaceships. It is not so difficult to approach it and even minimally keep an eye on it.[20]

Spinetta suggests that we change the perspective with which we relate to the cosmos ("keep an eye on it"), focusing on the harmony and synchronicity of the universe as a whole and our relationship with the world, connecting with that transcendent mystery. However, how do we understand the universe

---

19 Spinetta in Eliana Pirillo, Jorge Battilana, and Luis Alberto Spinetta, *Luis A. Spinetta: un vuelo al infinito* (Buenos Aires: Corregidor, 2014), p. 131.
20 Spinetta in Diez, *Martropía*, p. 157.

from a scientific perspective without losing this vision of mystery? We need to explore what the musician understands by the cosmological dimension.

For Spinetta, humanity and immensity must go hand in hand. There should be a balance between both, so that they each carry the same weight in the cosmos. The musician writes profound songs that highlight the tragedy of the human condition, which is the inability to communicate with other living species on the planet and our failure in the search for balance ("the sky crosses and does not let itself be known" ["el cielo se cruza y no se deja saber"], "La verdad de las grullas" [The Truth of the Cranes]).[21] He asserts, convinced, that "everything is nature. No matter what disaster we create, we are a product of it. We are not of any other nature than the same one we want to destroy".[22] However, he makes it clear that, for him, it is not nature that is in danger; rather, it is we who are the ones at risk, the human species is the one that could cease to exist. In "La verdad de las grullas", he denounces that most cities "advance until they die" ["avanzan hasta morir"] and "we are all distancing ourselves at once" ["todos nos estamos alejando en un momento"]. He suggests returning to the "organization of the jungle" ["organización de la selva"] and listening to "a truth that the cranes tell: do not venture beyond the mortal valley. They say that human beings gather there to capture and harm each other" ["una verdad que dicen las grullas: no te aventures más allá del valle mortal. Dicen que se juntan allí seres humanos para capturarse y hacerse todo tipo de mal"]. The analogy between the mortal valley and the organisation of the jungle is remarkable as a natural ecosystem, where death is part of the cycle of life. Venturing outside this balance is the closest thing to the current world view ("human beings gather there to capture and harm each other").

He suggests connecting with the whole through music:

> Music is a language that exists in the cosmos, just like everything else around us. The musician who connects with the cosmos, who knows how to explore it with love, who achieves communication with other beings and with God... that musician can take possession of and use that language as if reading a code that seems indecipherable to others.[23]

This quote is key to the argument that I am trying to sustain in this chapter, as it confirms the use of a language by the musician who relates to the cosmos that "for others seems indecipherable". It appears to be a particular way of storytelling, describing, communicating, which is, in truth, one of the earliest human needs.

In fact, the need of humans to tell the story of creation, the story of their relationship with the universe, has been present since the Palaeolithic

---

21 Spinetta, Silver sorgo (Universal/Interdisc, 2001).
22 Spinetta in Diez, *Martropía*, p. 29.
23 Spinetta in Eduardo Berti, *Spinetta. Crónica e iluminaciones* (Buenos Aires: Editora/12, 1988), p. 19.

period. This is demonstrated by both cave paintings and art during the times of Homer, Michelangelo, and Tolstoy. These artists used elements of traditional creation stories and religious visions of the universe as symbolic vehicles for their own visions. At the end of the twentieth century, several modern painters, musicians, and architects began to move away from work based on absolutes and began to celebrate what defines us as re-creators. It is not surprising that the theory of relativity and uncertainty emerged at the same time as the human need to tell a true story instead of repeating an old one. The characteristics of what we call modernism and postmodernism in art suggest that in the absence of valid symbols of power, the artist begins to focus on the process of producing art as the object of their work.[24] In summary, the art of modernists and postmodernists represents the myth of creation as a continuous process of which we are a fundamental and functioning part. Spinetta presents in his art his peculiar way of relating to the story of creation and the deep connection between everything that exists.

The stage of creation involves breaking the limits and coordinates imposed on us by education and society, and opening the mind to growth. The act of overcoming oneself, like a wall that prevents a wider view of the cosmos, is precisely the creative act, described by the musician in the following terms:

> The moment when borders appear is a neutral moment in the spirit, where everything is very open. It's a sleepwalking unconsciousness. And more than innocence, it's a very big change in reality that happens in an ephemeral way. When I want to remember it, I'm already working and my mind is too attentive to everything that needs to be done, rather than the moment when something occurred to me. That moment is generally quite unknown, and if I can bring it to reality and concretize it, even if it's just a sketch, it's very important because it can escape quickly. It has a bit of violence, of suffering, because it's something I'm pulling from somewhere I don't really know where it is. When I let myself flow and things happen to me, I try to play a worthy role in everything that comes to me from the world. That's why I give it the characteristic of energy delivery. It's an unconscious moment, something happened and left a little mark with which I later start to work. The work to complete a song is not like the moment of creating it. The moment of the idea is very impressive.[25]

This passage highlights the concept of spiritual birth as an act of breaking through societal and personal boundaries in order to achieve growth and creativity. The musician describes the creative process as a moment of unconsciousness, where ideas and inspiration flow freely, and which may require effort to bring to concrete reality. The process is often accompanied by a sense of violence and suffering, as the artist grapples with ideas that

---

24 These processes are observed in the paintings of Vincent Van Gogh, Jackson Pollock, and Salvador Dalí, for example.
25 Spinetta in Diez, *Martropía*, p. 80.

may be difficult to express or fully comprehend. Nonetheless, the musician seeks to capture and convey the energy of the moment and recognises the significance of the creative act as a fundamental aspect of human experience.

The album ends with "Las golondrinas de Plaza de Mayo" (Plaza de Mayo's Swallows), a reference, for those who want to see it this way, to the mothers of the plaza, although they are not directly named.[26] In addition, Spinetta himself clarified that this wasn't his idea when writing the lyrics of the song. However, and once again adhering to the interpretative freedom of the audience, the allusion to the well-known mothers worked for many precisely because those words echo in society, not only because of the context in which the text appears but also because of the parallel with the swallows: they function as a group ("from the same tree" ["desde el mismo árbol"]), they are constant in their marches ("they come and go" ["vienen y van"]), and they are unyielding ("they only fly freely" ["solo vuelan en libertad"]). How can we not think of the mothers and grandmothers today, when talking about the Plaza de Mayo?

The Garden of Those Present is perhaps the most political record of Spinetta's entire career. Enigmatic and encrypted, it is one of the most beautiful and hopeful of his albums, where Captain Beto only had power inside his ship, travelling alone and lost in the galaxy, and many Argentineans identified with him, "watering the geraniums of his cabin" ["regando los malvones en su cabina"], fuelling a glimmer of hope for the future. It is an album that lifts us above the evils of this world and asks us whether we could forgive.

As much as Spinetta publicly said that he refused to politicise with his music and wanted to create a parallel world with his songs, in the seventies the context was so oppressive that it became difficult to completely withdraw from the political environment. And while in some way such a thing might have been possible, perhaps it was unethical. How could anyone turn a totally deaf ear to what was happening? With this album, Spinetta achieves an aesthetic balance between political–social references that avoid censorship, the beauty of poetry, hope, and pain, which very few artists achieved at that time. Building a "garden" for those "present" is an act of unconditional love and, at the same time, a gesture of encrypted dissident criticism against governments (both the new and the previous one) and a smart way to avoid censorship.

---

26 The Mothers of the Plaza de Mayo is a well-known organised group, whose members started their marches in the square in front of the Pink House in Buenos Aires during the dictatorship, demanding answers from the regime about their disappeared children. They continue their work today.

Epilogue

"Forbidden things are open to the imagination"

—*Margaret Atwood,* The Testaments

Not being able to assert the exact meaning of a metaphor, an allegory, or a symbolic text can be seen as a dangerous thing by some—and a stimulating and liberating exercise by others. That is the power of language in song. Song can make you free.

Argentine rock is a compelling case of freedom in song. In its origin, it differs from its Anglo-Saxon predecessor by its birth in a context of restricted democracy and its subsequent growth in the shadow of the series of dictatorships that ruled the country. Therefore, it developed in limited and constrained spaces, and over the years it kept alive its search for freedom and justice.

The purpose of cultural analysis of these songs, following Bicknell, "might not be that of finding definitive answers to a finite number of questions, but rather that of posing an ever-expanding number of questions, based on an ever-widening understanding of the interrelationship of texts and contexts".[1] What is that "ever-widening", other than exercising freedom?

The cry for freedom emanating from the corpus of songs explored in this book does not end here. It is only the start of a bigger quest. Meaning in song requires the interactions between the lyrics, the performer, and the audience. Is it eternal? Can meaning in song be constructed again and again over time? We hope so.

Thanks to The Bird Making Machine, we are reminded that "with eyes closed, we can only see our nose" ["Cómo mata el viento norte"]. And with that, we also hope, as Luis Alberto Spinetta wished in one of his compositions, that Song finally reaches the Sun.

---

[1] Bicknell, *Philosophy*, p. 110.

Bibliography

AA.VV. *Grandes entrevistas de Rolling Stone. Íconos del rock nacional* (Buenos Aires: Publirevistas, 2006).

Abalos, Ezequiel. *Historias del Rock de Acá: primera generación* (Buenos Aires: Editora AC, 1995).

Alabarces, Pablo. *Entre gatos y violadores: el rock nacional en la cultura argentina* (Buenos Aires: Colihue, 1993).

Althusser, Louis. "Ideology and Ideological State Apparatuses (Notes towards an Investigation)." In *Lenin and Philosophy and Other Essays*. Translated by Ben Brewster (London: NLB, 1971).

Archetti, Eduardo P. *Masculinities: Football, Polo and the Tango in Argentina* (Oxford: Berg, 1999).

Arendt, Hannah. *The Human Condition* (Chicago: University of Chicago Press, 1998 [1958]).

Avellaneda, Andrés. *Censura, autoritarismo y cultura: Argentina 1960–1983*, 2 volumes (Buenos Aires: Centro Editor de América Latina, 1986).

Aznar, Pedro. Interview now excerpted via [TV channel] Volver, 28 October 2007. http://www.youtube.com/watch?v=j3NUybAPvpg.

Balderston, Daniel, et al. *Ficción y política: la narrativa argentina durante el proceso militar* (Buenos Aires: Alianza Editorial, 1987).

Bannister, Matthew. "Ladies and Gentlemen, The Beatelles! The Influence of Sixties Girl Groups on the Beatles." *Beatlestudies 3: Proceedings of the Beatles 2000 Conference*. Edited by Yrjö Heinonen, et al., 169–79 (Finland: University of Jyväskylä, 2000).

Benedetti, Sebastián, and Martín Graziano. *Estación imposible. Periodismo y contracultura en los '70: la historia de Expreso Imaginario* (Buenos Aires: Marcelo Héctor Oliveri Editor, 2007).

Berti, Eduardo. *Spinetta. Crónica e iluminaciones* (Buenos Aires: Editora/12, 1988).

—. "El Himno para todo público." *Página 12* (Buenos Aires), 28 October 1990.

—. *Rockología, documentos de los '80* (Buenos Aires: Beas Ediciones, 1994).

Bicknell, Jeanette. *Philosophy of Song and Singing: An Introduction* (New York: Routledge, 2015).

Blaustein, Eduardo, and Martín Zubieta. *Decíamos ayer: la prensa argentina bajo el Proceso* (Buenos Aires: Colihue, 2006).

Boixadós, Alberto. *Arte y subversión: arte, mistificación, política* (Buenos Aires: Areté, 1977).

Buch, Esteban. *O juremos con gloria morir: una historia del himno nacional argentino, desde la Asamblea del año XIII hasta Charly García* (Buenos Aires: Eterna Cadencia, 2013).

Caistor, Nick. "Whose War Is It Anyway? The Argentine Press during the South Atlantic Conflict." In *Framing the Falklands War: Nationhood, Culture and Identity.* Edited by James Aulich, 50–57 (Milton Keynes: Open University Press, 1992).

Calveiro, Pilar. *Poder y desaparición. Los campos de concentración en Argentina* (Buenos Aires: Colihue, 2001).

Chastagner, Claude. *De la cultura rock* (Buenos Aires: Paidós, 2012).

Chirom, Daniel, and Charly García. *Charly García* (Buenos Aires: Librería y Editorial El Juglar, 1983).

Cibeira, Juan Manuel. *La biblia del rock. Historias de la revista Pelo* (Buenos Aires: Ediciones B, 2014).

Ciccioli, Martín. *Rockeado: la historia detrás de las canciones de tu vida* (Buenos Aires: Emecé, 2010).

Citro, Silvia. "El rock como un ritual adolescente. Trasgresión y realismo grotesco en los recitales de Bersuit." *Trans. Revista transcultural de música* 12: n. p., 2008.

Clarín (Buenos Aires), 26 March 1976.

Clarín, suplemento especial (Buenos Aires), 24 March 1976.

Clarín, suplemento especial (Buenos Aires), 27 March 1977.

Cohen, Sara. "Men Making a Scene: Rock Music and the Production of Gender." In *Sexing the Groove: Popular Music and Gender.* Edited by Sheila Whiteley, 17–36 (New York: Routledge, 1997).

CONADEP. *Nunca Más (Never Again). Report of the National Commission on the Disappearance of Persons.* Translated by Writers and Scholars International Ltd (Buenos Aires: Editorial Universitaria de Buenos Aires, 1984). http://www.desaparecidos.org/nuncamas/web/english/library/nevagain/nevagain_001.htm.

Conde, Oscar. *Poéticas del rock* (Buenos Aires: Marcelo Héctor Oliveri Editor, 2007).

Constitución Nacional de la República Argentina (Capítulo Primero: Declaraciones, derechos y garantías). https://www.congreso.gob.ar/constitucionParte1Cap1.php.

De Amézola, Gonzalo. "La última dictadura militar en la escuela Argentina: entre la historia reciente y la memoria colectiva." *Revista de teoría y didáctica de las ciencias sociales* (17): 29–56, 2011.

Delbueno, Horacio. "Rock nacional: rebelde me llama la gente. Contexto socio-histórico." In *Yo no permito: rock y ética en Argentina durante la última dictadura.* By Ramón Sanza Ferramola and Horacio Delbueno, 9–32 (San Luis: Nueva Editorial Universitaria, 2009).

Delgado, Julián. "El show de los muertos: música y política en el grupo de rock argentino Sui Generis." *A contracorriente* 13 (3): 18–49, 2016.

Dente, Miguel Angel. *Transgresores: Spinetta / García / Páez* (Buenos Aires: Distal, 2000).

Di Cione, Lisa. "Rock y dictadura en la Argentina: reflexiones sobre una relación contradictoria." *Revista afuera* 10 (15): 1–9, 2015.

Di Pietro, Roque. *Esta noche toca Charly: un viaje por los recitales de Charly García (1956–1993)* (Buenos Aires: Gourmet Musical Ediciones, 2017).

Díaz, Claudio. *Libro de viajes y extravíos: un recorrido por el rock argentino, 1965–1985* (Unquillo: Narvaja, 2005).

Diez, Juan Carlos. *Martropía: conversaciones con Spinetta* (Buenos Aires: Aguilar, 2006).

Discovery Communications. "El karma de vivir al sur." *People & Arts* (2002).

Duizeide, Juan Bautista. *Luis Alberto Spinetta: el lector kamikaze* (Buenos Aires, 2017).

Favoretto, Mara. Personal interview with Hernán Invernizzi and Judith Gociol, Buenos Aires, 26 November 2007.

—. *Alegoría e ironía bajo censura en la Argentina del Proceso (1976–1983)* (Lewiston NY: Edwin Mellen Press, 2010).

—. "Charly García: alegoría y rock." *Musica popular em revista* 2 (1): 125–51, 2013.

—. *Charly en el país de las alegorías: un viaje por las letras de Charly García* (Buenos Aires: Gourmet Musical Ediciones, 2014).

—. *Luis Alberto Spinetta: mito y mitología* (Buenos Aires: Gourmet Musical Ediciones, 2017).

—. "Brothers in Rock: Argentine and British Rock Music during the Malvinas/Falklands Conflict." In *The Bloomsbury Handbook of Popular Music and Social Class*. Edited by Ian Peddie, 291–311 (New York: Bloomsbury, 2020).

Feitlowitz, Marguerite. *A Lexicon of Terror: Argentina and the Legacies of Torture* (New York: Oxford University Press, 1998).

Fernández Bitar, Marcelo. *50 años de rock en Argentina* (Buenos Aires: Sudamericana, 2015).

Flachland, Cecilia. *Desarma y sangra. Rock, política y nación* (Buenos Aires: Casa Nova Editores, 2015).

Fletcher, Angus. *Alegoría. Teoría de un modo simbólico.* Translated by Vicente Carmona González (Madrid: Ediciones Akal, S.A., 2002).

Foster, David William. *Violence in Argentinean Literature: Cultural Responses to Tyranny* (Columbia: University of Missouri Press, 1995).

Frith, Simon. *Sound Effects: Youth, Leisure, and the Politics of Rock* (London: Constable, 1983).

—. *Performing Rites: On the Value of Popular Music* (Cambridge MA: Harvard University Press, 1998).

García Canclini, Néstor, editor. *Cultura y pospolítica: el debate sobre la modernidad en América Latina* (México: Consejo Nacional para la Cultura y las Artes, 1995).

Gobello, Marcelo. *Banderas en tu corazón. Apuntes sobre el mito de los redondos* (Buenos Aires: Ediciones Corregidor, 2014).

Grinberg, Miguel David. *Cómo vino la mano: orígenes del rock argentino* (Buenos Aires: Gourmet Musical Ediciones, 2008).

Grinberg, Miguel, and Hoby De Fino. *Apasionados por el rock* (Buenos Aires: Editorial Atlántida, 2010).
Grossberg, Lawrence. "Another Boring Day in Paradise: Rock and Roll and the Empowerment of Everyday Life." *Popular Music: A Yearbook* 4: 225–58, 1984.
Guerrero, Gloria. "'El gordo Spinetta.' Entrevista a Luis Alberto Spinetta. *Rolling Stone* 4, julio 1998." In *Las mejores entrevistas de Rolling Stone. Iconos del rock nacional 1967–2007*, 125–41 (Buenos Aires: Publirevistas, 2006).
Hernández, José. *El gaucho Martín Fierro* (Buenos Aires: Imprenta de La Pampa, 1872).
Invernizzi, Hernán. *"Los libros son tuyos": políticos, académicos y militares: la dictadura en Eudeba* (Buenos Aires: Eudeba, 2005).
Invernizzi, Hernán, and Judith Gociol. *Un golpe a los libros: represión a la cultura durante la última dictadura militar* (Buenos Aires: Eudeba, 2005).
King, Martin. *Men, Masculinities and the Beatles* (Farnham: Ashgate, 2013).
Kreimer, Juan Carlos, Carlos Polimeni, Guillermo Pintos, and Gustavo Álvarez Núñez. *Ayer nomás: 40 años de rock en la Argentina* (Buenos Aires: Musimundo, 2006).
Kurlat Ares, Silvia. "El lenguaje de la tribu: los códigos del rock." *Revista iberoamericana* 73: 267–86, 2007.
La Nación. "A la Estratósfera." 30 September 2017 (accessed 27 March 2023). https://fb.watch/jwIybadvwg/.
Lévi-Strauss, Claude. *Myth and Meaning* (London: Routledge and Kegan Paul, 1978).
Lewis, George H. "The Meanings in the Music and the Music's in Me: Popular Music as Symbolic Communication." *Theory, Culture & Society* 1 (3): 133–41, 1983.
Lucena, Daniela, and Gisela Laboreau. "El rol del cuerpo-vestido en la ruptura estética de Virus durante los últimos años de la dictadura militar." *Música hodie* 15 (2): 192–202, 2015.
Ludmer, Josefina. *Aquí América Latina. Una especulación* (Buenos Aires: Eterna Cadencia, 2010).
Manzano, Valeria. "'Rock Nacional' and Revolutionary Politics: The Making of a Youth Culture of Contestation in Argentina, 1966–1976." *The Americas* 70 (3): 393–427, 2014.
Marchini, Darío. *No toquen: músicos populares, gobierno y sociedad: de la utopía a la persecución y las listas negras en la Argentina 1960–1983* (Buenos Aires: Catálogos, 2008).
Middleton, Richard. *Voicing the Popular: On the Subjects of Popular Music* (London: Routledge, 2006).
Mignone, Emilio Fermín. *Iglesia y dictadura* (Buenos Aires: Colihue, 2013).
Montanaro, Pablo. "Eudeba era muy peligrosa para los militares. Entrevista a Hernán Invernizzi." *Rio Negro Online* (Buenos Aires), 6 February 2006. https://www.rionegro.com.ar/columnistas/eudeba-era-muy-peligrosa-para-los-militares-DFHRN06020616061003.
Monteleone, Jorge. "Figuras de la pasión rocker. Ensayo sobre rock argentino." *Everba* 1 (Summer), 2002. http://everba.eter.org/summer02/figuras_jorge.htm.

O'Donnell, Pacho. *Breve historia argentina. De la Conquista a los Kirchner* (Buenos Aires: Aguilar, 2014).
Parui, Avishek. *Culture and the Literary: Matter, Metaphor, Memory* (London, New York: Rowman & Littlefield, 2022).
Piglia, Ricardo. *Crítica y ficción* (Barcelona: Anagrama, 1986).
Pintos, Víctor. *Tanguito. La verdadera historia* (Buenos Aires: Planeta, 1993).
Pirillo, Eliana, Jorge Battilana, and Luis Alberto Spinetta. *Luis A. Spinetta: un vuelo al infinito* (Buenos Aires: Corregidor, 2014).
Pitluk, Roberto. *El macho argentino: reflexiones sobre masculinidad empobrecida* (Buenos Aires: Ediciones Pausa para la reflexión, 2007).
Polimeni, Carlos. *Bailando sobre los escombros: historia crítica del rock latinoamericano* (Buenos Aires: Editorial Biblos, 2002).
Portela, Ignacio. "Spinetta trascendió el rock. Entrevista a Eduardo Berti." Todos estos años de Spinetta. *Revista Sudestada de colección*, número 11, pp. 18–21.
Prevéndola, Juan Ignacio. *Rockpolitik: 50 años de rock nacional y sus vínculos con el poder político Argentino* (Buenos Aires: Eudeba, 2015).
Pujol, Sergio. *Rock y dictadura: crónica de una generación (1976–1983)* (Buenos Aires: Booket, 2005).
—. *Las ideas del rock: genealogía de la música rebelde* (Rosario: Homo Sapiens Ediciones, 2007).
—. *Canciones argentinas (1910–2010)* (Buenos Aires: Emecé, 2010).
Ramos, Laura, and Cynthia Lejbowicz. *Corazones en llamas: historias del rock argentino en los '80* (Buenos Aires: Clarin Aguilar, 1991).
Risler, Julia. *La acción psicológica. Dictadura, inteligencia y gobierno de las emociones 1955–1981* (Buenos Aires: Tinta Limón, 2018).
Roffé, Reina. "Omnipresencia de la censura en la escritora argentina." *Revista iberoamericana* 51 (132): 909–15, 1985.
Sanchez, Nora. "García Y2K." 11 January 2000 (accessed 17 October 2018). https://www.clarin.com/espectaculos/garcia-y2k_0_r1vgdJ2gCYx.html.
Sarmiento, Domingo. *Facundo: civilización y barbarie* (Santiago: El Progreso de Chile, 1845).
Secul Giusti, Cristian. "Rompiendo el silencio: la construcción discursiva de la libertad en las líricas de rock-pop argentino durante el período 1982–1989." Doctoral dissertation (Buenos Aires: Universidad Nacional de La Plata, 2017).
Secul Giusti, Cristian, and Federico Rodríguez Lemos. "Si tienes voz, tienes palabras: análisis discursivo de las líricas del rock argentino en la 'primavera democrática (1983–1986)'." Dissertation (Buenos Aires: Universidad Nacional de La Plata, 2011).
Seoane, María, and Vicente Muleiro. *El dictador: la historia secreta y pública de Jorge Rafael Videla* (Buenos Aires: Sudamericana, 2016).
Sosnowski, Saúl. *Represión y reconstrucción de una cultura: el caso argentino* (Buenos Aires: Eudeba, 1988).
Taylor, Diana. *Disappearing Acts: Spectacles of Gender and Nationalism in Argentina's "Dirty War"* (Durham: Duke University Press, 1997).
Uriarte, Claudio. *Almirante Cero: biografía no autorizada de Emilio Eduardo Massera* (Buenos Aires: Planeta, 1991).

Verbitsky, Horacio. *Malvinas: la última batalla de la Tercera Guerra Mundial* (Buenos Aires: Editorial Sudamericana, 2002).

—. *Confessions of an Argentine Dirty Warrior: A Firsthand Account of Atrocity* (New York: New Press, 2005).

Vila, Pablo. "Argentina's 'Rock Nacional': The Struggle for Meaning." *Latin American Music Review / Revista de música latinoamericana* 10 (1): 1–28, 1989.

Vila, Pablo, and Paul Cammack. "Rock Nacional and Dictatorship in Argentina." *Popular Music* 6 (2): 129–48, 1987.

"Viola's Message to Youth." *La Nación* (Buenos Aires), 21 September 1981.

Warner, Marina. *Alone of All Her Sex: The Myth and Cult of the Virgin Mary* (London: Vintage, 2000).

Discography

Alejandro Lerner. *Todo a pulmón* (Raviol Records/Interdisc, 1983).
Almendra. *Hoy todo el hielo en la ciudad / Campos verdes* (RCA, 1968).
—. *Tema de Pototo / El mundo entre las manos* (RCA, 1968).
—. *Almendra* (RCA, 1969).
—. *Almendra II* (RCA, 1970).
Bersuit Vergarabat. *Bersuit* (Universal Music, 2006).
Celeste Carballo. *Mi voz renacerá* (Interdisc, 1983).
Charly García. *Pubis angelical / Yendo de la cama al living* (DG Discos/Interdisc/Universal Music, 1982).
—. *Clics modernos* (DG Discos/Interdisc/Universal Music, 1983).
—. *Piano bar* (DG Discos/Interdisc/Universal Music, 1984).
—. *Parte de la religión* (Sony BMG, 1987).
—. *Cómo conseguir chicas* (Sony BMG, 1989).
—. *Filosofía barata y zapatos de goma* (Sony BMG, 1990).
—. *La hija de la lágrima* (Sony BMG, 1994).
—. *Say no more* (Sony BMG, 1996).
—. *Demasiado ego* (Universal, 1999).
—. *Influencia* (EMI, 2002).
—. *Rock and roll yo* (EMI, 2003).
—. *Kill gil* (Sony Music/Del Ángel FEG, 2010).
Charly García & The Prostitution. *60x60* (EMI Music/DSX Films, 2012).
Ciro y los persas. *Espejos* (300 Producciones, 2010).
Dúo Fantasía. *El futuro es nuestro* (Sazam Records, 1983).
Fito Páez. *El jardín de los presentes* (CBS, 1976)
—. *Del 63* (EMI, 1983).
—. *Yo te amo* (Sony Music, 2013).
Juan Carlos Baglietto. *Baglietto* (EMI, 1983).
La Máquina de Hacer Pájaros. *La máquina de hacer pájaros* (Microfón/Sony BMG, 1976).
—. *Películas* (Microfón/Sony BMG, 1977).
León Gieco. *IV LP* (Music Hall, 1978).
Los Abuelos de la Nada. *Vasos y besos* (Interdisc, 1983).
Los Beatniks. *Rebelde / No finjas más* (Columbia Records, 1966).

Los Enanitos Verdes. *Simulacro de tensión* (Sony Music, 1986).
Los Fabulosos Cadillacs. *Yo te avisé* (CBS, 1987).
Los Gatos. *La balsa / Ayer nomás* (TNT, 1967).
Los Twist. *La dicha en movimiento* (SG Discos/Interdisc, 1983).
—. *Kamikaze* (Ratón Finta, 1982).
—. *Privé* (Interdisc, 1986).
—. *Silver sorgo* (Universal/Interdisc, 2001).
Miguel Abuelo. *Los solistas de Mandioca* (Talent, 1970).
—. *Buen día, día* (Interdisc, 1984).
Miguel Abuelo & Nada. *Miguel Abuelo & Nada* (Moshe-Naïm, 1975).
Miguel Cantilo. *Unidad* (Sazam Records, 1983).
Moris. *30 minutos de vida* (TNT, 1970).
Patricio Rey y sus Redonditos de Ricota. *Oktubre* (Del Cielito Records, 1986).
Pescado Rabioso. *Artaud* (Talent, 1973).
—. *Pescado II* (Talent, 1973).
Rata Blanca. *Rata Blanca* (Universal, 1988).
Raúl Porchetto. *Cristo rock* (Microfón, 1972).
—. *Metegol* (Music Hall, 1980).
—. *Reina Madre* (Interdisc, 1983).
Serú Girán. *Serú Girán* (Music Hall, 1978).
—. *La grasa de las capitales* (Music Hall, 1979).
Soda Stereo. *Soda Stereo* (CBS, 1984).
Sui Generis. *Vida* (Microfón/Sony BMG, 1972).
—. *Confesiones de invierno* (Microfón/Sony BMG, 1973).
—. *Pequeñas anécdotas sobre las instituciones* (Microfón/Sony BMG, 1974).
—. *Adiós Sui Generis I* (Microfón/Sony BMG, 1975).
—. *Adiós Sui Generis II* (Microfón/Sony BMG, 1975).
—. *Adiós Sui Generis III* (Microfón/Sony BMG, 1996 [recorded live in 1975]).
—. *Sinfonías para adolescentes* (Universal Music, 2000).
Sumo. *Divididos por la felicidad* (CBS, 1985).
Various Artists. *Por qué cantamos* (EMI, 1985).
Virus. *Recrudece* (DG Discos, 1982).
—. *Agujero interior* (CBS, 1983).
—. *Locura* (Music Hall, 1985).
Vox Dei. *La Biblia* (Disc Jockey, 1971).

Discography

Alejandro Lerner. *Todo a pulmón* (Raviol Records/Interdisc, 1983).
Almendra. *Hoy todo el hielo en la ciudad / Campos verdes* (RCA, 1968).
—. *Tema de Pototo / El mundo entre las manos* (RCA, 1968).
—. *Almendra* (RCA, 1969).
—. *Almendra II* (RCA, 1970).
Bersuit Vergarabat. *Bersuit* (Universal Music, 2006).
Celeste Carballo. *Mi voz renacerá* (Interdisc, 1983).
Charly García. *Pubis angelical / Yendo de la cama al living* (DG Discos/Interdisc/Universal Music, 1982).
—. *Clics modernos* (DG Discos/Interdisc/Universal Music, 1983).
—. *Piano bar* (DG Discos/Interdisc/Universal Music, 1984).
—. *Parte de la religión* (Sony BMG, 1987).
—. *Cómo conseguir chicas* (Sony BMG, 1989).
—. *Filosofía barata y zapatos de goma* (Sony BMG, 1990).
—. *La hija de la lágrima* (Sony BMG, 1994).
—. *Say no more* (Sony BMG, 1996).
—. *Demasiado ego* (Universal, 1999).
—. *Influencia* (EMI, 2002).
—. *Rock and roll yo* (EMI, 2003).
—. *Kill gil* (Sony Music/Del Ángel FEG, 2010).
Charly García & The Prostitution. *60x60* (EMI Music/DSX Films, 2012).
Ciro y los persas. *Espejos* (300 Producciones, 2010).
Dúo Fantasía. *El futuro es nuestro* (Sazam Records, 1983).
Fito Páez. *El jardín de los presentes* (CBS, 1976)
—. *Del 63* (EMI, 1983)
—. *Yo te amo* (Sony Music, 2013).
Juan Carlos Baglietto. *Baglietto* (EMI, 1983).
La Máquina de Hacer Pájaros. *La máquina de hacer pájaros* (Microfón/Sony BMG, 1976).
—. *Películas* (Microfón/Sony BMG, 1977).
León Gieco. *IV LP* (Music Hall, 1978).
Los Abuelos de la Nada. *Vasos y besos* (Interdisc, 1983).
Los Beatniks. *Rebelde / No finjas más* (Columbia Records, 1966).

Los Enanitos Verdes. *Simulacro de tensión* (Sony Music, 1986).
Los Fabulosos Cadillacs. *Yo te avisé* (CBS, 1987).
Los Gatos. *La balsa / Ayer nomás* (TNT, 1967).
Los Twist. *La dicha en movimiento* (SG Discos/Interdisc, 1983).
—. *Kamikaze* (Ratón Finta, 1982).
—. *Privé* (Interdisc, 1986).
—. *Silver sorgo* (Universal/Interdisc, 2001).
Miguel Abuelo. *Los solistas de Mandioca* (Talent, 1970).
—. *Buen día, día* (Interdisc, 1984).
Miguel Abuelo & Nada. *Miguel Abuelo & Nada* (Moshe-Naïm, 1975).
Miguel Cantilo. *Unidad* (Sazam Records, 1983).
Moris. *30 minutos de vida* (TNT, 1970).
Patricio Rey y sus Redonditos de Ricota. *Oktubre* (Del Cielito Records, 1986).
Pescado Rabioso. *Artaud* (Talent, 1973).
—. *Pescado II* (Talent, 1973).
Rata Blanca. *Rata Blanca* (Universal, 1988).
Raúl Porchetto. *Cristo rock* (Microfón, 1972).
—. *Metegol* (Music Hall, 1980).
—. *Reina Madre* (Interdisc, 1983).
Serú Girán. *Serú Girán* (Music Hall, 1978).
—. *La grasa de las capitales* (Music Hall, 1979).
Soda Stereo. *Soda Stereo* (CBS, 1984).
Sui Generis. *Vida* (Microfón/Sony BMG, 1972).
—. *Confesiones de invierno* (Microfón/Sony BMG, 1973).
—. *Pequeñas anécdotas sobre las instituciones* (Microfón/Sony BMG, 1974).
—. *Adiós Sui Generis I* (Microfón/Sony BMG, 1975).
—. *Adiós Sui Generis II* (Microfón/Sony BMG, 1975).
—. *Adiós Sui Generis III* (Microfón/Sony BMG, 1996 [recorded live in 1975]).
—. *Sinfonías para adolescentes* (Universal Music, 2000).
Sumo. *Divididos por la felicidad* (CBS, 1985).
Various Artists. *Por qué cantamos* (EMI, 1985).
Virus. *Recrudece* (DG Discos, 1982).
—. *Agujero interior* (CBS, 1983).
—. *Locura* (Music Hall, 1985).
Vox Dei. *La Biblia* (Disc Jockey, 1971).

Index

AAA (Anti-communist Argentine Alliance) 19, 151
abnormality 74, 129–30
Abonizio, Adrián 115
Abuelo, Miguel 16–17, 20
Actas del Proceso 40
Acusticazo festival 18
Adiós Sui Generis (three albums) 25, 143
adultery 61
Agosti, Orlando 45, 56
"Águila de trueno" (Spinetta) 101
Agujero interior (Virus) 111
"Ah! Basta de pensar" (Spinetta) 101
"Alarma entre los ángeles" (Spinetta/Invisible) 152–3
Alfonsín, Raúl 108, 112–14, 119
"Algo de paz" (Porchetta) 105
"Alguien en el mundo piensa en mí" (García) 136
allegorical texts 30, 56, 80
allegory 3–4, 11–13, 159
 and censorship 53
 García's use of 28, 30, 82–3, 85, 90–1
 Moris' use of 18
Almendra 3, 6, 21, 24, 32–6
Althusser, Louis 42
"Amigo vuelve a casa pronto" (Sui Genesis) 27
"Ana no duerme" (Almendra) 34
Anglophone rock music 9–11, 13, 16
 banned from Argentine radio 5–6, 94, 110

anti-Argentine campaign 72, 74
arbitrariedades legitimadas 40
Archetti, Eduardo 141–2
Arendt, Hannah 77
Argentina
 allegorical description of 90
 coup d'état of 1976 25, 56
 gender in 31, 140–2
 military dictatorship of 1966–73 *see* Revolución Argentina
 military dictatorship of 1976–83 *see* National Reorganisation Process
 national anthem of 131–2
 neoliberal period in 119–21
 political instability of 14
 threefold crisis in 11–12
Argentine being *see ser nacional*
Argentine Constitution 40–1, 43
Argentine rock 159
 in 1990s and early 2000s 119–25
 after the PRN 107–9
 as counterculture 13–16
 dissidence in 53–4
 during PRN 77
 emergence of 9–13
 and the Malvinas/Falklands War 5–6, 94–9, 105–6
 and politics 18–21
 songs of freedom 114–19
 stardom in 129–30
 transition songs 6, 109–14, 118
Argentine rock lyrics 1–3, 5–6, 9
 in 1960s 11, 13, 16
 of Almendra 32, 35

anti-war 98–9
and Catholic Church 56
of García's solo albums 129, 139
gender in 141, 143–4
of La Máquina de Hacer Pájaros 82
of neoliberal era 125
post-dictatorship 109
of Sui Generis 24, 26, 28–9, 31
under PRN 37, 53–4, 75, 77
armed forces, in PRN rhetoric 56, 58–9, 67, 71, 74
authoritarianism 3
authors, permitted 51
Avellaneda, Andrés 38, 41, 122
"Ayer nomás" (Moris) 18
Aznar, Pedro 91

BA Rock Festival 18, 110
Baglietto, Juan Carlos 115–16
Balderston, Daniel 38
Banade archives 47–8
barbarism 68, 71, 132
the Beatles 12, 102, 130, 140–1
Benedetti, Mario 115
Bersuit Vergarabat 121–5
Berti, Eduardo 148
Bicicleta (Serú Girán) 89
Bignone, Reynaldo 104
Biravent, Moris *see* Moris
birth, spiritual 156
blacklists 4, 46, 49, 91, 152
Blanca, Rata 105
"Blues del levante" (García) 143
Boixadós, Alberto 78, 142
Bolatti, Guillermo 65
Bonermann, Elsa 51
books
  banning 47
  burning 68, 152
borders 156
"Botas locas" (Sui Generis) 25–6, 37
Buarque, Chico 10
Buch, Esteban 131–2

Cabildo 78, 142
Calveiro, Pilar 55n1

Cammack, Paul 2
Cámpora, Héctor 19, 29
cancer, as metaphor 4, 55, 57, 59
"Canción de Alicia en el pais" (Serú Girán) 89–92
"Canción de dos por tres" (García) 102–3
"Canción para mi muerte" (Sui Generis) 25
Cantilo, Miguel 18–19, 111
Carballo, Celeste 111
Carcavallo, Francisco 38
carnival 121–2
Carroll, Lewis 90
Carta Política 43
"Casa vacía" (García) 133, 145
Cassandra 30
castaways 14–16
Catholic Church
  and the PRN 43–5, 60
  and *ser nacional* 68–9
Catholic literature, censorship of 52
Catholic publishing houses 50
Cavallo, Domingo 120
celebrities 111, 119–20, 122, 124
censorship 1–6, 12, 16, 20–1
  in Argentina 1, 38–9, 47, 53, 148
  boomerang effect of 52–4
  of children's literature 51–2
  end of 107, 109–10
  and *Expreso Imaginario* 80
  during Malvinas/Falklands War 98, 106
  PRN's methods of 38–42, 46–50
  and Serú Girán 86, 89
  Spinetta avoiding 148, 157
  and Sui Generis 27, 29
  as surgery 57–8
censorship committees 49
The Century Indignation 24
"Cerca de la Revolución" (García) 112, 130
Chastagner, Claude 10
children, death of 63
children's literature 51
"Chipi Chipi" (García) 134
Chirom, Daniel 30

INDEX

Christian values
  in Massera's speeches 45
  PRN rhetoric of 4–5, 38, 41, 50, 53, 112
  and *ser nacional* 57, 69
Ciro y los persas 105
citizen responsibility 68
Clarín
  Catholic Church in 43
  Charly García in 132
  and the disappeared 73
  and Malvinas/Falklands conflict 74
  theme of union in 63, 66
  women in 62
the Clash 102–3
Clics modernos (García) 110
coded language 3, 5, 12, 15, 75
  Sui Generis and 26, 29
colonisation 47, 88
"Color humano" (Almendra) 34
COMFER (Comité federal de Radio diffusion) 98
common enemy 56, 69–70, 74
Communication Triangle 80
communism
  iconography on album covers 119
  rhetoric against 4, 16, 40, 55, 102
Cómo conseguir chicas (García) 144
"Cómo mata el viento norte" (La Máquina de Hacer Pájaros) 83, 159
CONADEP (Commission on the Disappearance of Persons) 6, 44, 46n39, 108, 111
concentration camps 46, 55n1, 57
Confesiones de invierno (Sui Generis) 27–9
Conquest of the Desert 67–8
consumerism 119, 128
cooptation 6, 128–9
Cordera, Gustavo 124
Correa, Alejandro 24
corruption 20, 111, 120, 124–5
"Cosmigonón" (Serú Girán) 86, 88
counterculture 13, 16, 75
  magazines of 79–80, 82
  right-wing on 78
creation stories 155–6

Cristo rock (Porchetto) 57
Crosby, Stills, Nash & Young 26
Crow, Joseph 142
"Cuando comenzamos a nacer" (Sui Generis) 27
"Cuervos en la casa" (Páez) 116–17
cultural repression 48
culture
  false 98
  memory and representation in 149

Dalí, Salvador 156n24
"De ahí soy yo" (Bersuit Vergarabat) 122–4
de la Rúa, Fernando 120
de los Santos, Lalo 115
"De nada sirve" (Moris) 18
death flights 137
death squads 30, 46, 57, 110, 151
"Deberías saber por qué" (García) 136
Del 63 (Páez) 116
Demasiado ego (García) 137, 139, 145
"Demoliendo hoteles" (García) 111, 129
deoxidisation 84–5
Derisi, Octavio 44n27
detention centres 46, 49
devastation 29, 34
Díaz, Claudio 11–12, 20
Diez, Juan Carlos 32
dirty war 62, 68, 95
the disappeared 46–8, 72–5, 91
  and the Catholic Church 43–4
  mothers and wives of 62–3
  and Spinetta's music 151
disappearing technique 4, 46–9
dissidence, and censorship 11, 41, 53
divided literature 52–3
Dongji, Tulio Halperín 39
"Doscientos años" (Spinetta/Invisible) 153
DPG (Dirección General de Publicaciones) 48
Due Obedience Law 114
Duhalde, Eduardo 121
dulce de leche 35–6

Dúo Fantasía 111
Dylan, Bob 10, 26, 148

eclecticism 32
"El anillo del capitán Beto" (Spinetta/Invisible) 152
"El Banquete" (Virus) 99
El Club del Clan 11–12, 16
El Jardín de Los Presentes (Spinetta/Invisible) 145, 151–7
"El mundo entre las manos" (Almendra) 33
"El oso" (Moris) 18
"El Show de los Muertos" (Sui Generis) 30
"El tuerto y los ciegos" (Sui Generis) 30
"Ella es bailarina" (García) 144
EMGE (Estado Mayor General del Ejército) 48
"En las cúpulas" (Almendra) 36
encryption, aesthetics of 11
endurance, culture of 121
the enemy
  and the disappeared 72–5
  language of 94, 98
  music of 98, 106
  in PRN rhetoric 57, 69–72, 95
ERP (Popular Revolutionary Army) 17
"Escúchame entre el ruido" (Moris) 18
eternity 35, 133–8, 154
Eudeba (Editorial Universitaria de Buenos Aires) 48–50, 67
euphemisms 46, 56
exceptionality 133–4
exemplary measures 41–2
exile 15, 35, 39, 84, 112, 152
existentialism 7, 18, 27, 148
Expreso Imaginario 79–81

"Fabricante de mentiras" (Sui Generis) 143
FAEDA (Argentine Federation of Anti-communist Democratic Entities) 16

Falú, Juan 148
family
  in PRN rhetoric 57, 59–63
  and *ser nacional* 68
Fandermole, Jorge 115
Favero, Alberto 115
Feitlowitz, Marguerite 58, 66
Fernández Capello, "Vicentico" 114
Festival of Latin American Solidarity 94–6, 98, 103
FIFA World Cup 1978 63–6, 72
"Figuración" (Almendra) 34
Foster, David William 38
Francis of Assisi, Saint 88
freedom
  Charly García on 131, 140–5
  of expression 4
  interpretative 157
  in song 159
  of speech 29, 107
"Friday 3AM" (Serú Girán) 89
Frith, Simon 128
Frondizi, Arturo 14
Full Stop Law 114

Gabriela 18
Gallardo, Fabián 115
Galtieri, Leopoldo 92–4, 96, 100, 104
García, Charly 3, 6–7, 21, 36, 125
  anti-war music 100, 102–3
  censorship of 5, 37
  collaboration with Spinetta 23–4
  and Fito Páez 116
  gender and freedom 140–4
  later bands of 82–92
  as parodic rock star 127–30, 133–40, 144–5
  and PRN government 79
  statue of 24, 132
  and Sui Generis 24–5, 27–31
  transition music of 110–12
  version of Argentine national anthem 131–2
García, Rodolfo 79
Gardel de Oro award 138
Garré, Silvina 115
Gatti, Juan 28–9

Gelly y Obes, María 67
gender
    in Argentine rock 18, 31
    Charly García and 140–4
gender equality 31
genocide 67–8, 153–4
Gente 62, 66, 97
"Gente del sur" (Blanca) 105
ghost juries 39, 42
Gieco, León 18, 79, 94–5, 100, 104, 145
GIT 109
Giusti, Secul 109, 118
Gociol, Judith 39–41, 45
Goldin, Rubén 115
Gonzalez, Angel 120
Gordillo, Lucrecia 62
Greek mythology 30
Grinbank, Daniel 79, 98
Grinberg, Miguel 13, 81, 150
Grondona, Mariano 43
Grossberg, Lawrence 128–9
grotesque realism 121–2, 125
Guerrero, Gloria 153
guerrilla groups 17, 55, 69, 112
Guevara, Che 14, 50, 112
guilt 74, 112, 132, 135, 154
Guzzetti, César A. 55

hairstyles 5, 11n7, 14, 82, 141
Haley, Bill 9
half-words 41
Harguindeguy, Albano 46n38
hedonism 109
hegemony crisis 11
"Héroes de Malvinas" (Ciro y los persas) 105
hippies 11, 13–14, 16, 18, 88
historical allegories 66
Holy Week 1987 114
"Hombres de hielo" (Almendra) 34
homosexuality 142, 144
"Hoy todo el hielo en la ciudad" (Almendra) 33
human rights 16, 31
    Catholic Church on 44n27
    PRN rhetoric of 53, 62, 65–6

Human Rights Commission *see* Inter-American Commission on Human Rights

Illia, Arturo Umberto 13–14
immensity 34, 149, 151, 155
impact theory 4, 46
impunity 46, 119, 121, 125
INAMU (National Institute of Music) 148–9
"Inconsciente colectivo" (García) 102
indigenous history 48–9, 67–8, 101
individualism 132–3
indoctrination 51, 62
Inquisition 39
instinct 19, 33
Instituciones see Pequeñas anécdotas sobre las instituciones (Sui Generis)
Inter-American Commission on Human Rights 46, 65–6, 70
"Interferencia total" (García) 112
Invernizzi, Hernán 4, 39–41, 45–6, 46n40, 48–50, 71
Invisible (band) 149, 151
irony 12, 28, 53, 75, 106, 109, 111

John Paul II, Pope 97
"Juan Represión" (Sui Generis) 25

Kamikaze (Spinetta) 100–2, 104
Kill gil (García) 137–8
Kirchner, Néstor 114, 121
Koffman, Ethel 115

"La Argentinidad al palo" (Bersuit Vergarabat) 124
"La aventura de la abeja reina" (Spinetta) 101
"La balsa" (Nebbia/Tanguito) 15
La Biblia (Vox Dei) 56
"La canción del soldado y Rosita Pazos" (Paez) 105
La Cueva bar 13
La grasa de las capitales (Serú Girán) 88
"La isla de la buena memoria" (Lerner) 105

La Máquina de Hacer Pájaros 5, 79, 82–6, 159
"La muralla verde" (Los Enanitos Verdes) 113
La Opinión 55, 58, 64, 69, 73
La Perla bar 13–14
La Razón 62, 69
La Trova Rosarina 115–18
"La verdad de las grullas" (Spinetta/Invisible) 155
Lanusse, Alejandro 17, 28–9
"Las golodrinas de Plaza de Mayo" (Spinetta/Invisible) 157
Las Manos de Filippi 124
Lebón, David 18, 79
Leguizamón, Miguel 120
Lennon, John 98
Lerner, Alejandro 105
Levingston, Roberto Marcelo 17, 28
Lewis, George 128
literary texts 53, 151
Locura (Virus) 118
loneliness 32, 34, 59
looting 119–20
López Rega, José 19n36, 91
Los Abuelos de la Nada 110–11, 115
Los Beatniks 12–13, 18
Los Enanitos Verdes 113
Los Fabulosos Cadillacs 114
Los Gatos 20, 24
"Los libros de la buena memoria" (Spinetta/Invisible) 152
"Los Sobrevivientes" (Serú Girán) 88
Los Twist 109–10
"Love is Love" (García) 134
Ludmer, Josefina 148
Luna, Félix 108

macho culture 18, 120, 141, 143
magic 153
Malvinas/Falkland Islands War 5, 93–6
  aftermath of 104–5
  media presentation of 96–7
  and military rhetoric 74
  songs associated with 100–4, 119

"Mambrú se fue a la guerra (no sé cuándo vendrá)" 35
Manal 24
Manfroni, Carlos 78, 142–3
manhood 31–2
Manichaeism 71
Mar del Plata 24, 132
Maradona, Diego 65
Marchini, Darío 79
Maresma, Olimpo Santiago 71
marginal spaces 109
"Mariel y el capitán" (Sui Generis) 31
"Mariposas de madera" (Abuelo) 17
marriage 26, 30, 144
  same-sex 142
Martínez de Perón, María Estela (Isabel) 19, 91
martyrs 58
Marxism 42–3, 51, 57, 70
masculinity 18, 140–2
Masiello, Francine 39
mass media 42, 48, 67
Massera, Emilio Eduardo 5, 45–6, 56, 58n12
  and the enemy 69–71, 73
  and family metaphor 59–61
  and Malvinas/Falklands War 97, 105
materiality 149, 151
"Me tiré por vos" (García) 135
medical metaphors 4, 55, 57–8, 84, 87, 128
mediocrity 53
"Mejor no hablar de ciertas cosas" (Sumo) 113
memory, good and bad 152
memory studies 149
Menem, Carlos 25n8, 114, 119–20
Menéndez, Luciano Benjamín 73
Merlo, Antonio Luis 64
messianic expressions 43, 45, 56–7, 67, 96, 119
Mestre, Nito 24, 27–9, 79, 132
metaphors 7, 11–13, 159
  Abuelo's use of 20
  basic 15, 150

García's use of 83–5, 110, 128
PRN's use of 56–7
Serú Girán and 88–9
Spinetta's use of 17, 151
women as 140
see also medical metaphors
military Junta *see* National Reorganisation Process
military rhetoric 74, 98
military service 25, 37
Molinari, Edelmiro 18
Monjeau, Federico 148
Monteleone, Jorge 133
Montoneros 17
moral law 67
morality leagues 42
Morello-Frosch, Marta 39
Moris 12, 18
Mothers of the Plaza de Mayo 53, 62–3, 137, 140, 157n26
Movimiento de Sacerdotes del Tercer Mundo 44
"Mr Jones o pequeña semblanza de una familia tipo americana" (Sui Generis) 31
"Muchacha ojos de papel" (Almendra) 34
Multipartidaria 96
Muñoz, José María 65
music festivals 18–19
música beat 10–12, 16, 24

Nacht und Nebel 47
narrating machine 85
"Natalio Ruiz, el hombrecito del sombrero gris" (Sui Generis) 31
National Day of the Musician 3, 145, 148
National Defence Law 1966 40
national identity 2, 4–5
National Reorganisation Process 2–3
  and the Catholic Church 43–6
  censorship under 37–41
  Charly García and 82, 84
  cultural policy of 47–50, 52
  and the disappeared 46–7
  education policy of 50–2

  end of 104–6
  rhetorical pillars of 4–5, 55–74
  rock music under 77–9
  trials and pardons of leaders 112–14, 119
  and war 93–5
  see also Malvinas/Falkland Islands War
national rock *see* rock nacional
national union 60, 63, 96, 131
Nazi Germany 47–8
Nebbia, Litto 14, 18
neoliberalism 48, 119–20, 125
New York, Charly García in 110
"No bombardeen Buenos Aires" (García) 102–3
"No puedo verme" (La Máquina de Hacer Pájaros) 83–4
"No soy un extraño" (García) 144
"No te animás a despegar" 136
"No te dejes desanimar" (La Máquina de Hacer Pájaros) 84
"Noche de perros" (Serú Girán) 88
nonsense 11–13, 53, 86–8, 103
nueva canción Argentina 16
nueva ola 11, 16
"Nunca podrán sacarme mi amor" (Páez) 117–18

"Obertura 777" (La Máquina de Hacer Pájaros) 85
Oktubre (Patricio Rey y sus Redonditos de Ricota) 118–19
Olivera, Alfredo 79, 92
Olivera, Héctor 38
Onganía, Juan Carlos 14, 17, 28, 40, 91
Operación Claridad 50–1

Paez, Fito 105, 115–17
"Para quién canto yo entonces" (Sui Generis) 30–1
Para Ti 59n15, 62, 72
paracensorship 39, 42, 52
para-musical texts 5
paranoia, and censorship 39–40

"Parte de la religión" (García) 132
party, perpetual 121–2
Parui, Avishek 149
paternalistic rhetoric 59
Patricio Rey y sus Redonditos de Ricota 109, 118–19
peace
 flags of 72
 songs of 100–4
Películas (La Máquina de Hacer Pájaros) 85
Pelo 79, 81–2
"Pensé que se trataba de cieguitos" (Los Twist) 110
Pequeñas anécdotas sobre las instituciones (Sui Generis) 5, 29–32, 141
Pequenino, Eddie 10
"Perdonado (niño condenado)" (Spinetta/Invisible) 154
Perlanda Gómez, Felipe 44
permeability 122
Perón, Juan Domingo 17, 19–20, 112
Peronism 14, 18–19, 108, 112
Piano bar (García) 111, 129–30
Piglia, Ricardo 58, 85
Pistocchi, Jorge 79–80
Pitluk, Roberto 141–2
"Plegaria para un niño dormido" (Almendra) 35
"Podrías entender" (García) 133
political power 13, 45
Pollock, Jackson 156n24
pop artists 13
popular music
 discursive practices around 2
 resistance through 10
Por qué cantamos 115–16
Porchetto, Raúl 18, 56–7, 100, 103–5
post-autonomous literature 148
postmodernism 119, 156
Prima Rock festival 78
privatisation 120
PRN (Process of National Reorganisation) *see* National Reorganisation Process
progressive music 11, 142

"Promesas sobre el bidet" (García) 112, 129
protest songs 38, 148
Pujol, Sergio 38, 79, 85

"Qué se puede hacer salvo ver películas" (La Máquina de Hacer Pájaros) 85–6
"Que ves el cielo" (Spinetta/Invisible) 153
"Quedándote o yéndote" (Spinetta) 101

"Rap del exilio" (García) 112
"Raros peinados nuevos" (García) 130
recuperation, process of 58
red berets 35
Reina Madre (Porchetto) 100, 103
repression 57, 59, 73, 88, 150
reproductive laws 142
Revolución Argentina 19, 28–9
"Rezo por vos" (García/Spinetta) 23–4
rhetorical strategies 3
Ripoll, Daniel 82
Risler, Julia 38
rituals 119, 121, 124
"Rock and Roll" (La Máquina de Hacer Pájaros) 84
Rock and roll ya (García) 137–8
Rock Around the Clock 9
rock chabón 109, 121
rock concerts
 during the dictatorship 53–4, 94
 politicisation of 18–19
 reporting on 82
 by Serú Girán 86, 91
 by Sui Generis 25
rock culture 75, 121, 130, 150
rock festivals 18, 110
rock magazines 5
 communication via 79–82
rock music 1–2
 and popular culture industry 128–9
 see also Argentine rock

rock nacional 6, 53, 98, 105, 107
rock stars 6, 127–30, 134–5, 137–8, 144–5
Rodríguez, Jesús 114
Rodríguez, Silvio 10
Rodríguez Sáa, Adolfo 120–1
Roffé, Reina 39
"Rojo como un corazón" (Páez) 117
Rolanroc 19, 79
Rosario 115, 117
"Ruido de magia" (Spinetta/Invisible) 153
rupture 20, 109, 122

Sabina, Joaquín 138
Sarlo, Beatriz 39, 41–2
Sarmiento, Domingo 68
Sasiaiñ, Juan Bautista 73–4
scandals 128, 135, 137–8
self-censorship 4, 39, 42, 45, 51–2, 80
self-destruction 153–4
self-promotion 137
self-referentiality 109
"Seminare" (Serú Girán) 25, 87–8
ser nacional 41, 50, 57, 66–9, 74, 132
Serú Girán 5, 79, 82, 86–92, 103
sexism 18
sexualised bodies 121, 125
"Shisyastawuman" (García) 144
sick bodies 55–9
SIDE 16
Simon & Garfunkel 26
SNM (Say No More) 130, 132, 136, 145
soccer
 culture of 121
 in PRN rhetoric 63–5
 see also FIFA World Cup 1978
social abandonment 121, 125
social chaos 119–20
Soda Stereo 109, 118
Solari, Carlos "Indio" 119
"Solo le pido a Dios" (Gieco) 94, 100, 104
song-poems 148
Spanish language
 future tense 86

 gender in 31
 pronouns in 60
 rock music in 3, 12–13, 16
Spinetta, Luis Alberto 3, 6–7, 10, 21, 125, 159
 and Almendra 32–6
 anti-war music 100–2, 104
 birth date of 145, 148–9
 collaboration with García 23–4
 image and personality 147–8
 and the Malvinas/Falklands War 94
 manifesto of 1973 19, 32–3
 and PRN government 79
 song-poetry of 17, 149–57
 on Spanish and English languages 12, 16
Spiritual Power 45
"Sr Cobranza" (Las Manos de Filippi) 124
state ideological apparatus 42
Strassera, Julio César 60
subversion
 and censorship 4, 46
 and cultural policy 49–50, 49n49
 and educational policy 51
 and the enemy 69–70, 72–3
 medical metaphors for 57–9
 PRN's campaign against 38, 41, 56, 69–70, 74–5
 and state killings 19n37
 women and 61–3
Sui Generis 3, 6, 21, 24–32, 111
 commemorated with statues 132
 women in lyrics of 143
Sumo (band) 109, 113
supra-constitutional acts 40
surgery, metaphor of 4, 55, 57–9, 111
surrealism 13, 34, 53, 150
symphonic rock 82

Tagore, Rabindranath 148
tango 1
 and Argentine rock 97, 102
 Carlos Menem dancing 120
 in Charly García's music 138
 and gender 140

and La Trova Rosarina 115
  lyrics of 139
  in Montevideo and Buenos Aires
    124
"Tango en segunda" (Sui Generis)
  29–30
Tanguito 14, 15n24
Tato, Miguel 58
Taylor, Diana 3
"Te hacen falta vitaminas" (Soda
  Stereo) 118
team, allegory of 63–5
Teatro Abierto 4
"Tema de Pototo" (Almendra) 32
terror
  lexicon of 5
  rhetoric of 55
terrorism 37–8, 57, 73–4, 112
  state 88, 95, 107
Thatcher, Margaret 100
"Tirando piedras al río" (Abuelo) 20
To Walk Spanish (band) 24
"Todas las hojas son del viento"
  (Spinetta) 17
toma de posesión 13
"Toma un tren hacia el sur"
  (Almendra) 35
Tornadú, Noemí 52
Tortolo, Adolfo 58–9
torture 5, 38, 44, 46, 58, 112
tradition 41, 51–2, 66, 86
"Transformation" (García) 134,
  137–9
transgression, rituals of 122
"Tratando de crecer" (Baglietto) 116
30 minutos de vida (Moris) 18
"Tribulaciones, lamentos y ocaso de
  un tonto rey imaginario, o no"
  (Sui Generis) 28
triggering language 153
Tupac Amaru II 101
"Tuve tu amor" (García) 112
the two Demons 112

UBA (University of Buenos Aires) 13
"Un rosarino en Budapest" (Páez)
  117

unawareness 41
Unidad (Cantilo) 111
union, in PRN rhetoric 57, 63–6
unity 65–8, 74, 111
the universe, in Spinetta's poetry
  147–8, 150, 154–6
University of San Martín 128

Van Gogh, Vincent 156n24
Vaquero, José Antonio 49n49
Verbitsky, Horacio 72, 97, 138
vice 135
Vida (Sui Generis) 26–7
Videla, Jorge Rafael 45, 92
  and the disappeared 73
  on the enemy 70
  and family metaphor 60, 62–3
  rhetoric of 56–7
  and *ser nacional* 67–8
  and soccer 64–5
Vila, Pablo 2
Vilas, Acdel Eduardo 72
Viola, Roberto 74, 78–9, 92
Virgin Mary 61
Virus (band) 99, 109, 118
Vox Dei 56
"VSD" (García) 138

war terminology 95
Warner, Marina 61
Washington consensus 119
weapons of the weak 3, 12
Western values 50, 57, 65, 69, 112
Williamson, John 119
women
  beautiful 120, 124
  in Charly García's music 140–4
  in macho culture 18
  in PRN rhetoric 59, 61–3
  and sport 65

"Y tu amor es una vieja medalla"
  (Spinetta) 101
Yendo de la cama al living (García)
  100, 102, 110
"Yo no me sentaría en tu mesa" (Los
  Fabulosos Cadillacs) 114

"Yo no quiero volverme tan loco" (García) 102
"Yo soy tu bandera" (Los Abuelas de Nada) 115
youth culture 4, 94, 128
　PRN and 78–9

youth identity 5, 79, 114
youth solidarity 26

Zaguri, Pajarito 12
Zas 109

Printed in the USA
CPSIA information can be obtained
at www.ICGtesting.com
LVHW011836041124
795688LV00004B/566